US ARMY SPECIAL WARFARE

Its Origins

US ARMY SPECIAL WARFARE

Its Origins

Psychological and Unconventional Warfare, 1941-1952

by

Alfred H. Paddock, Jr.

University Press of the Pacific
Honolulu, Hawaii

US Army Special Warfare,
Its Origins: Psychological and
Unconventional Warefare, 1941-1952

by
Alfred H. Paddock, Jr.

ISBN: 0-89875-843-2

Reprinted from the 1982 edition

University Press of the Pacific
Honolulu, Hawaii
http://www.universitypressofthepacific.com

CONTENTS

FOREWORD

It has been said that the future can only be approached clearly and wisely if the path leading to the present is known. In assessing national security policy choices, decisionmakers often do not have available the clarifying perspective provided by history. Recognizing this problem, the National Defense University has encouraged selected history-oriented research to complement our other topical publications on national security issues. This first volume in our new Military History Series is by Colonel Alfred H. Paddock, Jr., USA, on the origins of the US Army's special warfare capability.

As the most senior of our military services, the Army has undergone many organizational and doctrinal changes since its inception as a small militia force in 1775. But the year 1945 marked the beginning of an era of dramatic change. The new global realities of the post-World War II period suggested the need for an Army able to respond to a spectrum of conflicts. This led to the building of a "special warfare" capability encompassing psychological and unconventional warfare as a response to military challenges at the lower end of the conflict spectrum.

Colonel Paddock traces the origins of Army special warfare from 1941 to 1952, the year the Army's special warfare center was established. While the Army had experience in psychological warfare, the major recent US experience in unconventional warfare had been in the Office of Strategic Services, a civilian agency, during World War II. Many Army leaders, trained and experienced in conventional warfare, hesitantly accepted psychological warfare as a legitimate weapon in the Army's wartime arsenal, but questioned the validity and appropriateness of the Army's adoption of unconventional operations. The continuing tensions of the cold war and hostilities in Korea resolved the ambivalence in favor of coordinating in a single operation the techniques of both types of warfare.

Colonel Paddock's extensively documented work traces a portion of a brief episode in our Nation's military history, but an instructive one. For the historian and military scholar, it provides the necessary backdrop for understanding the subsequent evolution of the Army's special warfare capability. For the national security policymaker, it suggests the value of the innovative impulse and the need for receptivity to new ideas and adaptability to change.

Thus, this new NDU Press Military History Series will aid us look forward to effect change by reminding us of the lessons of past military efforts.

JOHN S. PUSTAY
Lieutenant General, USAF
President

PREFACE

The original intent of this study was to analyze how the US Army, which was developed to fight conventional wars, attempted to cope with the demands of low-intensity warfare after World War II. The primary focus for the investigation was to be the evolution of the Army's John F. Kennedy Center for Military Assistance at Fort Bragg, North Carolina, from its inception in the early 1950's through the Vietnam years. I still intend, as a future project, to accomplish that original goal. My preliminary research, however, revealed that the story of how and why the Army decided to undertake such a quest in the first place has not been adequately told. This study is intended to fill that void in our military history. Specifically, it examines the Army's activities in psychological and unconventional warfare during and after World War II to determine the impetus for, and origins of, the formal "special warfare" capability created in 1952 with the establishment of the Psychological Warfare Center (later the Center for Military Assistance). An understanding of these historical roots should provide a more enlightened perspective from which to assess the subsequent evolution of "special warfare" in the Army.

I am indebted to Professor I. B. Holley of Duke University for first suggesting this topic and for his constructive advice. The comments and insights provided on the outline and manuscript by my mentor, Professor Theodore Ropp of Duke, were invaluable. The long talks with Professor John K. Mahon, University of Florida, during his year with the US Army Military History Institute, were most appreciated, as were the comments on the manuscript by Professor Harold Deutsch of the Army War College faculty. For their expert, willing assistance during my research, I am particularly indebted to William Cunliffe and Ed Reese of the National Archives, Miss Hannah Zeidlik of the US Army Center of Military History, Miss Joyce Eakin and Dr. Richard Sommers of the Military History Institute, and Mrs. Beverly Lindsey of the John F. Kennedy Center for Military Assistance. My sincere gratitude goes to my wife, Theresa, for her patience, initiative, and thoroughly professional typing of the manuscript. Paul Taborn, The Adjutant General's Office, Department of the Army, was most understanding and helpful in the interagency processing of my personal notes, documents from the National Archives, and the final manuscript. Timely completion of the study would not have been possible without the encouragement, assistance, and scholarly environment provided by the Army War College and Strategic Studies Institute.

Finally, this study is dedicated to my wife and three children, who know better than anyone the sacrifices it required.

A. H. P., JR.

THE AUTHOR

Colonel Alfred H. Paddock, Jr, was born 11 February 1937 in Moscow, Idaho; enlisted in the US Army in September 1957; and was commissioned through the Infantry Officer Candidate School in September 1958. He earned his B.A. degree in political science from Park College, and holds M.A. and Ph.D. degrees in history from Duke University. Colonel Paddock is a graduate of the US Army Command and General Staff College and the US Army War College.

His military career has included command and staff assignments in Korea, Laos, Okinawa, Vietnam, and the United States. He served three combat tours with Special Forces units in Southeast Asia. He was an instructor in strategy and strategic studies at the Command and General Staff College, Fort Leavenworth, Kansas; served in the Politico-Military Division of the Department of the Army Staff in Washington, DC; commanded the 6th Psychological Operations Battalion at Fort Bragg, North Carolina; was both a faculty instructor for the Department of National and International Security Studies and a Strategic Research Analyst, Strategic Studies Institute, at the US Army War College, Carlisle Barracks, Pennsylvania; and commanded the 4th Psychological Operations Group, Fort Bragg, North Carolina, from November 1979 to May 1982.

Colonel Paddock is the author of "Does the Army Have a Future? Deterrence and Civil-Military Relations in the Post-Vietnam Era" which appeared in the September 1978 issue of *Parameters*. He was a co-author of *Organization, Missions and Command and Control of Special Forces and Ranger Units in the 1980's*, published by the Strategic Studies Institute in April 1979.

Colonel Paddock is Chairman, Department of National and International Security Studies, US Army War College, Carlisle Barracks, Pennsylvania.

I

INTRODUCTION

In the first half of the twentieth century, American leaders employed US Armed Forces to support American foreign policy in "conventional warfare" against the organized, uniformed forces of enemy nations. Although the size and nature of the forces varied in two world wars and Korea, in each of these conflicts the US Army performed its role with regularly organized divisions and without the use of nuclear weapons. Whether infantry, mechanized infantry, armored, or airborne, the division was the basic formation of the Army, the key organization by which strength was measured in conventional war. After World War II, political and military leaders began to consider other forms of conflict in which US forces might be engaged. Organization, equipment, and doctrine were reexamined in view of the possibility of nuclear war, but in this process the division remained a fundamental military organization. Simultaneously, however, a few thinkers began to consider the possibility of forces capable of operating at the opposite end of the conflict spectrum from nuclear war, below the level of conventional war—to consider, in short, a capability to conduct guerrilla, or "unconventional" warfare. Regular divisions were never designed or equipped for unconventional warfare, so special units, training, and doctrine would be necessary for such a task.

In 1952 the Army created the first formal unconventional warfare force in its history, the 10th Special Forces Group, assigned to the Psychological Warfare Center, an institution created that same year at Fort Bragg, North Carolina. From that year to the present, this institution, known consecutively as the Psychological Warfare Center, the Special Warfare Center (1956), and finally the John F. Kennedy Center for Military Assistance (1969), has constituted the headquarters for Army "special warfare."

Secretary of the Army Elvis J. Stahr, Jr., defined "special warfare" in 1962 as "a term used by the Army to embrace all military and paramilitary measures and activities related to unconventional warfare, counter-insurgency, and psychological warfare."[1] *Unconventional warfare* primarily encompassed guerrilla operations and subversion to be carried out within enemy or enemy-controlled territory by indigenous personnel, supported and directed by US forces. *Counterinsurgency,* on the other hand, included all actions, military and political, taken by the forces of the United States alone or in conjunction with a legal government to *prevent or eliminate* subversive insurgency. *Psychological warfare* encompassed those activities planned and conducted to influence the opinions, emotions, attitudes, and behavior of the enemy, the indigenous population, and neutral or friendly foreign groups to help support US objectives.[2] Unconventional warfare, counterinsurgency, and psychological warfare, then, comprised the key elements of special warfare, which according to Secretary Stahr included the capability to fight "*as* guerrillas as well as *against* guerrillas and also involves the employment of psychological devices to undermine the enemy's will to resist."[3]

Secretary Stahr's words came from the early 1960's when special warfare, then symbolized by the Special Forces "Green Berets," enjoyed its zenith under the Kennedy administration. During the next decade, the goals of special warfare changed somewhat in form and emphasis, and the concept receded in importance within the Army. The special warfare historian might be excused for noting that that more recent period is reminiscent of the 1950's, when the idea of special warfare struggled for survival. The story of special warfare, then, is a story of the Army, hesitantly and reluctantly groping with concepts of an "unconventional" nature.

To understand the evolution of special warfare, particularly its embryonic existence in the early 1950's, one must grapple with the questions of how and why it all began. An examination of the original organization of the Psychological Warfare Center in 1952 reveals that its major subordinate elements—the Psychological Warfare School (divided into psychological operations and special forces instructional departments), the 6th Radio Broadcasting and Leaflet Group, and the 10th Special Forces Group—all involved two of the three components of special warfare; that is, psychological and unconventional warfare.[4] The third component, counterinsurgency, appeared later with US involvement in Southeast Asia. In addition, the 1952 organization of the Fort Bragg center seemed to favor psychological warfare over unconventional warfare; after all, it was the *Psychological* Warfare Center and the *Psychological* Warfare School.

The apparent dominance of psychological warfare was also evident in the official unclassified literature of the day, particularly the semiannual Department of Defense reports for 1952. The 1 January–30 June 1952 report, for example, although highlighting the establishment of the Psychological Warfare Center, made no mention of the concomitant creation of the 10th Special Forces Group, the first unit of its type in Army history.[5]

Why, in 1952, did the Army decide, for the first time in its history, to begin a special warfare capability by establishing the Psychological Warfare Center at Fort Bragg? What were the roots of psychological and unconventional warfare in US Army experience, and why were these concepts physically embodied in the same location in 1952? Finally, why did psychological warfare achieve ascendance over unconventional warfare? Answers to these questions lie in the history of psychological and unconventional warfare from World War II to creation of the Psychological Warfare Center in 1952.

II

PSYCHOLOGICAL WARFARE IN WORLD WAR II

With the outbreak of World War II, the United States had virtually no organized capability to conduct psychological and unconventional warfare. That situation changed on 11 July 1941, when President Franklin D. Roosevelt established the Office of Coordinator of Information (COI) and designated Colonel William J. Donovan as the first director. Thus was begun a bold idea: through COI and its successor, the Office of Strategic Services (OSS), the United States began "its first organized venture into the fields of espionage, propaganda, subversion and related activities under the aegis of a centralized intelligence agency."[1]

The Coordinator of Information

Ironically, the creation of COI came largely from recommendations following Colonel Donovan's fact-finding trips to the Middle East and Great Britain. He had been impressed by the British method of combining—in agencies called the Political Warfare Executive and Special Operations Executive—propaganda efforts with the "unorthodox" operations of sabotage, subversion, and guerrilla warfare. He had been impressed as well by the British system of intelligence and counter-intelligence, as conducted by their Secret Intelligence Service, and by their ability to coordinate intelligence activities with psychological warfare and special operations. Donovan thus proposed to Roosevelt the creation of a single agency to centralize the intelligence gathered by several un-coordinated offices in Washington, combining the functions of psychological warfare and special operations on the British model.[2] According to Corey Ford, Donovan's biographer, the President welcomed "the suggestion of a single agency which would serve as a clearinghouse for all intelligence, as well as an organ of counterpropaganda and a training center for what were euphemistically called 'special operations.'"[3]

As often happens to those who recommend measures of a far-reaching nature, Donovan was "invited" by the President to head the agency that he had proposed.[4] Initially COI contained two major divisions, Research and Analysis (R&A) and the Foreign Information Service (FIS), plus secret intelligence and sabotage branches for training. Dr. William L. Langer, a Harvard historian, became director of R&A, the division designed to evaluate all incoming intelligence. Robert E. Sherwood, a playwright and confidant of President Roosevelt, became head of FIS, the psychological warfare division. As William F. Daugherty has written, FIS "undertook to spread the gospel of democracy . . . and to explain the objectives of the United States throughout the world except in Latin America."[5] To carry out these aims, FIS used information from the wire services as propaganda on its 11 commercial shortwave stations, which transmitted in several languages. After Pearl Harbor, Sherwood's organization broadcast more than 300, 15-minute programs a week in Europe and Asia.[6]

Donovan's concept of psychological warfare was all-encompassing. The first stage would be "intelligence penetration," with the results, processed by R&A, available for strategic planning and propaganda. Donovan called propaganda the "arrow of initial penetration" and believed that it would be the first phase in operations against an enemy. The next phase would be special operations, in the form of sabotage and subversion, followed by commando-like raids, guerrilla actions, and behind-the-lines resistance movements. All of this represented the softening-up process prior to invasion by friendly armed forces. Donovan's visionary dream was to unify these functions in support of conventional unit operations, thereby forging "a new instrument of war."[7]

To carry out this concept, Donovan believed that COI should become a supporting agency for the Joint Chiefs of Staff (JCS) once JCS had been created in February 1942. The military services' de facto control over personnel and materiel made it necessary, he believed, to place COI under JCS authority. He realized pragmatically that the COI could not carry out secret activities without the concurrence and support of theater commanders, and that those commanders also must coordinate any such secret activities with conventional military operations. For several months he argued with Roosevelt for COI to be brought under the JCS, and for FIS foreign propaganda to be more closely coordinated with the intelligence activities of the military services.[8] But his arguments were unsuccessful.

OSS and OWI

Donovan's comprehensive concept of psychological warfare was not shared by everyone. On 11 June 1942, less than a year after COI's creation, President Roosevelt ordered that FIS be transferred to the newly established Office of War Information (OWI). By the same Executive order, Roosevelt also dissolved COI and supplanted it with a new organization, the Office of Strategic Services, with Donovan continuing as its head.[9] The change, however, did put OSS under JCS authority, as recommended by Donovan on 8 June.[10] In effect, as Edward Hymoff succinctly states, "COI became OSS and FIS became a division of the Office of War Information."[11]

Roosevelt's decision to reorganize the psychological warfare effort was apparently motivated by several factors. First, the increasing number of Government information agencies had created problems of overall coordination, and a need existed to consolidate wartime information and psychological warfare activities.[12] There was also growing recognition that COI had become unwieldy, and the President preferred that US wartime propaganda be separated from, rather than combined with, strategic intelligence and subversive operations.[13] Then there was the problem of personalities. Donovan and Sherwood, Chief FIS, had different views on the role of FIS as a part of COI. According to Corey Ford, "Colonel Donovan believed that, once a state of war existed, the propaganda arm should be exploited as a weapon of deception and subversion, and should be under military supervision," while Sherwood "held that propaganda broadcasts should stick scrupulously to the facts, and let the truth eventually prevail." Sherwood believed that "the American image overseas would suffer . . . if we emulated Axis methods and resorted to lies and deceit." He also believed that FIS should remain under civilian direction, and he clashed with Donovan over his proposals to put COI and FIS under JCS jurisdiction. These differing views were hardening into personal animosity between the two men; since both Donovan and Sherwood had the respect of the President, Roosevelt evidently felt that it would be wise to separate their responsibilities.[14] Perhaps the most important factor, however, was the opposition of Harold D. Smith, Director of the Budget. Smith submitted a memorandum to the President on 7 March 1942, proposing a reorganization of war information services that resulted in the formation of OWI.[15] Thus, for many reasons, the President shifted the major responsibilities for psychological warfare to the newly created OWI.

The creation of OWI, however, neither solved the problems of coordination nor delimited responsibilities for psychological warfare, even with a highly respected Columbia Broadcasting System reporter like Elmer Davis as its first director. Although most existing information services were transferred to OWI, Donovan's agency continued to keep its fingers in the propaganda pie. Having lost the battle to keep FIS under his direction in COI, Donovan continued to assume some psychological warfare functions for OSS.

Eventually the lines of responsibility were more clearly drawn and accepted by the two agencies. In addition to its intelligence and special operations activities, OSS retained responsibility for "black" propaganda operations, which were essentially covert activities using information issued from a concealed or falsified source to lower the enemy's morale.[16] OWI, on the other hand, controlled all propaganda in the United States and all "white" propaganda—information, official or otherwise, plainly issued from a known source—outside the United States with the exception of the Western Hemisphere; that remained a responsibility of the Office of Coordinator of Inter-American Affairs (CIAA) in the State Department.[17] In March 1943, another Executive order more clearly identified OWI's responsibilities for conducting foreign information and overt propaganda operations, and also decreed that its activities be coordinated with plans of the military services.[18]

The Army's Psychological Warfare Branch

When the European war broke out, the Army, like other agencies, was ill prepared to understand psychological warfare, much less plan for and conduct it. During World War I, the Army had given psychological warfare token recognition by establishing the Psychological Warfare Sub-Section of G-2 in the War Department, and the Propaganda Section, G-2, General Headquarters (GHQ), American Expeditionary Forces. However, from 1918 to 1941 no psychological warfare office existed at the War Department. The lessons of experience were lost, and by 1941 only one officer on the War Department staff had had psychological warfare experience in the previous war. He was Colonel Charles H. Mason who, as Chief of the Intelligence Branch, Military Intelligence Division (MID) from November 1940 to July 1941, had tried to reestablish a branch for psychological warfare planning and operations. His attempts failed, however, and Mason "complained that his efforts were met with indifference and opposition within the War Department."[19]

The first positive steps toward creation of a psychological warfare capability were a result of the personal interest of John McCloy, who had recently been appointed Assistant Secretary of War. Influenced by the effectiveness of German propaganda, he suggested in June 1941 that a special study group be organized by Brigadier General Sherman Miles, Acting Assistant Chief of Staff, G–2, to plan for future psychological warfare operations.[20] McCloy's action illustrates a theme that recurs at critical points throughout the history of special warfare—important governmental civilians intervene to prod hesitant and cautious uniformed Army leaders into taking action on concepts of an "unconventional" nature.

The special group suggested by McCloy was established on 25 June 1941 as the Psychologic Branch, with Lieutenant Colonel Percy Black as its chief. A great deal of secrecy surrounded its creation. Curiously, the only officer with World War I psychological warfare experience, Colonel Mason, was not even informed of its existence. Black's initial study examined all agencies—official and private—engaged in psychological information or propaganda, and concluded that "there was no effort to study the effect of propaganda on various groups, or relate propaganda plans to the plans of the military high command." This embryonic office attempted the following tasks: liaison with the Foreign Monitoring Broadcast Service of the Federal Communications Commission to obtain daily and weekly summaries of foreign broadcasts, completion of surveys for the Office for Coordination of Commercial and Cultural Relations and for the Council for Democracy, initiation of a weekly telegram service to military missions with a brief summary of national defense progress, and purchase of copies of *Newsweek* and *Life* for distribution to selected missions in Europe to counteract the pictorial propaganda of Germany.[21] These initial efforts by the Army were obviously modest.

To protect its strict security, the Psychologic Branch changed its name to the Special Study Group. An advisory committee of civilian psychologists felt that it was inadvisable to use terms like "propaganda," "control of opinion," and "psychiatry." Thus the name Special Study Group "would be far less revealing than any reference to psychology or propaganda." Later, in March 1942, the name changed to Psychological Warfare Branch, G–2, primarily because the growing number of personnel involved made strict secrecy difficult and because this same secrecy impeded coordination with other offices. Colonel Black was succeeded by Colonel Oscar M. Solbert, who remained chief of the branch until 26 July 1942. His successor was Colonel C. Blakeney, who continued as chief until the branch was dissolved in December 1942.[22]

The Special Study Group/Psychological Warfare Branch expanded upon the activities begun under the Psychologic Branch. One of its most important jobs was to produce a daily analysis of Axis propaganda, over 300 issues of which were circulated for guidance to the Office of Facts and Figures, CIAA, the National Broadcasting Corporation, and the Bureau of Public Relations. Since the War Department did not control radio broadcasting, the branch was limited to making suggestions. These ranged from suggested items for use in speeches by the Chief of Staff, to suggested broadcasts containing definite objectives for use by COI. The branch also helped plan leaflet operations in strategic and combat phases, and developed the *Combat Propaganda Bulletin*, a record of lessons learned and recent activities for distribution in Washington and to the military theaters.

In December 1942 the first psychological warfare units were created with the formation of the 1st and 2nd Radio Service Sections. Each section had an authorized strength of 3 officers and 39 enlisted men. Together the two formed the 1st Combat Propaganda Company. When the Psychological Warfare Branch was dissolved on 31 December 1942, the company was transferred from the Military Intelligence Service (MIS) to OSS, then back to MIS on 2 March 1943. At this point, the company was reorganized into combat propaganda teams, equipped with radio transmitters, sound trucks, and language personnel, and then sent to Europe.[23]

Concurrently, a draft training manual, *Combat Propaganda Company,* was developed in the autumn of 1942. It was based on an existing pamphlet, *Military Intelligence Propaganda—Confidential,* written by Major P. M. Robinett in December 1940. The manual proved useful in organizing propaganda companies in Europe during 1943–45.[24] The activities of the Army's Special Study Group/Psychological Warfare Branch during 1941–42 were varied but certainly not "center stage" at the War Department.

Dissolution of the Psychological Warfare Branch

Dissolution of the Psychological Warfare Branch in December 1942 grew from the problem of defining psychological warfare, a problem that persisted throughout the war, and from interagency battles over responsibilities in this new field. The Joint Chiefs of Staff had created a Joint Psychological Warfare Committee (JPWC) in March 1942 (JCS 12) to plan psychological warfare in combat theaters and enemy-controlled areas.

The committee was reconstituted on 21 June 1942 (JCS 68), after OSS and OWI were established as two separate agencies. Membership was made up of general and flag officers from the Army's G-2, the Office of Naval Intelligence (ONI), the War Department General Staff (WDGS), and the Commander in Chief, US Fleet. Colonel Donovan served as chairman. Established at the same time were a Joint Psychological Warfare Subcommittee, a Supporting Committee on Psychological Warfare within OSS, and a Joint Psychological Warfare Advisory Committee with Donovan as chairman. This last committee was formed to coordinate the psychological warfare activities of agencies outside the jurisdiction of the JCS, such as Nelson Rockefeller's CIAA, Henry Wallace's Board of Economic Warfare, OWI, and the State Department.[25]

To tackle the problem of defining psychological warfare, a "Basic Estimate of Psychological Warfare" was prepared by the OSS Supporting Committee and approved by the JPWC on 7 September. The fine hand of Donovan is seen in the definition of psychological warfare contained in this Basic Estimate:

> [Psychological warfare] is the coordination and use of all means, including moral and physical, by which the end is attained—other than those of recognized military operations, but including the psychological exploitation of the result of those recognized military actions—which tend to destroy the will of the enemy to achieve victory and to damage his political or economic capacity to do so; which tend to deprive the enemy of the support, assistance or sympathy of his allies or associates or of neutrals, or to prevent his acquisition of such support, assistance, or sympathy; or which tend to create, maintain, or increase the will to victory of our own people and allies and to acquire, maintain, or to increase the support, assistance and sympathy of neutrals.

The Basic Estimate further specified that propaganda, subversion, combat propaganda companies, and intelligence secured by research and espionage were the tools needed to carry out this broad concept of psychological warfare.[26] The OSS Supporting Committee had spent 6 months trying to develop a salable definition. But the JPWC, after having approved it, did not forward the Basic Estimate to the JCS for approval as a doctrine statement.[27]

This difficulty of defining psychological warfare was linked to OSS' groping while trying to find its niche as a new agency. The *War Report of the OSS* states the problem: "A contributing factor to the whole situation was a definite resentment of OSS, as such, which found its strongest expression in Donovan's colleagues on the JPWC. This resentment seemed to be based, in part, upon the fact that OSS was a civilian agency, and, in part, upon the position of OSS as an agency of the JCS and fear that it might encroach upon the functions of G-2 and/or ONI." [28] At any rate, the existing psychological warfare committee system proved to be ponderous, confusing, and generally unworkable.

Finally, on 23 December 1942, the JCS issued JCS 155/4D, which abolished the JPWC and made OSS responsible for "planning, developing, coordinating, and executing the military program of psychological warfare" and for "the compilation of such political, psychological, sociological, and economic information as may be required by military operations." [29] Concurrent with the reorganization of the JCS psychological warfare machinery, the Army decided to abolish its Psychological Warfare Branch. The decision was announced in Military Intelligence Service Memorandum 147, 31 December 1942, which explained that "since the Office of Strategic Services was responsible for propaganda, there appeared to be no need for the Branch." [30]

At this point the Army's participation in psychological warfare appeared to be minimal. Such was not the case overseas, however, for JCS 155/4D, which had precipitated the demise of the Army's Psychological Warfare Branch, also gave theater commanders control of psychological warfare in their jurisdictional areas. [31] In effect, the War Department, as Paul Linebarger states, considered "the theaters in this respect as autonomous, and [left] to the respective Theater Commanders the definition of their relationship with OWI and OSS, and their use of each." [32]

Theater Psychological Warfare

Most of the Army's operational work in psychological warfare took place at the theater level, where the responsible organization was normally designated a Psychological Warfare Branch (PWB). The largest of these, the PWB at Allied Forces Headquarters (PWB/AFHQ), was activated in North Africa in November 1942 at the order of General Dwight D. Eisenhower, and then expanded in February 1944 to the Psychological Warfare Division, Supreme Headquarters, Allied Expeditionary Force (PWD/SHAEF). [33] PWD/SHAEF defined psychological warfare as "the dissemination of propaganda designed to undermine the enemy's will to resist, demoralize his forces and sustain the morale of our supporters." [34] With this definition, then, and the overall objective of controlling and coordinating psychological warfare in the area of continental Europe controlled by the Supreme Commander, the specific missions of PWD were the following:

1. To wage psychological warfare against the enemy.

2. To use the various media available to psychological warfare to sustain the morale of the people of friendly nations occupied by the enemy and to cause the people of these countries to acquiesce in the wishes of the Supreme Commander.

3. To conduct so-called consolidation propaganda operations in liberated friendly countries. [Consolidation propaganda was that directed toward a military force and designed to insure compliance with the instructions promulgated by the commander of the occupying force.]

4. To control information services in Allied-occupied Germany.[35]

To carry out these tasks, PWD used psychological warfare tools such as British Broadcasting Corporation and OWI transmitters, front-line loudspeaker broadcasts, and large-scale leaflet dropping operations. PWD even provided leaflets to be dispersed by the novel method of specially designed artillery shells.[36]

The basic Army field operating unit for psychological warfare was the Mobile Radio Broadcasting (MRB) Company. Early MRB units had served with the Military Intelligence Service in December 1942 and, after being transferred for a brief period to OSS, went back to the Army in March 1943. The equipment for these units was unlike anything conventional soldiers had seen in the field—public address systems, radios, monitoring sets, loudspeakers, typewriters, mobile printing presses, and leaflet bombs. MRB units were usually divided by the separate Army groups and field armies into small teams, often to work in direct support of frontline conventional combat units. One MRB company commander, Major Edward A. Caskey, described his responsibilities as primarily tactical, or combat, propaganda efforts. His company used short-range radio broadcasts as well as tactical leaflets printed on the spot, then delivered to enemy lines through the use of modified artillery smoke shells. He also maintained prisoner-of-war interrogation teams that worked with G-2. Caskey explained: "Both Germans and Italians (prisoners) stated that the content of the leaflets had greatly influenced their decision [to surrender]. They all insisted that they were mostly impressed with the veracity of our leaflets."[37]

Five such companies eventually served under PWD/SHAEF. Although these units were the result of improvisation in 1943 and 1944, the doctrinal and organizational concepts they embodied reappeared in the psychological warfare units formed during the Korean conflict.[38]

Taken together, then, several diverse organizations in PWD, both civilian and military, somehow had to be fused into a common psychological warfare organization. According to an account prepared by the PWD staff, PWD/SHAEF "was the first agency, military or civilian, to coordinate successfully in Western Europe the efforts of the numerous military and civilian agencies which had waged Anglo-American psychological warfare since the beginning of the war." The chief of PWD, Brigadier General Robert A. McClure, was assisted by four deputies, each representing a civilian agency that contributed personnel to PWD. Two of those agencies were American—OWI and OSS; two were British—the Political Intelligence Department of the Foreign Office and the Ministry of Information. General McClure's name will reappear, for he was to figure prominently in establishing the Psychological Warfare Center at Fort Bragg in 1952.[39]

Not everyone was enamored with PWD operations. It was, by conventional unit standards, a rather strange collection of personnel, equipment, and activities. A survey report in August 1943 by the Inspector General, Major General Virgil L. Peterson, described the PWB in North Africa (forerunner of PWD/SHAEF) as "a heterogeneous group of some 468 writers, psychologists, economists, linguists, and world travelers," whose efforts "were somewhat lacking in coordination and control, until they were all assembled in one building and placed under command of an American Army officer." General Peterson concluded his report with a compliment, stating that his survey group "was much impressed with the industry and enthusiasm of the people engaged in these psychological warfare activities." But he also added a caveat about the new organization: "The survey group does not feel qualified to arrive at any conclusions regarding their value to the Theater, or the Army as a whole."[40]

Professor Saul K. Padover, a PWD combat intelligence officer, was later to recall that "at first PWD was not much appreciated; hard-bitten regular Army men referred to the psychological warriors as 'feather merchants.'" But Padover noted, as the war progressed, the organization's effectiveness received more respect from "formerly suspicious commanders," particularly at the tactical level. And at the end, even generals like George Patton were asking for frontline support because "it was definitely recognized that the loudspeakers helped to persuade the enemy to come over with arms in the air."[41]

The Propaganda Branch, G–2

The success of the PWB in North Africa provided much of the impetus to reestablish a psychological warfare branch at the War Department. General McClure's deputy, C. D. Jackson, OWI, returned to the United States for a visit in June 1943. During his trip he talked with John J. McCloy, Assistant Secretary of War, who in 1941 had displayed the interest in psychological warfare that led to the creation of the Psychologic Branch. Still deeply interested, Secretary McCloy proceeded to staff papers left with him by Jackson. These papers contained a proposal for a central psychological warfare branch at the War Department to direct and coordinate the work of the theater PWB's.[42] The seed had been planted.

Prior to this, on 9 March 1943, the continuing difficulty of clearly defining the propaganda responsibilities of OSS and OWI had resulted in Executive Order 9312. That order gave OWI responsibility for planning, developing, and executing all foreign propaganda activities "involving the dissemination of information" (open, or "white," propaganda). This necessitated a revision of JCS 155/4D, which in December 1942 had given OSS responsibility for military propaganda and which had been the major reason for dissolution of the War Department's Psychological Warfare Branch. The revised directive, JCS 155/7D, issued on 4 April 1943, simply omitted any reference to OWI and propaganda.[43] Thus a major, albeit largely self-imposed, constraint was lifted, allowing the Army to re-create a psychological warfare branch in Washington.

By August 1943, the papers Jackson had left with Secretary McCloy were beginning to have an impact. In addition to proposing a central psychological warfare branch at the War Department, the papers described the system by which propaganda planning and control were being carried out in the North African theater. In a memorandum to the Secretary to the General Staff, Colonel Otto L. Nelson, Brigadier General J. E. Hull, Acting Assistant Chief of Staff, Operations, and Plans Division (OPD), commented that "although the value of propaganda may not be as great as its proponents claim, it is a recognized instrument of modern war which can be useful." After this rather ambivalent endorsement, he stated that the principles contained in the PWB North African papers were sound and recommended that they be circulated to theater commanders.[44] A letter dated 20 August 1943 to all major commanders forwarded the papers "in the event you desire to establish similar agencies." One of the papers, signed by Colonel C. B. Hazeltine, strongly advocated a mixed civilian-military team as "a must for maximum results in a PWB organization."[45] Yet, it was this civilian influence and interaction that made psychological warfare and unconventional warfare suspect to many conventionally minded Army officers.

Meanwhile, General Peterson's survey report on the PWB in North Africa was now in circulation, and the report contained the complaint from General McClure "that there was no corresponding agency established in the War Department, through which he could channelize his correspondence." Also at about this time, the JCS began to require theaters to submit plans for psychological warfare. Both of these matters were discussed at the 23 August 1943 meeting of the Army's General Council. General McNarney, the Deputy Chief of Staff, recognized the responsibility of OWI "for most of this work," and was not prepared to decide "whether or not the War Department should establish an agency primarily for dealing with these matters or attempt to coordinate by liaison with OWI." Thus he directed the Operations Division and G-2 to "get together and submit recommendations."[46]

The immediate result of this directive was a report to the Joint Intelligence Committee on 8 September 1943 signed by the Assistant Chief of Staff, G-2, and the Assistant Chief of Staff, OPD. The report outlined the agencies primarily responsible for preparing and disseminating foreign propaganda, and concluded that a War Department agency for control of propaganda should be established and have a direct channel through the JCS to the Combined Chiefs of Staff (CCS). Recognizing the Army's deficiencies in this area, the report also noted that "the abolition of the Psychological Warfare Section of G-2 (in December 1942) has seriously reduced the War Department's ability to supply appropriate material to propaganda agencies." Finally, the report included this assessment of the value of psychological warfare:

> Although the proponents of psywar are prone to exaggerate its importance, the military value of propaganda in recent operations involving American Forces has been clearly discernible and propaganda has also been used by our enemies with marked success. It is a powerful weapon for influencing men's minds and, therefore, cannot be neglected.[47]

Again we see a lukewarm endorsement of this new field, but an endorsement nevertheless. Momentum had gathered for a new psychological warfare branch in the War Department.

By the middle of October, Major General T. T. Handy, the G-3, and Major General George V. Strong, the G-2, had submitted a more detailed study to General McNarney recommending the establishment of a central authority within the War Department for propaganda plans, policies, and releases. The report was approved by General McNarney and the Secretary of War on 26 October.[48] The matter appeared to be settled. But neither General Strong nor General Handy wanted the responsibility of the new function. In a memorandum to General Handy on 6 November 1943, General Strong, the G-2, attached a study prepared by G-3 that concluded that the new branch should be in the Operations Division because that division "has the greatest interest in operational propaganda and a direct channel to the Joint and Combined Chiefs of Staff on all operational subjects."[49] Not to be outdone, General Handy, the G-3, acknowledged on 10 November that G-3 did have an interest in operational propaganda. He suggested that the new branch should be under the G-2's direction because his positions as a member of the Emergency Combined Propaganda Committee and as a Joint Chief of Security Control gave him close touch with War Department coordination and control of propaganda.[50] The matter was finally resolved by referring to the original recommendations approved by General McNarney on 26 October, which had specified that the new propaganda agency be established in the Military Intelligence Division (G-2).[51]

The dialogue between G-2 and G-3 over a new function provides insight into attitudes toward psychological warfare. General staff divisions normally do not avoid or give up a function considered to be important—if it has "high visibility." General Handy's and General Strong's reluctance to accept an activity that was new, difficult to understand, and considered by many officers as a minor side show in the war effort, illustrates a theme that recurs throughout this study—the story of an Army hesitant and reluctant to accept concepts of an "unconventional" nature.

Creation of the new Propaganda Branch in G-2 was formally announced on 15 November 1943 by Military Intelligence Division Directive No. 78. During the General Council meeting held the same day, General Kroner, the G-2 representative, stated that the head of psychological warfare activities in North Africa, General McClure, had indicated that there was no corresponding agency in the War Department to consider psychological warfare problems "at the proper level." General Kroner concluded that "this is indicated as a need for this very important branch."[52] The seed, planted 6 months earlier by Jackson in his discussions with Assistant Secretary of War McCloy and by McClure's own statements during the intervening period, had finally borne fruit.

The primary responsibility of the new branch was to coordinate propaganda functions for the War Department. It prepared propaganda items for use by OWI, CIAA, and other nonmilitary organizations. It advised the G-2 on all propaganda problems presented by theater commanders. It coordinated propaganda matters brought before the JCS and the CCS by the War Department. It shepherded OWI and CIAA plans through the JCS, and it coordinated with similar branches in the Navy and State Department. Finally, the branch chief served as the Army member of the JCS liaison with OWI and CIAA.[53]

At the end of the war, a few senior officers recognized the need to build upon the Army's experience and retain a capability for psychological warfare. In a December 1945 letter to the War Department, Major General L. L. Lemnitzer, then head of the Joint Strategic Survey Committee of the JCS, stated:

> To avoid a repetition of the PWB mistakes we made in World War II and to take full advantage of the experience gained in that war, I recommend that a comprehensive study be made of this subject at an early date with a view of:
> 1. Analyzing all available PWB material of World War II, including particularly the PWB reports from the various theaters of operations to establish sound PWB principles, techniques, organization, equipment and procedures for future employment of this weapon.
> 2. Establishing short courses in our staff schools to provide future commanders and staff officers with a general understanding and appreciation of this new weapon of warfare.
> 3. Examining the feasibility of establishing a small PWB section in the War Department to provide continuing study of this subject, or failing that, to assign this responsibility to an existing section or agency best prepared to assume it.[54]

The Propaganda Branch had foreseen the need for such a study. In May 1945 letters had been sent to theater PWB's requesting the appropriate historical materials.[55] The branch continued in existence until January 1947, when the responsibility for psychological warfare activities was transferred from G-2 to the Plans and Operations Division.

Appraisal

It is impossible to discuss the evolution of Army experience in psychological warfare during World War II without acknowledging the impact of the major civilian agencies that had an interest in this activity. First, the Coordinator of Information, then its successor, the Office of Strategic Services, and, finally, the Office of War Information—all influenced the Army's development of a psychological warfare capability as they engaged in interagency struggles to sort out responsibilities in the new field. In many respects, it was the confusion generated by this profusion of agencies that forced the War Department to reestablish a Propaganda Branch in November 1943. Through this office and the theater Psychological Warfare Branch, the Army worked closely with these agencies, and in particular OWI, for the duration of the war.

This reliance on civilian agencies did not sit well with many military professionals. A quotation from the unsigned letter of an officer with Headquarters, Western Task Forces, in 1942 illustrates this attitude:

> I still believe we could get along far better without the OWI. The psychological situation is far too complex to be handled by poets and gentlemen of the press in Washington and even the German Propaganda Machine worked in reverse in the face of actual military operations. The only propaganda which can achieve results is the propaganda of deeds not words. One U.S. medium tank has proved far more effective than all the bag of trick gadgets, which merely offend good taste and give nothing concrete where want is great.

The officer ended his letter with the conclusion, "I believe that such agencies as the OWI and OSS can be profitably eliminated in the future." [56]

Ironically, it was a civilian—Assistant Secretary of War John McCloy—who pushed the Army into developing a branch at the War Department for planning and coordinating psychological warfare activities, initially in June 1941 and again in November 1943. And it was a civilian—C. D. Jackson of OWI—who, as General McClure's deputy, provided Assistant Secretary McCloy with the PWB/AFHQ organizational papers that stimulated resurrection of a psychological warfare branch in 1943. The initiative shown by influential civilians to urge conservative Army leaders to venture into a new and uncertain field is a theme we shall see throughout our investigation of the origins of a special warfare capability for the Army.

Certainly Brigadier General McClure was an exception to this theme. The civilian-military team that he headed, first in North Africa PWB/AFHQ, then later in PWD/SHAEF, served as the model for successful Army psychological warfare operations during the war. The Mobile Radio Broadcasting companies employed in Europe were the first tactical propaganda units in Army history. McClure himself strongly urged establishment of a central psychological warfare agency in the War Department. All in all, he was the most important Army officer in this new field during World War II.

Although small throughout, the Propaganda Branch, G-2—and its predecessors, the Psychologic Branch, the Special Study Group, and the Psychological Warfare Branch—performed a low-key, but valuable service. Its "principal success," states *A History of the Military Intelligence Division,* "was in the guidance it gave to operational units in the field, and as an agency for the coordination of propaganda activities with military operations."[57] While the MID history may somewhat overstate the extent of this success, nonetheless, that such an agency was deemed necessary was demonstrated by the creation of the Propaganda Branch 10 months after dissolution of the Psychological Warfare Branch.

Army personnel employed in psychological warfare in all theaters probably never totaled more than 2,000 at any one time,[58] a minuscule number when compared to many other activities. Despite the often less-than-enthusiastic manner in which the Army embraced it, psychological warfare gained respectability. Formal organizations and procedures were developed that eventually bestowed this new endeavor with a degree of legitimacy.

The impact of psychological warfare is always difficult to assess. But General Eisenhower, at least, thought the European experiment useful:

> In this war [he wrote in PWD/SHAEF's account of its operation], which was total in every sense of the word, we have seen many great changes in military science. It seems to me that not the least of these was the development of psychological warfare as a specific and effective weapon.
>
> The exact contribution of psychological warfare toward the final victory cannot, of course, be measured in terms of towns destroyed or barriers passed. However, I am convinced that the expenditure of men and money in wielding the spoken and written word was an important contributing factor in undermining the enemy's will to resist and supporting the fighting morale of our potential Allies in the occupied countries.

Without doubt, psychological warfare has proved its right to a place of dignity in our military arsenal.[59]

Thus, World War II saw the Nation—and the US Army—develop the foundation for a modern psychological warfare capability. What it would do with this foundation, so painfully acquired, remained to be seen.

III

UNCONVENTIONAL WARFARE IN WORLD WAR II

The task of tracing the origins of unconventional warfare in the US Army is complicated by the fact that in the early 1960's several World War II "elite" units were included in the official lineage of Special Forces. One of these was the 1st Special Service Force, a joint United States-Canadian unit formed in 1942 at Fort William Henry Harrison, Montana, and commanded by Major General Robert T. Frederick. Also included in the official lineage were US Army Ranger battalions, the first of which was formed on 19 June 1942 at Carrickfergus in Northern Ireland, under the command of Colonel William O. Darby. A similar organization, Brigadier General Frank Merrill's 5307th Composite Unit (Provisional), better known as "Merrill's Marauders," was not officially a part of Special Forces lineage but has been informally adopted by Special Forces.[1]

Whatever the "official" lineage, however, none of these units by definition was an unconventional warfare organization. According to the *Dictionary of U.S. Military Terms,* unconventional warfare "includes the three interrelated fields of guerrilla warfare, evasion and escape, and subversion . . . conducted within enemy or enemy-controlled territory by predominately indigenous personnel usually supported and directed by personnel from an outside country."[2] The 1st Special Service Force, the Ranger battalions, and "Merrill's Marauders" did not fit this description; they were primarily long-range penetration organizations that specialized in reconnaissance, raiding, and commando operations. British Royal Marine Commandos and Orde Wingate's Raiders performed similar tasks for the British throughout the Second World War. Yet the author himself remembers standing in a mass formation with the 77th Special Forces Group at Fort Bragg in early 1960 when the 1st Special Service Force was reconstituted and consolidated with the Ranger battalions, then activated as the parent unit of all Special Forces Groups; it was a memorable day, as retired Major General Frederick came down from Canada to preside over the conferral of 1st Special Service Force and Ranger unit colors, lineage, and honors to the Army's Special Forces.

Looking back on that scene, one wonders why Special Forces felt it necessary to adopt the lineage of units that were not true forerunners of unconventional warfare. An argument could be made that a few individuals from those units became early members of Special Forces, and that some of the tactics and techniques of their former units were incorporated into Special Forces training. But these alone are insufficient explanations. Apparently the answer was simply that the Army had no true unconventional warfare units of its own; therefore, someone in authority took the best alternative and borrowed the lineage of some well-known "elite" special-purpose units of World War II fame. While the lineage of those units undoubtedly adds to the luster of Special Forces, little is served by dwelling on their history as forerunners of a US Army unconventional warfare capability.

OSS and Unconventional Warfare

Personnel of the Office of Strategic Services (OSS), however, did participate in unconventional warfare activities during World War II, and the US Army contributed officers and men to this unique organization. OSS bore the stamp of its first chief, William Joseph Donovan, an imaginative, forceful man nearing 60, known since his youth as "Wild Bill." Donovan was a highly decorated World War I hero who had become a millionaire Wall Street corporate lawyer. President Roosevelt selected him, as one critic of OSS expressed it, "to direct the New Deal's excursion into espionage, sabotage, 'black' propaganda, guerrilla warfare, and other 'un-American' activities."[3] Established to meet the special conditions of World War II, OSS was the first agency of its kind in the history of the United States. Largely because of the imagination and foresight of General Donovan, OSS "undertook and carried out more different types of enterprises calling for more varied skills than any other single organization of its size in the history of our country."[4] Such disparate tasks required a potpourri of talent, with Americans from all walks of life participating. OSS strength had been estimated at 12,000 to 30,000; the official *War Report of the OSS,* however, released in 1976, placed the agency's maximum strength in December 1944 at 13,000 personnel, approximately 7,500 of whom were stationed overseas.[5]

Donovan's agency was divided into intelligence, special operations, and training functions. Intelligence and special operations were each further subdivided into several branches: Research and analysis, secret intelligence, and counterespionage, for example, fell under intelligence; and sabotage, guerrilla warfare, and psychological warfare fell under special operations. Psychological warfare bore the deceiving title "Morale Operations" (MO); that branch was responsible for creating and disseminating "black," or covert propaganda.[6]

In January 1943, during one of his several reorganizations of OSS, Donovan established the post of Deputy Director, Psychological Warfare Operations (PWO) to supervise the activities of both the Special Operations (SO) and Morale Operations branches. In May 1943, he organized a third branch, the Operational Group (OG) Command, to direct guerrilla warfare, and placed it under the Deputy Director, PWO. Later, he simplified this title to Deputy Director, Operations, with SO, MO, and OG as subordinate branches.[7] Through all this confusion of seemingly interchangeable organizational titles and activities, Donovan, even after losing the responsibility for overt, or "white," propaganda to the Office of War Information (OWI) in March 1942, continued throughout the war to perceive a close interrelationship between psychological warfare and what in later years became known as unconventional warfare.

OSS and the Army

Although its role in strategic intelligence was important, the aspect of OSS most applicable to a discussion of unconventional warfare was "special operations," a term that covered, according to Harry Howe Ransom,

> espionage, counterintelligence in foreign nations, sabotage, commando raids, guerrilla and partisan-group activity . . . various other forms of psychological warfare and underground operations. In essence, OSS assumed operational responsibility in a field previously ignored and scorned by many diplomats and military professionals.[8]

The last point is significant; OSS was not a military organization, but personnel from the military services did participate in its activities. The Army contributed the most military personnel during the war—4,097 by November 1943 and 8,360 by May 1945.[9]

As early as 10 October 1941, when he had created a "Special Activities" section in the Coordinator of Information (COI), Donovan had seriously considered the idea of special operations, including the formation of guerrilla units. He had been impressed by the organization and methods of Great Britain's Special Operations Executive (SOE). Moving quickly, by December he had proposed to the President that the United States organize "a guerrilla corps, independent and separate from the Army and Navy, and imbued with a maximum of the offensive and imaginative spirit." By early 1942 he had requested training areas from the Department of Interior and instructional personnel from the War Department. Lack of a War Department allotment, however, impeded initial recruiting efforts for the projected guerrilla groups.[10]

Predictably, the military services had misgivings about a guerrilla corps "independent and separate from the Army and Navy." During the period after Pearl Harbor, before the Joint Chiefs of Staff (JCS) had been organized, US Forces were in disarray. Furthermore, Donovan had not prepared the bureaucracy for his innovative proposal. As William R. Corson observes: "For Donovan to think, even with FDR's endorsement, that such an organization could be brought to pass in the face of the military's obvious objections was, charitably, an act of lunacy on his part."[11]

Aside from the bureaucratic sensitivities involved, many senior military leaders had serious reservations about the practicality of Donovan's ideas. Major General Strong, Army G-2, commenting on a memorandum from COI in June 1942 (by this time COI had been dissolved and Donovan was Director, OSS) on "Organization of Guerrilla Warfare Command," regarded the proposal as "essentially unsound and unproductive." Strong believed that most of the operations envisaged for such a force should be carried out by specially trained regular troops; therefore, "to squander time, men, equipment, and tonnage on special guerrilla organizations and at the same time to complicate the command and supply systems of the Army by such projects would be culpable mismanagement." Although he recognized the value of sabotage and subversive activities to military operations, Strong questioned the feasibility of directing such forces from Washington. In his opinion, guerrilla warfare, if conducted at all, was a function of regular Army task forces whose operations would "take the form of raids and are practically identical with commando operations."[12] Strong's last statement reveals a fundamental, but not uncommon, misunderstanding of the nature of guerrilla warfare.

Despite the reluctance of the military services, one benefit of placing OSS under the direction of the Joint Chiefs of Staff was the issuance of JCS 155/4D on 23 December 1942. That directive gave OSS responsibility for the organization and conduct of guerrilla warfare, and specified that

personnel employed in guerrilla warfare be limited to "organizers, fo-
menters and operational nuclei of guerrilla units."[13] Thus OSS had a
charter. While Donovan's initial ideas for a "Guerrilla Group," comprised
of 10 "Guerrilla Battalions," did not survive intact, he did ultimately create
a variety of unconventional warfare activities that depended heavily on
participation by Army personnel.

Probably the best known unconventional warfare operation in which
US Army personnel participated was that of Detachment 101 in Burma,
commanded by Colonel W. R. Peers. Detachment 101 organized and
trained native Kachin tribesmen to conduct successful guerrilla warfare
operations against the Japanese in 1943–45. One former OSS member
suggested in a conversation with the author that 101 "represented a sort of
microcosm of the entire range of OSS capabilities."[14] The Kachins, led by
101, performed a variety of unconventional warfare missions in support of
Allied conventional operations. For example, they gathered intelligence,
aided escape and evasion efforts for downed US fliers, undertook espionage
and counterespionage missions, and attacked Japanese communications
lines.[15] Almost 700 US Army officers and enlisted men contributed to 101's
operations in Northern Burma over a 3-year period. Total guerrilla
strength surpassed 10,000 by February 1945. After the completion of its
mission in Burma, Detachment 101 received the Presidential Unit Cita-
tion.[16] According to one student of OSS history, Detachment 101 performed "the most successful OSS guerrilla operations of the war."[17]

While Detachment 101 may have enjoyed the most spectacular tactical combat success, the major OSS effort during the war was directed at
France.[18] Here, US Army personnel made a significant contribution to the
three groups of OSS operational units that worked behind enemy lines in
direct support of the French Resistance. The first group consisted of 77
Americans who worked in civilian clothes as organizers of secret networks,
as radio operators, or as instructors in the use of weapons and explosives.
Thirty-three members of that group were active in France before 6 June
1944, D-day. The second group consisted of 78 Americans who were members of the "jedburgh teams," organized in Great Britain or Algiers and
parachuted into France beginning on D-day. Jedburgh teams were
composed of a British or American officer, a French officer, and a radio
operator. These teams, usually working in uniform, coordinated and legit-
imatized Maquis activities under the aegis of Supreme Headquarters,
Allied Expeditionary Force (SHAEF), obtained supplies for the resistance
groups, reported significant intelligence, and as a secondary role engaged in guerrilla warfare and attacks on German lines of retreat or
communication.[19]

The largest OSS group in France consisted of some 356 Americans who were members of OSS "Operational Groups" (OG's). All recruits for the OG's were French-speaking volunteers from US Army units, primarily infantry and engineer (for demolition experts). Medical technicians were procured from the Medical Corps, radio operators from the Signal Corps.[20] Working in uniform, these teams parachuted behind the lines after D-day to perform a variety of missions. They cut and harassed enemy communication lines; attacked vital enemy installations; organized, trained, and sustained the morale of local resistance groups; and furnished intelligence to the Allied armies. Interestingly, Donovan distinguished between the missions of Rangers and Commandos and those of the OG's, even though some aspects of their tactical operations were similar. The crucial difference in his mind was that the OG's "fitted into the pattern of OSS activities behind the enemy lines."[21]

Actually, the mission of the OG's was distinct not only from that of the Rangers and Commandos but also from that of other OSS activities. The OG Branch had been established on 4 May 1943; then, on 27 November 1944, the OG Command was activated as a separate entity within OSS. In addition to basic military training, OG recruits received specialized instruction on such subjects as foreign weapons, operation and repair of enemy vehicles, enemy espionage organizations, communications, demolitions, organization and training of civilians for guerrilla warfare, parachute jumping, and amphibious operations. Their basic function was to organize resistance groups into effective guerrilla units, equip them with weapons and supplies, and lead them into attacks against enemy targets, in concert with orders from the theater commander. As for how the concept of their mission differed from those of other Special Operations activities, an OSS general orientation booklet published in 1944 described it this way: "OG personnel activate guerrillas as military organizations to engage enemy forces. They always operate in uniform as military units and are not primarily concerned with individual acts of sabotage." Clearly, the OG's were primarily designed for guerrilla warfare, and the principles that they embodied were to significantly influence the Army's effort to develop a similar capability in later years.[22]

Another pertinent aspect of the OG concept was its basic operational unit, the section, composed of 2 officers and 13 enlisted men. Eight years later the first formal unconventional warfare unit formed in the US Army—the 10th Special Forces Group—was to adopt this same structure for its basic operational detachment. Also significant is the fact that the first commander of the 10th Special Forces Group was Colonel Aaron Bank, an Army officer who had served with OSS in France. Even the name

"Special Forces" is reminiscent of the combined headquarters formed in 1943 by OSS and SOE which in 1944 was renamed "Special Forces Headquarters" (SFHQ).[23]

"Throughout France," states the *War Report of the OSS,* "before and after D-day, SFHQ supplied, directed, and communicated with the Maquis in the largest resistance uprising in history."[24] A less enthusiastic analysis of the role of SFHQ, and in particular of OSS, was rendered by the G-2 Division, War Department General Staff (WDGS), in a "Summary of French Resistance, 6 June-31 August 1944." The opening paragraph of that summary reads as follows:

> It must be borne in mind that so-called resistance activities in France were the combination of the efforts of the local French themselves under the organization and direction of American, British, and French agents of SFHQ infiltrated from the United Kingdom and North Africa. In the majority of cases, the specific acts of sabotage were committed directly by the local French; and it is to them, for their courage and daring, that the greater portion of credit for the end results accomplished must be given. However, it is not at all out of place for OSS in general, and SO particularly, to take credit for its share in the planning and directing of the overall scheme of sabotage.[25]

Once again, this evaluation reveals more about the low regard accorded unconventional activities in general, and the OSS in particular, by many Army officers, than it does about the value of the resistance itself.

While the success of OSS and SOE efforts in France is difficult to estimate, General Eisenhower, commenting on how effectively the Maquis cut enemy lines of communication in support of the Normandy landings, stated that the French Resistance forces were worth 15 divisions to him in his invasion of the Continent.[26]

Guerrilla Warfare in the Philippines

One large unconventional warfare operation not directed by OSS, but in which US Army personnel played a key role, was the Philippine Campaign, 1941-45. When the Japanese overran the islands, several Army officers escaped to the mountains, where they established extensive intelligence networks and guerrilla forces. In Northern Luzon, Lieutenant Colonel Russell Volckmann equipped, trained, and commanded five Philippine regiments that successfully engaged the Japanese in combat both immediately before and during the landing of US forces at Lingayen in January 1945. On Mindanao, Lieutenant Colonel Wendell Fertig eventually consolidated some 37,000 guerrilla troops and held 90 percent of the island until the end of the war.[27] Both Volckmann and Fertig were to figure prominently in the activation of the Army's Special Forces in the early 1950's.

Attitudes Toward Unconventional Warfare

Near the end of World War II, President Roosevelt had foreseen the need for a permanent strategic intelligence organization for the postwar period, and asked General Donovan to give some thought to its possible structure. Replying with a "Memorandum for the President," Donovan proposed the "establishment of a central intelligence authority," which would report directly to the President, "with responsibility to frame intelligence objectives and to collect and coordinate the intelligence material required by the Executive Branch in planning and carrying out national policy and strategy." Donovan also urged the President to keep the trained, specialized personnel of OSS from being dispersed after the war so that they could contribute to this proposed organization.[28]

When someone in the Federal bureaucracy leaked a copy of Donovan's memorandum, the resultant public furor over what the *Chicago Tribune* called a proposed "Super-Spy System for Postwar New Deal" forced Roosevelt to tell Donovan that he "would wait out the storm and submit the proposal at a more propitious moment." That was in February 1945. In April the President died, and with his death the fortunes of OSS were dealt a severe blow.[29] Whereas Donovan had enjoyed the confidence of Roosevelt, Edward Hymoff charges that Truman "had no concept of OSS as an organization nor what it represented for the future of American foreign policy decisionmaking."[30]

President Truman ordered that the OSS be disbanded on 1 October 1945. One scholar has suggested that Truman was motivated

> apparently because of pressures from the armed services, the Federal Bureau of Investigation [FBI], the Department of State, and the Bureau of the Budget. Another influence was undoubtedly Mr. Truman's own apparent prejudice against cloak and dagger operations by the United States. To continue an international spying organization in peacetime seemed somehow un-American in the atmosphere of the immediate postwar period.[31]

It is instructive to dwell on this analysis for a moment. First, one must not fall into the trap of exaggerating the success of OSS unconventional warfare operations. It may be true, as one historian has suggested, that the most significant long-range work was done in strategic intelligence by the much less publicized and romanticized "college professors, lawyers, and others who worked tirelessly in the research units, in the analysis of economic objectives, and in other operational analysis and technical groups within OSS." It was these groups who contributed much data on which successful wartime operations were based, and who developed techniques useful to contemporary intelligence research and analysis.[32]

Moreover, the unconventional warfare operations of OSS actually constituted a small portion of the overall US war effort, and many OSS resistance activities were haphazard, poorly organized, and uncoordinated with overall operations. Yet, one World War II participant has written that "unconventional warfare operations (not necessarily those sponsored by OSS) during World War II reaped a substantial strategic harvest," citing as examples the accomplishments of Soviet, Yugoslav, Albanian, and French partisans in immobilizing large numbers of German and Italian divisions.[33] The point of this discussion, however, is not to judge the success or failure of OSS unconventional warfare operations, but to illustrate—as another resistance participant, Charles Thayer has done—that the first American experience with modern, sophisticated, large-scale guerrilla movements took place during World War II, and furthermore, that a civilian-led US agency, the OSS, and not the military services, stepped in to capitalize on the potential for guerrilla warfare.[34]

In providing leadership in that area, General Donovan's infant organization incurred the wrath of other governmental agencies, including the military services. Opposition to the intelligence and special operations efforts of OSS was so intense that Dr. William Langer, head of Research and Analysis, later observed that "perhaps Bill Donovan's greatest single achievement was to survive." Even after being placed under the direction of the JCS in 1942, Donovan insisted on OSS independence and freedom from subservience to any single agency or military service.[35] It was this independence of OSS that was especially resented by "the traditionalists in the armed forces," claims Edward Hymoff in *The OSS in World War II*, primarily because "they had been plagued during the war by citizens in uniform who had become officers only because they were in OSS." In addition, "even more frustrating for the military professionals were the irreverent individuals in OSS who constantly flouted both authority and standard operating procedures."[36] Hymoff himself was a member of OSS, and perhaps best typifies the attitude of many Donovan "operatives" by his statement that one of the things he liked best about the unorthodox agency was that "it was so unmilitary."[37] Donovan protected his "irreverent individualists" by reportedly often saying, "I'd rather have a young lieutenant with guts enough to disobey an order than a colonel too regimented to think and act for himself."[38]

One of the most consistent and outspoken opponents of OSS, Major General George V. Strong, Chief of Army G-2 (Intelligence), felt from the outset of COI that Donovan's organization conflicted with Army interests. Strong also argued that "Wild Bill's" independence would make him ineffective as a "team player." Later, when OSS came under the direction of the JCS and was struggling for survival, General Strong, according to Corey Ford, "refused to exercise his authority so that OSS could obtain the supplies and personnel of which it was desperately in need." In fact, 6 months passed before the JCS gave Donovan's organization any operational instructions or official directives about its responsibilities. The logjam broke only after President Roosevelt learned of the delay and told General George C. Marshall, Chairman of the JCS, to "give Bill Donovan a little elbow room to operate in."[39]

In the face of such determined opposition, Donovan survived only because of the personal backing of Roosevelt. As Stewart Alsop and Thomas Braden noted in *Sub Rosa: The OSS and American Espionage,* the major adversaries of OSS—the Army, the Navy, and the FBI—"were fully conscious of Donovan's close friendship with Roosevelt," and therefore were aware that "if it came to a showdown, the back door of the White House was always open to William J. Donovan and a special plea."[40] The parallel between Roosevelt's support of OSS and John F. Kennedy's vigorous promotion of Special Forces in the face of reluctant foot-dragging by some senior military leaders[41] will not be lost on students of special warfare history, particularly when one considers that both organizations lost influence after the deaths of the two presidents.

Although the services—particularly the Army—contributed personnel to OSS, some commanders were reluctant to use OSS teams in their areas of responsibility. Detachment 101, for example, was initially prevented from operating in Burma because General Joseph Stilwell, commander of American forces in China, Burma, and India, was "fervently prejudiced against the 'irregular' military activity proposed by OSS," and "disparaged guerrilla tactics as 'illegal action' and 'shadow boxing.'"[42] Stilwell eventually relented and later praised the contributions of 101, but General Douglas MacArthur steadfastly refused to permit OSS to operate in the South Pacific throughout the war, even when General Donovan offered a plan to support guerrilla operations in the Philippines.[43]

In addition to the personal rivalry, bureaucratic antipathy, and jealousy that were provoked by General Donovan's organization, the operations of OSS may have antagonized military leaders of the "regular" US Army who, by training and experience, were conditioned to think in terms of conventional warfare. Some of these leaders, therefore, may well have looked askance at what they considered the unorthodox and unnecessary OSS guerrilla warefare activities. Charles Thayer, in his book *Guerrilla,* claims that many general officers "harbor a deep-seated aversion to guerrillas, apparently because they fit no conventional pattern and their underhanded clandestine tactics have little in common with the military code of honor and chivalry which career soldiers . . . like to associate with their profession."[44] In another attempt to explain why so many US military leaders opposed unconventional warfare, Franklin Mark Osanka, a student of guerrilla activities, offers this more convincing rationale:

> Guerrilla warfare has not been an American forte because in most its wars . . . the United States has not had to rely upon guerrilla warfare. American experience with guerrilla warfare has been limited by the strength of American arms. The United States has been able to mobilize overwhelming economic and military power and to bring it to bear directly on the enemy, attacking him not where he was weakest but where he was strongest, because we are stronger still. American military doctrine has reflected this experience.[45]

Despite opposition from the military, however, by the end of the war OSS had developed a nucleus of officers trained and experienced in guerrilla warfare. According to Thayer, serious efforts were made to persuade the Pentagon to retain this nucleus for future war, but "these recommendations were to no avail on the ostensible ground that such 'elite' groups were incompatible with the democratic tradition."[46] While this explanation of the Pentagon's refusal may seem extreme, a respected military historian, Russell Weigley, states in his *History of the US Army* that the Army has a "long-standing suspicion of elite forces."[47] Certainly this "suspicion" may explain the Army's reluctance to create an "unconventional warfare" capability in the immediate postwar period, particularly when memories of OSS-Army rivalry were still fresh. Thayer does point out that while most of the personnel trained in guerrilla warfare were discharged, a nucleus of psychological warfare experts was retained, "largely as a result of the newly acquired respectability of this technique in the course of World War II."[48] What Thayer fails to mention is that the Army possessed its own formal staffs and units charged with the responsibility for psychological warfare. In other words, psychological warfare had an identity, however tenuous, within the Army, an identity that guerrilla warfare did not share because most of the officers and men who operated in that area were assigned to OSS—an organization certainly not considered part of the Army. At any rate, psychological warfare "survived" in the immediate post-World War II Army, although just barely, while the Pentagon apparently gave little consideration to building on the nucleus of OSS-trained officers to create a formal unconventional warfare capability.

Dissolution of OSS

Dismemberment of OSS took place quickly with President Truman's order dissolving the agency in October 1945. By this time General Donovan had retired to civilian life, and the remains of his former organization were dispersed to the unreceptive State and War Departments. Carefully trained personnel drifted away to other jobs outside Government. Portions of the Secret Intelligence and Special Operations branches joined the War Department's newly established Strategic Services Unit (SSU), which, according to Corey Ford, "was nothing more than a caretaker body formed to preside over the liquidation of the OSS espionage network." Brigadier General John Magruder, formerly assistant director of OSS, and head of SSU until February 1946, resigned in protest over the agency's continuing loss of highly trained personnel. For all practical purposes, any formal US capability for guerrilla warfare disappeared. Only a few secret intelligence and analysis personnel remained, and there was little need for their skills in the immediate postwar period.[49]

Appraisal

The only true unconventional warfare organization in the United States during World War II was the Office of Strategic Services, a civilian agency. Although a few Army officers participated in non-OSS directed guerrilla operations in the Philippines, most of the Army's experience in unconventional warfare came from providing personnel to serve with OSS. Of particular note were the OSS Operational Groups that were recruited entirely from the Army and employed extensively in Europe. In terms of organization, training, and job description, the OG's presaged the basic operational detachment adopted by the Army's 10th Special Forces Group upon its creation in 1952. Thus, for the Army the true roots of a modern unconventional warfare capability lay in its association with OSS.

Clearly, the central figure in unconventional warfare during World War II was Major General William Donovan. Edmond Taylor, a former member of COI/OSS, vividly describes in his book *Awakening From History* Donovan's vision of the potential of unconventional warfare:

> The paramilitary and guerrilla aspects of the OSS mission probably interested him more than any other. By combining unlimited nerve, Yankee ingenuity, and self-reliance, the American tradition of frontier warfare, and the most advanced twentieth-century science or technology, Donovan believed that effectively unconventional solutions could be found to almost any strategic problem. Above and beyond his other, sometimes mutually incompatible goals, Donovan, I think, hoped to demonstrate through OSS that the normally untapped reserves of individual courage and resource, and the dynamism of the individual will to win constitute the basic raw materials of victory, and that in an increasingly mechanized world, human dignity is still not only a moral but a strategic quantity.[50]

Taylor, an unabashed admirer of Donovan ("I stayed in OSS, though sometimes attached to it by nothing more tangible than the invisible presence of Donovan in my mind") offers a moving personal opinion about the general's dedication to unconventional warfare: "As far as I was concerned General Donovan's demonstration was conclusive, and it made an abiding contribution to the development of my personal outlook on the unending struggle for survival among nations and civilizations, institutions and ideologies, that we call history."[51]

Without question, Donovan inherited many of his ideas from the British. But only a man of his stature, perseverance, and personal dynamism could have successfully applied those unorthodox concepts in the face of the intense opposition and competing bureaucratic interests that marked US interagency efforts during the war. Thus, while some of the Army officers detailed to OSS were to play important roles in the creation of the 10th Special Forces in the early 1950's, Donovan must be considered the spiritual father of Army unconventional warfare.

Actually, Donovan's influence on the Army extends beyond unconventional warfare; it also embraces psychological warfare. As discussed earlier, the initial idea behind formation of the Coordinator of Information, at least as conceived by Donovan, included combining intelligence, special operations, and propaganda functions in the same agency. Indeed, his all-encompassing concept of "psychological warfare" included all the elements—and more—of what the Army was later to call "special warfare" (with the exception of counterinsurgency). Probably Donovan's greatest disappointment was losing the responsibility for open, or "white," propaganda, to the Office of War Information in 1942 when COI became OSS. Even after this setback, Donovan continued to stress throughout the war the close interrelationship of psychological warfare and special operations (unconventional warfare). It is the author's belief that this interrelationship, so firmly espoused by Donovan, influenced General McClure's ideas about combining psychological and unconventional warfare functions at both the Army Staff and the Psychological Warfare Center in the early 1950's. COI, then, can be considered a common point of origin for both unconventional and psychological warfare in modern American experience, and William Donovan can also legitimately be considered the spiritual father of a "special warfare" capability for the Army.

Looking at the Army's experience with both psychological and unconventional warfare during World War II, one is struck by the similarities of institutional responses to those two relatively new activities. To many military professionals, both were unorthodox, untried activities, heavily influenced by civilians. Together they never involved more than 10,000 Army personnel at any one time—a minor sideshow, thought many, compared to the overall "conventional" war effort. The military response to both was at times hesitant, skeptical, indifferent, and even antagonistic.

Psychological warfare, however, gradually gained greater acceptance within the Army. The crucial difference was that formal staff sections and units were developed by the Army to employ this weapon. There was still a heavy reliance on civilians, but military men were in command and made the final decisions as to its use, particularly in the virtually autonomous theaters. Thus psychological warfare acquired a measure of legitimacy within the Army and survived as a formal activity after the war.

Unconventional warfare, on the other hand, remained the province of a civilian agency, the OSS. Although Donovan's outfit relied heavily on Army personnel and was subject to JCS direction, it nonetheless remained a separate and distinct organization. The tensions created by this independent, "unconventional" posture are perhaps best described in the final portion of the *War Report of the OSS:*

> An agency engaged in secret and unorthodox activities is peculiarly susceptible to difficulties in its relations with other agencies and departments of its government. Secrecy inevitably creates a psychological attitude of distrust and suspicion on the part of others. In many instances, this attitude is aggravated by the clash with established procedures and regulations which the performance of irregular and unorthodox activities often entails.[52]

As a result of this independence, OSS—and unconventional warfare—did not gain within the Army the degree of acceptance ultimately enjoyed by psychological warfare. Lacking solid institutional roots, OSS failed to survive with the war's end. Its demise meant the disappearance of any formal US capability for unconventional warfare. Only the legacy of William Donovan and the experience of the OSS personnel who remained were left to build on for the future. Both would be drawn upon with the coming of the cold war.

IV

THE INTERWAR YEARS, PART I: PSYCHOLOGICAL WARFARE

"It is hard now to remember how menacing the Soviet encroachments appeared," wrote Ray Cline in 1976.[1] Cline, a former Deputy Director of the Central Intelligence Agency (CIA), was speaking of the 1947-48 period, during which American concerns about Soviet intentions were gathering in intensity. The situation was such that in March 1948 the Commander in Chief, European Command (EUCOM), Colonel Lucius Clay, cabled Washington: "I have felt a subtle change in Soviet attitude which I cannot define but which now gives me a feeling that it [war] may come with dramatic suddenness."[2] The Soviet Union's expansion into Eastern Europe; pressures on Greece, Turkey, and Iran; the Berlin Blockade; the fall of China to the Communists; the U.S.S.R.'s detonation of an atomic device in 1949; and the Korean war in 1950—these were just some of the developments that gradually hardened the attitudes of US policymakers and shattered American dreams of a post-World War II peace.

These attitudes emerged from what Daniel Yergin has called the "two commanding ideas of American postwar foreign policy—anti-Communism and a new doctrine of national security." The results, says Yergin, were policies that "included containment, confrontation and intervention, the methods by which US leaders have sought to make the world safe for America."[3] As our policymakers struggled to find effective means to respond to the perceived military and ideological threats, they examined ways to improve US capabilities in intelligence and psychological and unconventional warfare. The first result of this quest was the creation of the CIA, but it was also to have an impact upon the military services, particularly the Army. To understand the origins of a special warfare capability for the Army, we first must sketch the early history of the CIA, for the two are inextricably interwoven.

Creation of the CIA

Three months after he disbanded the Office of Strategic Services (OSS), President Truman on 22 January 1946 created the Central Intelligence Group (CIG)—the direct predecessor of the CIA. Truman had realized the need for a centralized body to gather and coordinate intelligence information and to eliminate friction among competing military intelligence services. By the spring of 1946, the War Department's Strategic Services Unit was transferred to CIG, giving it the remnants of an OSS clandestine collection capability. This led to the formation of the Office of Special Operations (OSO), which was responsible for espionage and counterespionage. By June 1946, CIG had a strength of approximately 1,800, of which about one-third were overseas with OSO.

With the passage of the National Security Act in July 1947, CIG became an independent department renamed the Central Intelligence Agency. The major tasks assigned to the agency were the following: (1) to advise the National Security Council (NSC) on matters related to national security, (2) to make recommendations to the NSC about the coordination of intelligence activities of the departments, (3) to correlate and evaluate intelligence and provide for its dissemination, (4) to carry out "services of common concern," and (5) "to perform such other functions and duties related to intelligence affecting the national security as the NSC from time to time direct." The CIA also assumed the previous functions of CIG— clandestine and overt collection, production of national current intelligence, and interagency coordination for national estimates.

Although the original discussions about the creation of both CIG and the CIA had focused on the problem of intelligence coordination, within a year of the 1947 act the CIA was charged with the conduct of covert psychological, political, paramilitary, and economic activities. On 14 December 1947, the National Security Council adopted NSC 4/A, which gave the CIA responsibility for covert psychological operations; on 22 December, the Special Procedures Group was set up within the CIA's Office of Special Operations to carry out psychological operations. By June 1948, NSC 10/2 had broadened that authority for covert operations to include political and economic warfare and paramilitary activities (such as sabotage and support to guerrillas). The Special Procedures Group was replaced by the Office of Special Projects, which shortly was renamed the Office of Policy Coordination (OPC). Its head was Frank Wisner, the former OSS station chief in Rumania. By the end of 1948, the CIA had a limited covert action capability.

The capability for covert action expanded as a result of the Korean war and the CIA's participation in paramilitary activities in the Far East. OPC's strength rose from 302 in 1949 to 2,812, plus 3,142 overseas contract personnel, in 1952; its budget, from $4.7 million to $82 million; and its number of overseas stations, from 7 to 47 during the same period. Another stimulus for CIA/OPC's expansion was NSC 68, issued on 14 April 1950, which called for a nonmilitary offensive against the Soviet Union, including covert economic, political, and psychological warfare to foster unrest in U.S.S.R. satellite countries. Similarly, NSC 10/5, which on 21 October 1951 had replaced NSC 10/2, again called for intensified covert action and reaffirmed the CIA's responsibility for its conduct. Finally, in August 1952, the clandestine collection and secret intelligence functions of OSO merged with the covert action capabilities of OPC. The resulting amalgamation was called the Directorate of Plans, with Frank Wisner of OPC in charge and Richard Helms from OSO as his second in command. Thus by 1953 the CIA was six times the size it had been in 1947, and the clandestine services had become by far the largest component in the agency.[4]

This brief overview has only highlighted the CIA's early history, but a few points should be emphasized. First, there was the influence of OSS. Corey Ford, Donovan's biographer, states that the CIA "was the direct outgrowth of Donovan's World War II organization, and was based on fundamental OSS principles."[5] Allen Dulles, the first civilian director of the CIA, states in his *The Craft of Intelligence* that Truman based his establishment of the CIA on the controversial recommendations offered by Donovan before Roosevelt's death in 1945, and that "much of the knowhow and some of the personnel in OSS were taken over by the Central Intelligence Agency."[6] In fact, in 1949 one-third of the CIA's personnel had previously served with OSS.[7] In its first year, however, the agency was so intelligence-oriented that people with World War II "special operations" experience were not recruited. But by the latter part of 1948, a growing number of former OSS personnel with guerrilla warfare experience had joined the intelligence agency. That influx continued throughout the 1940's, and when the Korean war began, even more former OSS personnel joined the CIA.[8]

The CIA's first years were also influenced by the preoccupation of US policymakers with the Soviet threat, a preoccupation that is difficult to exaggerate. The impetus of the cold war provided an environment of fear that fostered renewed interest in psychological and unconventional warfare. As the Senate Select Committee's report on intelligence activities states, "Decisions regarding US sponsorship of clandestine activities were gradual but consistent, spurred on by the growing concern over Soviet intentions."[9] Finally, the growth of the Office of Policy Coordination was important, for it was this part of the CIA with which the Army would have to interact most as it groped to develop its own capability for psychological and unconventional warfare.

Army Demobilization

During 1945–46, Army psychological warfare staffs and units dissipated with the general demobilization of the military establishment. To be sure, a few senior officers recommended that the Army profit from its experience in that relatively new field. In December 1945 Major General Lemnitzer urged that the Army remember its wartime lessons and develop a psychological warfare capability for the future. He also recommended that the service schools include instruction "to provide future commanders and staff officers with a general understanding and appreciation of this new weapon of warfare."[10]

General McClure, the key World War II figure in Army psychological warfare, echoed the sentiments expressed by General Lemnitzer in a letter to the Propaganda Branch, War Department, in early 1946: "I urge that a comprehensive document on the subject of psychological warfare be produced and used in the National War College and the Command and General Staff School." McClure concluded by pronouncing the following verdict: "The ignorance, among military personnel, about psychological warfare, even now, is astounding."[11] And at a higher level, the Chief of the JCS Historical Section, Major General E. F. Harding (USA), recommended in February 1946 that the JCS employ a civilian professional to write a history of World War II psychological warfare. To make his point about the necessity of such a study, Harding reminded the JCS that the Army's World War I experience in this activity had not been recorded, and argued the importance of psychological warfare in modern total war.[12] Despite these entreaties, the nation longed for prompt return to normalcy. The military services, faced with the problems of rapid demobilization, gave little attention to the relatively minor subject of psychological warfare.[13]

Some Army personnel did, of course, have grave reservations about Soviet intentions, even though the U.S.S.R. had been a major ally in war. As a Senate report on US intelligence activities states, "American military intelligence officers were among the first to perceive the changed situation."[14] In a lengthy letter written in January 1946, Major General W. G.

Wyman, the G-2 of Army Ground Forces (AGF), prefaced his views on the ideological threat, both domestic and international, posed by the U.S.S.R. with this statement: "The confusion of mind and the inconsiderate thinking of the soldiers of the Ground Forces in the United States is illustrative of similar thought which exists amongst troops of occupation and the civilian population of the United States." Alarmed about the problems associated with demobilization, he asked rhetorically, "Where is the mental penicillin that can be applied to our loose thinking to insure the wholesome thought that is so urgently needed in our country today?" Launching into a comparison of communism and democracy, he outlined several areas of the world under Soviet domination or pressure—"the tentacles of communism"—and then addressed the domestic scene: "Our troubles of the day—labor, demobilization, the discontented soldier—these things are the sores on which the vultures of communism will feed and fatten."

Having given an overview of the ills, Wyman then turned to his prescription:

> There must be some agency, some group either within or outside our national security forces, which can interest itself in these matters. There must be some weapon by which we can defend ourselves from the secret thing which is working at our vitals—this cancer of modern civilization. . . . A new government policy is desperately needed to implement the psychological effort indicated. . . . We must combat this creeping shadow which is in our midst.

General Wyman concluded his letter by urging that the War Department, "in the interest of national security," recommend to the President that:

1. Federal intelligence agencies concentrate on collecting information on activities subversive to our government at home and abroad.

2. A government agency be selected to wage a psychological war against these activities.

3. A policy be established to publicize such subversive activities and expose them to our people.[15]

This remarkable analysis vividly portrays the mood of the times. While General Wyman's views may today appear somewhat extreme, in 1946 they represented the genuine concerns and fears of a segment of American society, both in and out of uniform. A larger part of the population, however, desired peace and a return to normalcy, and it was these conflicting pressures that policymakers struggled with in the immediate postwar period. Those same conflicting pressures also affected the evolution of psychological warfare in the Army.

Psywar to Plans and Operations Division

In May 1946 the Intelligence Division, G-2, began work on a recommendation that War Department responsibility for psychological warfare be moved from G-2 to a special staff division created for this activity. However, both the Chief of Information, Major General M. S. Eddy, and the Director, Plans and Operations (P&O) Division, Major General Lauris Norstad, felt that such a special staff division was not justified in peacetime, so the recommendation was withdrawn in late June. General Norstad did express the view that his division should be responsible for the planning and policy guidance for psychological warfare, but only if the propaganda branch personnel from G-2 were transferred to him with the function.[16]

At the same time, General McClure, who was in Germany as Director, Information Control, responded to a request from Colonel D. W. Johnston, Chief, Propaganda Branch, for his recommendations about the proper place for psychological warfare agencies "within the staff structure of all appropriate echelons." Using his wartime experience as an example, McClure argued strongly that psychological warfare should not be under G-2:

> A great part of my difficulty in carrying out what I felt was my mission was with G-2. The G-2's all felt that they had a monopoly on intelligence and were reluctant in the earlier stages to give any of that intelligence to Psychological Warfare knowing that it would be broadcast or used in print.

He believed that an association of psychological warfare with G-3 would be more productive: "My greatest contacts were with G-3 and it was with the operational phases and even long-range operational plans . . . that I feel we did our best work."

McClure's clear preference, however, was for a separate, special staff section:

> I am firmly convinced that an activity as important and as ramified as Psychological Warfare is one which should have the personal attention of the Chief of Staff and that the Director of Psychological Warfare should likewise have access to the Chief of Staff and even to the Commander himself.

Here General McClure found the opportunity to promote one of his favorite themes:

> I had that relationship with the Chief of Staff and the Supreme Commander [Eisenhower] throughout the war and even then it was not as satisfactory as it should have been because of our failure in peace-time to indoctrinate Commanders and Staff Officers with the capabilities and limitations of Psychological Warfare.

He concluded by recommending again that "Psychological Warfare be a separate Staff Section reporting directly to the Chief and Deputy Chief of Staff with the closest liaison with the *G* Sections as well as with other Special Staff Sections."[17] (It was to be another four and a half years before the special staff section that McClure recommended would come to fruition on the Army Staff, and he would be its first head.)

Colonel Johnston realized that any attempt to create a special staff section for psychological warfare at that time would be futile. Nonetheless, he attempted to move the function out of the Intelligence Division. On 22 August 1946, he recommended the establishment of a "Psychological Warfare Group" under Plans and Operations (P&O) in the War Department General Staff (WDGS). Relying heavily on General McClure's arguments, Johnston emphasized that psychological warfare was "primarily operational in nature and does not fall readily within the scope of the Intelligence Division." Perhaps the most interesting aspect of Johnston's rationale for his proposed change was his belief that the new line of authority would eliminate future interference by civilians:

> In the event of a future emergency, while overall political and psychological warfare policies will stem from the White House and the State Department, the existence of a nuclear organization within the War Department possessing a complete plan for military psychological warfare and the technical means for implementation, would avoid the situation of World War II, wherein theater commanders had thrust upon them civilian agencies to conduct psychological warfare within their theaters, with resultant conflict of authority and lack of control over training standards and performance.[18]

Here again we see evidence of the resentment that many regular officers felt toward what they considered unwarranted civilian interference.

A decision on Colonel Johnston's recommendations was delayed until October, and it probably differed from what he had envisaged. The original paper had picked up some additional facets, and what the Acting Chief of

Staff approved on 3 October 1946 was a series of War Department recommendations to the State-War-Navy Coordinating Committee (SWNCC) "to give early consideration to, and make prompt recommendations concerning Psychological Warfare Policy," and to "consider informing the U.S. public of foreign subversive activities within U.S."[19] In those recommendations, particularly those concerning subversive activities, the influence of General Wyman's January letter can be seen. With regard to the initial recommendation to establish a Psychological Warfare Group in P&O, however, the decision was that certain psychological warfare operations would be moved to other divisions and agencies, but that P&O would provide overall planning and policy guidance.[20]

Some footdragging followed until, during an informal conversation on 6 November 1946 between General Hodes and General Lincoln, General Hodes agreed to take over immediately the psychological warfare functions of G-2 and to absorb its Propaganda Branch.[21] The Propaganda Branch was formally discontinued by Intelligence Division Memorandum No. 100 on 29 November 1946, and the branch personnel assigned to the Policy Section, P&O.[22] A minor era in the evolution of War Department bureaucracy thus ended. Psychological warfare, which from 1941 had been a G-2 responsibility, passed to the operations side of the house.

Actually, the responsibility for psychological warfare had been diluted in the process. While War Department Memorandum No. 575-10-1, issued on 10 January 1947, charged the Director of P&O with the responsibility for general supervision of Army psychological warfare activities, several other War Department agencies were given pieces of the pie. These included the Director of Intelligence, who retained responsibility for collection, evaluation, and interpretation of sociological and psychological information, and the analysis of foreign propaganda; the Director of Organization and Training; the Director of Service, Supply, and Procurement; the Director of Research and Development; and the Chief of Public Information.[23] Real centralization of psychological warfare activities did not occur until January 1951, when the Office of the Chief of Psychological Warfare (OCPW) was formed, with General McClure as its head.

Eisenhower and McClure

At about the time that responsibility for psychological warfare passed to P&O, some interest in the field emerged at a higher policy level. Apparently initiated by the interest of Secretary of War Robert Patterson, discussions about covert operations as a future form of war took place in SWNCC. As an offshoot, in December 1946 an SWNCC subcommittee formulated guidelines for the conduct of psychological warfare in peacetime and wartime. Then, in April 1946 an SWNCC subcommittee was formed to plan psychological warfare; in June 1947 it was renamed the Special Studies and Evaluation Subcommittee.[24]

In a memorandum dated 19 June 1947 Army Chief of Staff Eisenhower indicated to the Director of P&O his desire for the War Department "to take those steps that are necessary to keep alive the arts of psychological warfare and of cover and deception and that there should continue in being a nucleus of personnel capable of handling these arts in case an emergency arises."[25] At the same time, the former World War II Supreme Allied Commander asked his former Chief of the Psychological Warfare Division, SHAEF, for comments on the subject.

McClure emphasized in his reply that "psychological warfare must become a part of every future war plan." He lamented the dispersion of people with World War II experience, and specifically recommended that:

1. A mixed civilian-military group, on a voluntary basis, be charged with studying psychological warfare policies and practices during this war.

2. Research be undertaken, at once, into the effectiveness of PW (psychological warfare).

3. A PW Branch of the Director of Information be established.

4. A PW Reserve, of limited number, be established.

5. Training for PW be undertaken at the General Staff College and the National Defense College.[26]

In light of the strong views that he had expressed earlier about the desirability of a Special Staff section for psychological warfare, McClure's recommendation to put this function under the Chief of Information appears strange. Perhaps he had decided that such a proposal was futile because of the previous resistance to this idea shown by the War Department staff. Perhaps his post-World War II experience in information had convinced him that this was the proper course. As he explained in his memorandum to Eisenhower: "It [psychological warfare] is more than intelligence; it is more than operations . . . it *is* information—secured and disseminated to friend and enemy."[27]

Little resulted from General McClure's recommendations. According to the Director of P&O in the staff reaction requested by Eisenhower, General McClure's first two recommendations had been followed: A civilian historian, Dr. E. P. Lilly, had been employed by the JCS to write a history of psychological warfare for World War II. But the War Department staff believed that the responsibilities for psychological warfare should remain as outlined in War Department Memorandum 575-10-1, and not be a function of the Chief of Information. Nor was the establishment of a psychological warfare reserve believed practical. With regard to McClure's final recommendation, the Director of P&O, General Norstad, simply replied that the subject of psychological warfare was included in the curriculum of the National War College, the Command and General Staff College, and the Air War College.[28]

Another senior officer who was unhappy with the progress of US psychological warfare was General Wyman. He wrote to General Norstad on 14 June 1947, and, with his usual intensity, declared, "I believe that the SWNCC group that has been set up is not sufficiently powerful to accomplish the urgent national requirement in this field. Such a group must have no diverting duties to take them away from this very extensive subject which is so important to us." He went on to state that a national psychological warfare objective must be established, and that the Army needed an interim directive so that it could "bring an aggressive program to bear on appropriate objectives without further delay." He concluded by reaffirming the necessity for action at the highest level: "I am convinced that a national agency must be set up, using SWNCC perhaps, but stirred up and goaded far beyond any present concept to immediate action."[29]

In his reply, Norstad agreed on the need for a national agency, but reminded General Wyman that the overall direction and control of peacetime activities was primarily a State Department function. He informed Wyman that two officers from P&O were members of the SWNCC Subcommittee on Psychological Warfare, which was primarily a contingency planning organization that should not engage in the day-to-day business of "selling democracy." He proceeded to draw a distinction between the peacetime activity of "selling democracy," an information function, and "psychological warfare," which "should apply only to wartime or pre-belligerency and have as its frank objective the coercion as well as the provision of thought."[30] Wyman agreed with Norstad's distaste for the term "psychological warfare," but felt that there was "a great need for a synonym which could be used in peacetime that would not shock the sensibilities of a citizen of democracy."[31]

The problem was not new. During World War II, agency differences over "open," "white," or "overt," as opposed to "closed," "black," or "covert" propaganda had been a source of continuing difficulty. In fact, those differences had been one of the primary factors in the dissolution of COI and the division of psychological warfare responsibilities between OWI (overt) and OSS (covert). But this was a new kind of war—a "cold war"—in which most Americans desired peace. Many military men wanted to have nothing at all to do with psychological warfare; it was not "real soldiering." Even those who felt that psychological warfare was important were understandably perplexed about the proper role of the military in this multifaceted and unorthodox activity. The correspondence between General Norstad and General Wyman mirrored the dilemma faced by concerned professionals.

Norstad asked the Chief of Information, General Eddy, for his informal views on this sensitive subject. Eddy's reply, in a lengthy memorandum written in October 1947, provides some valuable insights. He began by concurring "in the need to undertake without delay an extensive campaign of psychological warfare, in both overt and covert phases, as a matter of national necessity to offset the effectiveness of the growing PW campaign launched against the United States by the U.S.S.R." But then he discussed the importance of carefully presenting such a campaign to the American public and the role of the military in such an effort:

> Although the success or failure of such a PW campaign will be of the most vital military concern, the political structure of the U.S. precludes making PW a military effort. In fact, the political considerations are so sensitive in this field that the whole program may be defeated at its inception—no matter who assumes the initiative—if the entire question of ways and means of broaching the subject to the President, the Congress, the people—particularly the press—is not minutely examined by the best brains available and handled with the utmost tact, finesse and discretion. Otherwise, the American people and the Congress will misunderstand and disapprove the project at the outset.

Eddy believed that covert psychological warfare would not be accepted by the American people "without a great deal of preliminary education and groundwork," and emphasized that it should be conducted "under the aegis of an agency not directly connected with the armed forces." On the other hand, the public and Congress would probably accept overt psychological warfare, but only if they were fully informed as to its need and methods. That, Eddy said, would require the voluntary cooperation of the information media. Terms such as "psychological warfare," "propaganda," and "subversion" would have to be carefully explained "so as not to arouse public indignation or fear of 'gestapo-ism' and authoritarianism in our own country." And as for the military's role in this endeavor, Eddy thought that "the entire subject should be sponsored by civilians—not members of the military establishment—both in and out of the government. Publicly recognized military participation should be limited to advice, concurrence, and such performance as may be delegated to it."[32]

General Eddy's views vividly portray the murky and politically sensitive area that was psychological warfare in the early years of the cold war. The extreme caution he advocated undoubtedly contributed to the ambivalent attitudes of many senior Army officers toward this "grey area" activity during the interwar period.

General McClure, however, was not ambivalent, and rarely missed an opportunity to press for a strong Army role in psychological warfare. Responding to a request from Eisenhower for a small number of civilian candidates for a psychological warfare reserve, McClure in early November 1947 recommended a group of eight for policy planning and outlined how they could be used. He then added:

> Although activities of this group would have to be coordinated with other armed services and with the State Department, it appears to me that the Army is privileged to take the initiative in securing U.S. Government coordination of Psychological Warfare activities since the Army is the principal implementing agency in four occupied countries and a contributing agency through its Military Attache and Military Mission systems.[33]

McClure was correct; the Army was heavily involved in civil affairs, information control, and "reorientation" activities in several occupied countries. No one was more aware of that than the former Chief of PWD/SHAEF, who had left that position after the war to become Director of Information Control in Germany, and who was, at the time of this memorandum to Eisenhower, Chief of the War Department New York Field Office, Civil Affairs Division.

One of the men recommended by McClure for the psychological warfare reserve group was William S. Paley, Chairman of the Board of the Columbia Broadcasting System. Paley came to see General Eisenhower shortly after the McClure memorandum and expressed his willingness to help in psychological warfare planning, but said he preferred to do so as a civilian consultant rather than in uniform. In a memorandum to Secretary Forrestal, Eisenhower agreed with Paley's preference "inasmuch as the sense of the discussion among interested agencies has been to the effect that civilians should control and predominate in the current organization and planning."

Thus having established his acceptance of civilian leadership in psychological warfare planning, Eisenhower then made a case for a strong role for the military in the ongoing process:

> I realize that there are high-level committees considering the subject, but it seems to me that the military must give continued impetus to the organization and realistic functioning of this important activity. Further, the Armed Services should prepare plans now involving enunciation of policy and methods applying to actual war.

The argument for a military role in psychological warfare planning made, Eisenhower tactfully suggested that the Army, and specifically his former PWD/SHAEF chief, could provide the necessary leadership:

> I do not know whether the responsibility for this planning should be referred to the JCS or to an ad hoc committee under your immediate supervision. In the latter event, I could, if you so desire, detail as the head of a combined committee, a brigadier general (Robert A. McClure) who had extensive experience in this field during the war in Europe. He was closely associated with Bill Paley and others of similar qualifications. He is therefore in a position to crystallize the experience and knowledge acquired during the past war and should facilitate the development of a workable plan for the future employment of psychological warfare under conditions of actual war.

Ever the diplomat, Eisenhower closed his memorandum to the Secretary with supreme tact: "This note has no other purpose than to express readiness to be helpful. If the matter is completely in hand through the processes of the high-level committees, my suggestions may not be pertinent."[34]

The Chief of Staff's offer was not accepted, and McClure stayed at his post in New York. Nonetheless, Eisenhower's interest in psychological warfare was evident, and it was equally evident that Robert A. McClure carried some weight with the Chief. But the Army continued to feel its way gingerly in this ambiguous and politically sensitive field.

The Army's Reaction to NSC-4

The task of delineating agency responsibilities for psychological warfare proved difficult. In early November 1947, the Secretaries of Defense, the Army, the Navy, and the Air Force determined with the JCS that all propaganda—both overt and covert—should be a function of the State Department, in consultation with the CIA and a military representative. Accordingly, President Truman assigned psychological warfare coordination to the Secretary of State on 24 November, a decision that was reversed within 3 weeks. Secretary of State George Marshall opposed taking responsibility for covert actions that might embarrass the Department and discredit US foreign policy. He favored placing covert activities outside the Department, but still subject to guidance from the Secretary of State. Similarly, the military wanted to maintain some control over covert psychological activities without assuming operational responsibility. Unwilling to risk association with covert activities, the Departments turned to the CIA.[35] The result was NSC-4, entitled "Coordination of Foreign Intelligence Information Activities," a directive that in December 1951 "empowered the Secretary of State to coordinate overseas information activities designed to counter communism," and an annex, NSC-4A, which "instructed the Director of Central Intelligence to undertake covert psychological activities in pursuit of the aim set forth in NSC-4."[36] Shortly thereafter, on 22 December, the Special Procedures Group was established within the CIA's Office of Special Operations to carry out such covert operations.[37] Thus, responsibility for covert psychological warfare was fixed, or so it appeared. But much needed to be done to define agency responsibilities for the overt side.

The Army's first reaction to NSC-4 was an attempt to get its own house in order. A study was initiated in January 1948 "to determine what steps are required to strengthen and coordinate all domestic and foreign information measures of the Department of the Army in furtherance of the attainment of U.S. national objectives in compliance with NSC-4 and existing regulations." The study discussed the "insidious and destructive" Communist propaganda that "directly threatened" U.S. national security; advocated strong counterpropaganda measures, both foreign and domestic; and declared that "inasmuch as the use of propaganda as a *weapon* of either war or peace is of fundamental concern to the Department of the Army, it is believed imperative that Army efforts in this field be coordinated and directed."

An assertive posture was taken regarding the sensitivity of psychological warfare:

The fact that the American people and Congress do not like and/or are afraid of domestic propaganda, is no excuse for us to sidestep our responsibility. The responsibility of accepting the consequence of doing nothing is far greater. The American people have proved too many times that they can "take it" if they are told why.

The study also contained a lengthy discussion of opinion surveys from World War II—a cause for concern because they indicated "a lack of psychological conditioning of the soldier's mind before going to war." Thus the wish: "If the Army could engage in 'white' propaganda for civilian consumption, it would be beneficial as prior indoctrination of the future power of Army manpower."

The study emphasized that three Army Special Staff Divisions—Civil Affairs, Public Information, and Troop Information and Education—were engaged in dissemination of "white" propaganda, but that their efforts were uncoordinated. Furthermore, there was "little or no policy guidance or general supervision from P&O Division," as specified by War Department Memorandum No. 575-10-1, issued in January 1947. Since the study was prepared by Colonel Yeaton of P&O, this last conclusion was a rather candid and surprising admission.

In any event, to remedy the situation described, the study recommended the following:

That the Chief of Information be directed to supervise all current operations of the Department of the Army in the field of information, public relations, or education which have psychological or propaganda implications.

That all "white" propaganda, domestic and foreign, implemented by the Department of the Army and disseminated by the three (3) Special Staff Divisions (Civil Affairs, Public Information and Troop Information and Education) be coordinated by the Chief of Information.

That for psychological warfare or propaganda purposes, the Chief of Information receive policy guidance from the Director of Plans and Operations Division through appropriate and continuous liaison.

The Chief of Information agreed with the recommendations, but believed strongly that P&O should coordinate the overall psychological warfare effort. He also cautioned against casting the Chief of Information in a psychological warfare/propaganda role. P&O concurred with this, but saw "no danger if handled as suggested." On 18 December 1948, the study recommendations were approved by the Secretary of the Army.[38]

As we have seen, the Army's first reaction to NSC-4 produced little in the way of far-reaching measures, but rather an attempt to improve internal coordination of psychological and information activities. Those modest steps indicated the crosscurrents of uncertainty and caution, on the one hand, and a desire to "do something" about a perceived condition of national malaise and weakness, on the other. They reflected a sense of frustration by some with the lack of strong national direction in psychological warfare, and a feeling of uncertainty about the Army's leadership role in this politically sensitive area.

Another interesting facet of the Army's action was General McClure's role. Colonel Yeaton, who prepared the study for P&O, apparently felt that it was important to note for the Chief of Staff that the paper had been presented to McClure, "who gave complete concurrence."[39] Even from his office in New York, then, General McClure continued to influence the Army's thinking on psychological warfare.

McClure's influence continued to be felt at all levels of psychological warfare. A memorandum for the new Chief of Staff, General Omar Bradley, written in March 1948 by Lieutenant General A. C. Wedemeyer (who had replaced Norstad as Director of Plans and Operations), gave some indication about McClure's stature:

> In the last war this activity [psychological warfare] was not promptly or efficiently developed. Organization and functions were accomplished under duress. During the course of the war, many men became quite proficient in this unusual, but very vital work. I believe that Brigadier General Robert A. McClure should be brought to the War Department for consultation in the premises.[40]

The followup memorandum to that paragraph by the Assistant Chief, Plans and Policy Group, P&O, confirms the key role of McClure in policy matters:

> General McClure visited Washington before and after his trip to Europe. On the occasion of each visit, he spent considerable time in Policy. He was consulted on the provision of SANACC 304/6 and his recommendations are embodied in JCS 1735. He edited and approved our psychological warfare study now in the hands of the Joint Planners.

> General McClure now feels that close liaison has been established between P&O and himself. He has been of great assistance in the past, and his opinion will be sought in the future on all major psychological warfare issues.[41]

Further evidence of McClure's stature—and his close relationship with General Wedemeyer—was a June 1948 "Dear Bob" letter from Wedemeyer, thanking General McClure for his comments on an Army pamphlet entitled "Tactical Psychological Warfare" to be used at the Ground General School at Fort Riley:

> Your constructive views make it possible to improve these training publications. I hope that we can send similar material to you in the future, in order to obtain the continued benefit of your knowledge and experiences. Furthermore, I trust that you can find time to put down on paper more of your experiences and reflections on the broader aspects of psychological warfare, because we find ourselves short of seasoned, mature Army writing in this field.[42]

Switching to a higher policy level, McClure, in a "Dear Al" letter to General Wedemeyer in July 1948, laid out in considerable detail his concerns and recommendations for psychological warfare. He began by addressing a recent conversation with General Omar Bradley, who appreciated the value of psychological warfare during wartime but apparently felt that the Army should confine itself to planning and leave overall responsibility to the State Department. McClure had some misgivings about this approach:

> I am sure few people realize that today the Department of the Army is the foremost U.S. propaganda agency of our Government. Why, and how come, would require involved explanation to the uninformed. You and I know the answers. By default, State Department has not taken over its responsibilities in this field for many reasons—particularly appropriations.

Having stated his major theme, McClure supported it by presenting a tour d'horizon of the Army's activities. The Armed Forces radio networks, the *Overseas Stars and Stripes* newspaper, the Troop Education and Information program in Europe and the Far East, the Army's "complete responsibility for the propaganda to four occupied countries," the fact that the Army controlled more worldwide radio broadcasts than the State Department, the US Military Government newspapers published in 3 foreign countries, the 50 to 75 documentary films distributed each year, the world newsreels made in 3 languages each week, the control of all US commercial films shown in occupied countries, the cultural centers established in 60 cities of the occupied areas, the magazines published for foreign distribution ("We, the Army publish five while State publishes one") and the millions of pamphlets and leaflets printed for educational purposes in 4 occupied countries—all of this, and more, prompted McClure to declare, "I should say today that the Army has five times the outlet for projection of America that State has and probably a greater audience for its propaganda."

McClure also declared that the Army should not take a head-in-the-sand attitude about these activities, because, "Call it what you may, international information, propaganda, or psychological warfare, the responsibilities still rest with us." The responsibility for directing and coordinating propaganda was in line with clearly established US Government objectives and could not be ignored, but, McClure wrote, there was "no Army or National Defense Agency doing so." McClure used his own office—which was responsible for a sizeable portion of the program in occupied areas—to illustrate the lack of central direction and coordination: "In the year I have been in charge of the New York Field Office of Civil Affairs Division there has never been a conference outside of my own office on propaganda policy." That last statement startled someone—perhaps General Wedemeyer—for the handwritten exclamation "Wow!" appears next to it.

Continuing to beat the drum, McClure acknowledged that NSC-4 was a step in the right direction, but that "a great need for unity of purpose and central direction remained." With a touch of assertive pride, McClure added: "The Army has taken a major interest in this field and should be privileged to take the lead, if necessary."

Having laid his foundation, McClure then summarized his pleas to the Director of Plans and Operations:

The whole purpose of this letter to you is to urge:

1. recognition of the responsibility of the Army;

2. an organization in being within the National Defense setup to carry on the operations which the Army has assumed;

3. an organization to plan for and further psychological warfare;

4. a study of Psychological Warfare—its capabilities and short-comings;

5. utilization of those willing, experienced civilians, who are anxious to help a future Psychological Warfare organization.

Two pages of specific recommendations followed, including one for a national organization to handle both black and white propaganda ("the present separation of black and white propaganda between State and CIA is basically unsound.") Others addressed technical research and various studies needed, psychological warfare instruction for service schools, ways to improve the Reserve program for psychological warfare officers, and, an old theme, the "indoctrination of commanders in the capabilities and limitations of propaganda in warfare."

Apologizing for a lengthy letter, McClure closed by saying that he had written a personal, rather than official, communication since "much of this is outside of the field of my official responsibility."[43]

It was, in fact, an amazing letter, particularly since it was written by a man who admitted that much of what he wrote was outside his "official responsibility." In terms of breadth, scope, and imagination, it was one of the most comprehensive personal communications on the subject of psychological warfare written by an Army officer during the interwar years.

General Wedemeyer acknowledged McClure's dedication and expertise with a thoughtful, but delayed, reply in September: "I am deeply grateful, Bob, for your fine letter and the inclosures. I realize that you are unquestionably our outstanding authority on this very important subject, psychological warfare, and feel deeply indebted for your contribution." As a sidenote, he mentioned that Frank Wisner, Director of CIA's newly created Office of Special Projects (later renamed Office of Policy Coordination), had recently asked about the possibility of McClure "joining up with his team" because he recognized that "you are perhaps the most knowledgeable and experienced officer in the game."[44] McClure did not do so, however, and there is a certain irony in this minor episode in view of the conflicts that later arose between Wisner's "team" and that of General McClure as Chief of the Army's Office of Psychological Warfare in the early 1950's.

The essence of Wedemeyer's response to McClure's main argument for recognition of the Army's responsibilities and the need for a national psychological warfare organization was that the situation was out of the Army's hands. Until the NSC decided on several proposals before it for such an organization, he replied, not much could be done about policy, nor could Army plans for psychological warfare be made firm.[45]

Actually, Wedemeyer had given the subject more thought than his response to McClure may have indicated. In early August he had written a memorandum to General Bradley, the Chief of Staff, to offer "a few of my thoughts" on psychological warfare:

> Thus far in our planning, both within the Joint Staff and in P&O Division, we have been inclined to think of psychological warfare as a means which we should develop for giving further effect to strategic plans already developed. That is, we have considered it desirable to draw up a "psychological warfare annex" to each strategic plan. I am now inclined to think that this may be an unsound approach. It restricts psychological warfare activities within the narrowed limits of the strategic operations already determined without due consideration of the psychological problem.[46]

This was an important insight. What Wedemeyer was suggesting was that psychological warfare should be integral to the strategic planning process, rather than an afterthought to those plans. The lack of understanding by senior commanders and staffs of the crucial distinction between those two approaches has historically plagued the work of psychological warfare planners. Wedemeyer's tentative recognition of this conflict represented an important doctrinal advance, but one that was not always adhered to by his successors.

With that thought as background, Wedemeyer outlined for Bradley "a new approach" that the P&O was prepared to initiate:

1. We will select a small group of experienced, forward thinking, young planners and assign them the task of developing in broad outline a war plan based on the following single war objective: to cause the people of Soviet Russia to overthrow their present totalitarian government and to render them maximum practicable assistance in this undertaking.

2. It is expected that such a plan will develop to the greatest possible extent the full capabilities of a psychological warfare approach. It may produce a radically different scheme of military operations from that contemplated under the HALFMOON concept.

3. When this plan is developed, if it appears to have sufficient merit, we will then suggest that you present it to the Joint Chiefs of Staff for joint consideration.[47]

Despite its grandiose objective, Wedemeyer's proposal offered another important insight: the importance of assessing, and perhaps acting upon, the potential psychological vulnerabilities of a society.

Bradley's response was guarded, stating that while the proposal was "a good idea," it "might be impracticable as a line of action, but on the other hand it may not." He conceded that, in any event, "it would furnish some ideas for modification of HALFMOON." There is little indication, however, that much resulted from Wedemeyer's proposal, partly because he was unable to pry away from other divisions the caliber of planners needed for the task envisaged.[48]

While not enough to satisfy some like General McClure, some work had been done in Army psychological warfare, both at the staff level and in the field. In June 1947, based on a directive from the Director of Organization and Training, WDGS, an experimental "Tactical Information Detachment" had been activated at Fort Riley, Kansas. The detachment sent teams, equipped with loudspeakers and leaflets, to participate in Army field maneuvers in the continental United States, the Caribbean area, and Hawaii. (The Tactical Information Detachment was to be the only operational psychological warfare troop unit in the US Army when the Korean war erupted in June 1950.) Studies were started by Headquarters, AGF, for a cellular combat propaganda unit to replace the mobile teams of the MRB companies used in World War II. Psychological warfare extension courses were prepared by the Army General School at Fort Riley, primarily for specialists in the Military Intelligence Reserve.[49]

In September 1948, at the Department of the Army, P&O prepared a "tentative Psychological Warfare Plan (Army)" for wartime, which included estimates of Special Staff personnel needed at theater, army, and corps levels, as well as operating personnel needed to serve tactical units down to the level of regimental combat teams. Staffing of this tentative plan followed, but in late December 1948 it was determined that "no action is required or possible since, until higher authority has determined the degree of Army responsibility in PW [psychological warfare], the degree of Army need for TO&E units cannot be determined."[50] At the end of 1948, then, the Army was still gingerly feeling its way, waiting for "higher authority" to decide the extent of its role in psychological warfare.

In early 1949 some movement to provide for national overt psychological warfare planning began. In February, the NSC agreed that an organization for the peacetime planning of overt psychological warfare should be established within the State Department and directed the NSC staff to prepare a proposed directive on the subject. The directive established an organization consisting of a director appointed by the Secretary of State, consultants from the other agencies, as well as liaison from the CIA. The organization was to be charged with planning and preparation "for the coordinated conduct of foreign and domestic information programs and overt psychological operations abroad in the event of war or threat of war as determined by the President." A similar planning function previously assigned to the SWNCC Subcommittee on Special Studies and Evaluations was to be terminated, according to the directive. While there was some disagreement among the military services about certain revisions to the proposed directive, they were resolved—at least initially—to support it in the interest of expediting the action. As General Maddocks (who had replaced General Wedemeyer as director of P&O) penned on a memorandum to the Deputy Chief of Staff for Plans and Combat Operations, General Wedemeyer: "P.S. The important underlying factor in this matter is to get started. The directive can be amended as need therefor arises, after the group starts work." [51] To this, General McClure undoubtedly would have added, "Amen!"

The Carroll Report

One reason the Army moved rather hesitantly in psychological warfare was that the Secretary of the Army, Kenneth C. Royall, was himself concerned about Army involvement in this activity. He definitely opposed any association with covert operations, stating in June 1948 that he did not want the Army "even to know anything about it." [52] However, through the combined efforts of two civilian members of his staff—Under Secretary William H. Draper and Assistant Secretary Gordon Gray—and General Wedemeyer, Royall gradually relented at least to the point of allowing more participation by the Army in overt psychological warfare.

Under Secretary Draper started the ball rolling by employing a civilian consultant, Wallace Carroll, to prepare a study about the Army's role in current psychological warfare activities. Carroll's study, forwarded to Draper on 24 February 1949, recommended that a separate "unit" be established to take charge of the Army's psychological warfare responsibilities. The "unit" would be headed by a general officer or qualified civilian, who would coordinate with the Deputy Chief of Staff for Plans and Operations (who at this time was General Wedemeyer). [53]

Apparently, Draper made the results of Carroll's study available to Secretary Royall, because in a subsequent discussion between General Wedemeyer, the Secretary, and Assistant Secretary Gray, Wedemeyer reported that "Mr. Royall has changed somewhat in his view in that he accepts that we in the Department of the Army must participate a little; in fact, it was pointed out to him by Mr. Gray that we are actually participating in Europe. Mr. Royall wants this activity under a civilian Secretary and has designated Mr. Gray to supervise same."[54]

In this report to the Chief of Staff, General Bradley, Wedemeyer stated that Gray subsequently asked him (Wedemeyer) to propose to the Secretary an organization with Gray as head, a civilian assistant for psychological warfare, and a group of 8 to 10 officers in the Plans and Operations Division. Wedemeyer concluded by reminding the Chief that "Mr. Royall is very desirous that the uniformed services should not be involved too much in psychological warfare, but he does accept certain limited responsibilities in the Department." The Deputy Chief of Staff for Plans and Operations apparently thought that even this lukewarm endorsement represented progress since Royall had told him a year earlier that "the Army would have no part in psychological warfare and he admonished me definitely not to participate in such activity."[55]

Responding promptly to Gray's request, on 17 March 1949 General Wedemeyer forwarded to Secretary Royall the following memorandum:

1. Mr. Gordon Gray asked me to discuss Psychological Warfare with Mr. Carroll, a civilian consultant, whom Mr. Draper employed to investigate realistic and minimum Army participation. Mr. Carroll prepared a study which I have analyzed carefully. Further, I talked to officers who have had experience in the psychological field.

2. Last Saturday Mr. Gray and I had a discussion concerning Army participation that would be acceptable to you, and also that would insure a realistic and yet not embarrassing role for the Army.

3. I recommend that Psychological Warfare be supervised by Mr. Gray as a responsibility of his office. A small group of officers could be located in P&O where they would coordinate with the International Group and the Strategic Planning Group of that Division of the General Staff. Mr. Gray should have a civilian assistant whose primary function would be to handle all psychological warfare matters for him and to maintain appropriate contacts with the State Department. This latter Department in the final analysis should be responsible for all Psychological Warfare matters of policy and for the coordination of Psychological Warfare activities. The Army should do nothing except with the cognizance and at the request of the State Department. I had hoped to talk to you personally about the above matter; however, the Joint Chiefs of Staff are in almost continuous session and it has not been possible to do so. Mr. Gray asked me a few days ago to express my views to you concerning this subject; hence this memo.[56]

It was a masterful example of bureaucratic persuasion. Using the recommendation of an outside civilian consultant to pry an opening in Royall's opposition, Draper, Gray, and General Wedemeyer worked together to tactfully nudge the Secretary toward accepting some increase in Army psychological warfare planning. Royall's sensitivity on the subject undoubtedly influenced the Army's ambivalence toward psychological warfare. His resistance is the one notable exception during the period of this study of an important civilian Army official who adamantly opposed Army activity in psychological warfare. Indeed, the converse was more often the case; civilian officials frequently found it necessary to prod uniformed Army leaders into a greater effort in psychological warfare. Such was to be the case with Gordon Gray, who succeeded Royall as Secretary of the Army on 20 June 1949.

Gordon Gray—Revival of Interest

Not surprisingly, the emphasis on increased Army participation in psychological warfare urged upon Royall near the end of his tenure was continued by his successor. And with this apparent upswing in interest by the Army, again the advice of Brigadier General Robert A. McClure was sought. "Dear Bob," wrote the new Director of Plans and Operations, Major General Charles L. Bolte, on 7 July 1949:

> You will recall that some time ago we talked briefly about the dissolution or disappearance of adequate planning for other measures in the field of psychological warfare, since the war. I recall that you expressed some concern over the fact that this matter was not receiving adequate, if any, attention on the part of the appropriate authorities, at least in the Military Establishment.[57]

In view of McClure's consistent criticism to that effect since the end of World War II, this last assertion suggests considerable understatement.

Bolte continued:

> I think that you will be relieved to know that the matter is being revived and that some measures are to be taken to restore us to a more adequate position. In that connection I have been asked to suggest, or secure the suggestions of, some names of possible candidates for appointment to a civilian position in the Office of the Secretary of the Army. I thought possibly you might have in mind the names of some appropriate individuals.

McClure, who by now had moved from New York to Fort Ord, California, to be the Assistant Division Commander of the 4th Infantry Division, answered Bolte promptly. Grousing about having received unexpected orders transferring him to the Northern Military District of Vancouver Barracks ("The orders gave me only one week to pack up and move which shows the consideration which the Army usually gives to the domestic side of life"), McClure nonetheless applauded the apparent resurgence of interest: "I am very pleased with the contents of your letter and to realize that the D of A [Department of the Army] is at last waking up to the importance of one of its major weapons—a weapon which can be used without repercussions of an atomic bomb category." He went on to recommend several candidates for the civilian position, providing a thumbnail sketch of each person's qualifications.[58]

McClure's letter was en route to General Bolte when, on 11 July, a meeting was held in the Secretary of the Army's office to report on the progress of psychological warfare organization within the Department of the Army. This much was clear: (1) a civilian "supervisor" for psychological warfare would be located in the Office of the Assistant Secretary, (2) a small working group for psychological warfare would be established in P&O, and (3) a nucleus of information operators would be formed in the Office of the Chief of Information.

What was not clear, however, was the relationship between the civilian "supervisor" and the team of officers in P&O. General Wedemeyer's understanding was that the civilian "should not be in a position of authority within P&O nor violate the chain of command . . . but should merely 'monitor' the PW [psychological warfare] functions of P&O along with PW functions of other components of the Department of the Army." The Secretary's understanding of the matter was quite different, as reported in Wedemeyer's memorandum for record:

> Mr. Gray stated the matter more forcefully . . . [he] specifically indicated that the civilian "supervisor" was not merely to monitor but was to take a real part in the work concerning PW and he said, in essence, "if, as things develop, we run into a difficulty six or eight or twelve months from now, and if we *do* operate we are sure to run into a difficulty sooner or later, I want to be able to say that it was not just a military matter but that it was a fool civilian mixed up in it. I am thinking this way for the protection of the military."[59]

Another interesting aspect of this meeting was the advice provided by Professor Paul Linebarger, a civilian consultant and author of a recently published book on psychological warfare. Linebarger offered his views on desirable qualifications for the civilian "supervisor," suggesting that P&O could not fulfill its psychological warfare responsibilities unless the officers designated were assigned full time and given the opportunity for travel. General Bolte, Director, P&O, was reluctant to endorse this latter suggestion, indicating, "as he had indicated from time to time at other points in the conference, that the responsibility should be written out for P&O in full but that any external attempt to freeze or commit P&O personnel or structure would be unfortunate."[60]

The 11 July meeting provides a valuable snapshot of the state of psychological warfare at the Department of the Army in mid-1949: Gordon Gray, only a month into his new office, intensely interested in psychological warfare and forcefully exerting his authority in terms of organization, yet also alert to the political sensitivity of the subject; General Wedemeyer and General Bolte, interested in the subject but wary about its effect on traditional concerns of chain of command and lines of authority, and perhaps slightly resentful of civilian influence in this field, especially when a myriad of more familiar "purely military" problems competed for their attention (for example, General Bolte's resistance to "external" pressures on him to dedicate officers solely to psychological warfare); Professor Linebarger, the civilian consultant, naturally anxious to see this specialized subject receive greater attention, and perhaps just a little impatient with the less-than-total endorsement of psychological warfare by military leaders. Such was the range of emotions and attitudes on psychological warfare, all of which combined to portray a picture of hesitancy and slow progress within the Department of the Army 11 months before the Korean war would erupt.

Because many Army leaders still considered psychological warfare a new development, such hesitancy is understandable. Even though the Army had used psychological warfare in World War II, the Director of Organization and Training in May 1949 lumped it together with atomic warfare, radiological defense, biological warfare, guided missiles, and subversive warfare as "new developments [of warfare] or modifications of previous developments." General Bolte, Director of P&O, thought it premature to parcel out responsibilities for these topics to specific General Staff agencies until their roles and uses were better understood. Instead, he recommended that all General Staff divisions designate contact officers for discussions of the developments under P&O monitorship.[61]

Further, military service schools also were giving little attention to the subject of psychological warfare. A student committee report prepared at the Armed Forces Information School, Carlisle Barracks, Pennsylvania, in June 1949 concluded that there was no course in psychological warfare at any service installation adequate to provide the necessary knowledge for an Information and Education officer.[62] The Ground General School curriculum at Fort Riley offered 9 hours of instruction, the Command and General Staff School, 1 hour; tentative and draft field manuals were being used in schools and for extension courses; no training programs for Reserves were available or planned—all of which led to the admission in a P&O memorandum on 4 October 1949 that "much remains to be done if the Army is to be ready to fulfill its operational and mobilization responsibilities in the field of psychological warfare."[63]

By early 1950, Secretary Gray was beginning to suspect the same. He decided to query the new Chief of Staff, General J. Lawton Collins (who had succeeded General Bradley in August 1949), with a memorandum on 7 February 1950:

> As you know, I am keenly interested in the prompt and effective development of psychological warfare within the Army.
>
> I should like to have a report on the status of this matter by February 15th.
>
> In this connection, I am particularly interested in what consideration has been given to psychological warfare in conjunction with the current reorganization within the General Staff.[64]

There was not much progress to report to the Secretary of the Army. The opening paragraph of "Report on the Army Psychological Warfare Program," in fact, was a classic example of the type of bureaucratic gobbledygook often used to obfuscate an issue:

> While definite progress has been made in the last six months in the development and execution of a psychological warfare program within the Army, much remains to be accomplished. The establishment of a sound, comprehensive program and the effective carrying out of the many tasks and activities under such a program includes the solution of many problems which are interrelated and the solution of which is dependent upon the sequential and systematic development and completion of the more fundamental aspects of the overall program. An effort has been made, however, to meet the higher priority requirements in all important areas of the program as developed to date.[65]

Gray undoubtedly had to reread that paragraph, and even then probably wondered exactly what he had been told. In essence, the report stated that some progress had been made in operational planning, in the preparation of draft Tables of Organization and Equipment for troop units, and in nonmateriel research. Progress had been slow, however, in staff organization for psychological warfare, doctrine and techniques, personnel and unit training, training literature and training aids, materiel, and intelligence requirements. Most of the report, in fact, discussed problem areas and actions that needed to be taken. In this last category was the expressed need for a "school center for psychological warfare at which tactical doctrine, techniques, training literature and tactical studies can be prepared." [66] The Psychological Warfare Center, created almost 2 years later at Fort Bragg, would eventually fill that void.

Probably of greatest interest to the Secretary, however, was the report's statement that an increase in organization and staff personnel for psychological warfare would shortly be recommended—of interest, no doubt, because Gray had been waiting patiently since March 1949 for progress on this matter.

Finally, the report tactfully asked the Secretary to be patient and recognize the difficulties inherent in dealing with a new function: "For an appreciable period of time, the development and execution of a psychological warfare program will be essentially a 'pioneering' effort and will depend primarily upon initiative, constant direction, and follow-up provided by the General Staff and by Plans and Operations Division in particular." [67] The North Korean invasion was only 4 months away at the time of this report, and Gordon Gray was to leave his office within a month.

"Only a Start": Prelude to Korea

If the Army Staff thought that the new Secretary of the Army would lessen the pressure for more progress in psychological warfare, they were soon disabused of that notion. On 29 May 1950, within 5 weeks of replacing Gordon Gray, Frank Pace, Jr., sent the Chief of Staff a memorandum clearly outlining his interest in the subject:

> 1. On 7 February 1950, Secretary Gray requested a report on the status of psychological warfare development within the Army with particular reference to what organizational provision had been made within the Department of the Army for the direction and development of Army capability in this field. It is my understanding

that a plan to authorize the establishment of a Psychological Warfare Branch in G-3, Operations, and to provide adequate staffing
was approved on the condition that spaces be provided from within
G-3's current personnel ceiling.

2. Like Mr. Gray, whose views on the subject of Psychological Warfare are similar to mine, I believe the prompt development of the
capabilities of the various responsible agencies and departments of
the government to execute Psychological Warfare operations under
terms of reference established by the National Security Council is
vital to the national security. The Department of the Army, of
course, has a definite responsibility for psychological warfare development insofar as it affects national security and the conduct of
military operations.

3. Please keep me advised on the progress being made in the establishment of the contemplated branch to handle this activity for the
Department of the Army and in the procurement of necessary
personnel.[68]

Some, but not much, progress had been made. Shortly after the status
report to Secretary Gray in mid-February, a study forwarded to the Chief
of Staff recommended additional personnel for both psychological warfare
and special operations, and a separate branch, designated the Subsidiary
Plans Branch, in the Plans Group, P&O, for that purpose.[69]

A requirement had been established for approximately 16 officers with
specialized qualifications in psychological warfare and special operations
for assignment to Headquarters, Department of the Army; US Army,
Europe; Army Field Forces (AFF); and to the Command and General
Staff College, with the first 5 officers to be available July 1951. The
Personnel Division (G-1) was asked to provide a civilian graduate course
in international relations to furnish supplemental background in psychological warfare and special operations for the officers selected. A job description was designed, stating that the officers selected "must have had
direct experience in, or be thoroughly familiar with, the conduct of psychological warfare or of clandestine and paramilitary operations in support of
military operations." Letters were sent to major subordinate headquarters
announcing the program.[70]

G-3, Operations (the redesignated Plans and Operations Division)
initiated a series of conferences with Headquarters, AFF, in Fort Monroe,
Virginia, to discuss delineation of responsibilities for psychological warfare. The first conference was scheduled for 29 March 1950. One of the

items G-3 proposed for discussion at this conference is worthy of note: "Preparation and conduct of specialized school courses for Psychological Warfare student personnel, and of general indoctrination courses for all students, including consideration of the desirability of establishing a 'school center' (preferably as a part of, or as a section in, an existing Army school)."[71] While agreeing that psychological warfare deserved greater emphasis, AFF pointed out that personnel and fiscal limitations presented "a perplexing problem." The Tactical Information Detachment (2 officers and approximately 20 men) represented an encouraging start, as did the psychological warfare extension courses "now nearing completion," and the limited but valuable training material assembled. "But we admit that this is only a start," wrote Major General Robert Macon, Deputy Chief, AFF, to the G-3.[72]

"Only a start" also accurately described the situation at Headquarters, Department of the Army. In answer to Secretary Pace's primary question in his 29 May memorandum, the G-3 replied that the Psychological Warfare Branch would be activated "about 1 August" if necessary personnel savings were effected as a result of an ongoing G-3 survey.[73] Fifteen months and two Secretaries of the Army after Kenneth Royall's instructions to establish such a branch, the Army Staff was still searching for the necessary personnel spaces.

Thus, four-and-a-half years after General Lemnitzer and General McClure had urged continued development of psychological warfare, the Army was ill-prepared in terms of personnel, equipment, and organization. On the eve of the Korean war, it had made "only a start" toward development of a psychological warfare capability.

V

THE INTERWAR YEARS, PART II: UNCONVENTIONAL WARFARE

If the Army's capability to conduct overt psychological warfare was meager in June 1950, its unconventional warfare capability was non-existent. It was not supposed to have such a capability in peacetime; NSC 10/2 gave the responsibility for covert paramilitary activities to the Central Intelligence Agency (CIA) in June 1948. This is not to say, however, that the Army did not consider developing such a function. It did—and the story of the Army's tentative first steps in this field during the interwar years is an important link in the decisions that ultimately led to creation of the 10th Special Forces Group in early 1952.

The Airborne Reconnaissance Units

As we have seen, the impetus for the initiation of covert activities after World War II did not originate in the Central Intelligence Group, the forerunner of the CIA. Rather, it came from Secretary of War Robert Patterson in late 1946, prompting discussion among agencies initially on the subject of psychological operations.[1] Within the Department of the Army, Patterson directed in August 1946 that a letter be sent to the Commanding General, Army Ground Forces (AGF), indicating that "airborne reconnaissance agents" were successfully employed during World War II under the supervision of the Office of Strategic Services (OSS). Since the inactivation of OSS, the letter stated, no branch in the War Department was interested in the development of "airborne recon-naissance." AGF was therefore asked to prepare a study and submit recommendations on the desirability and organization of such a unit.[2] The War Department General Staff (WDGS) received the study in February

1947. Included in the study's recommendations was a request for an experimental unit of 6 officers and 35 enlisted men. The Military Intelligence Division (MID) within WDGS recommended approval of the study, noting:

> The airborne reconnaissance units are of a special type which is essential in war time and is one of the types developed by OSS. It is essential that such a unit be maintained in peace time to develop techniques and doctrines of employment and that the knowledge of this doctrine and technique be made known by teaching in appropriate schools.[3]

Concurring with MID's recommendations, the Director of Organization and Training approved the study in April and directed the Commanding General, AGF, to develop tactics, techniques, and training for the proposed unit. A Table of Organization and Equipment (TO&E) was also to be prepared and submitted to the War Department; the necessary personnel spaces would be provided when activation of the unit was directed.[4]

Events of the next 18 months, however, showed the difficulties that a military bureaucracy faces when trying to create a new entity, especially during periods of fiscal and personnel constraints. By the middle of 1948, staff officers from Headquarters, AGF, were corresponding with Colonel Ray Peers, former commander of Detachment 101, OSS, to seek advice on organizational concepts for "the Airborne Recon Company, or as we have named it, the Ranger Group."[5] The title "Ranger Group" demonstrated the confusion that often occurred when the Army grappled with creating an "unconventional" organization, particularly one with no formal predecessors in Army history. This is borne out in Major Ernest Samussen's letter to Colonel Peers, in which he noted that "we have strayed in many respects from your recommendations. This is largely due to our efforts to make a military organization which can be composed of cells of minimum size, and is thereby capable of being made into a TO&E."[6]

The confusion over what to call the new unit reflected differing ideas about how the unit would be used. A War Department paper discussed adding one "Ranger Group" to the General Reserve Troop Basis, noting that the proposed unit would not accomplish the purpose its author (apparently a Colonel Conrad) envisaged "if approved from an OSS point of view." This was in September 1948; Army Field Forces (formerly AGF) was still working on a TO&E for the Ranger Group that was not expected to be approved before January 1949.[7]

Circulation of the proposed TO&E among the staff at Army Field Forces did not clear up the confusion. The developing unit was a hybrid organization that combined Ranger and OSS concepts; witness the proposed Ranger group mission "to organize and conduct overt and covert operations behind enemy lines thereby assuming functions formerly performed by units of the OSS." The group of approximately 115 officers and 135 enlisted men would be attached to Army groups or armies or both to perform tactical missions. Its capabilities would include conduct of sabotage and surprise attacks in the enemy's rear areas; "black" psychological warfare and propaganda; collection of information by reconnaissance and espionage; development, organization, control, and supply of resistance groups; recruitment, training, and direction of foreign civilian agents; control of captured enemy agents and assisting intelligence staffs in counterespionage; and the organization and control of escape systems in enemy-held territory.[8]

From an "OSS point of view," this organizational concept should have been unacceptable. It attempted to lump together missions and capabilities of Rangers and Commandos with those of Special Operations and Operational Group elements of OSS. It combined the tactical with the strategic. The mission statement said "OSS," but the title was "Ranger"; the mission statement also said "tactical," but the capabilities belied OSS precepts, and General Donovan himself had drawn a distinction between the missions of Rangers and Commandos and those of the OSS.

Eventually Ranger units were formed and used in Korea, but they were not the OSS-type of "unconventional warfare" organizations that Secretary of War Patterson probably had in mind when he first raised the issue in 1946. The dialogue on "Airborne Reconnaissance Units/Ranger Groups" during 1946-48 clearly showed OSS' influence on Army thinking and presaged similar discussions in the early 1950's prior to the formation of the 10th Special Forces Group.

Another example of early Army thinking on unconventional warfare was a study of special and subversive operations done in late 1947 by the Organization and Training Division, Department of the Army Staff. Its stated purpose was "to study special and subversive operations to determine the desirability of including instruction and study of such operations in the school system."[9] It considered special operations to be the activities of US troops to activate or support both resistance groups and small unit operations behind enemy lines. Secret intelligence, morale operations ("black" propaganda), and psychological warfare were not included in the study.

Relying heavily on OSS historical data, including the seven volumes of the official *War Report of the OSS*, (which had not been approved for release at that time), the study concluded that "special operations of a subversive nature" offered great potential that "no commander should ignore" in his support of wartime military operations. The study's recommendations included providing 4 to 6 hours of instruction on the subject in appropriate service schools, continued study of the capabilities and desirable organization for special operations, and the creation of a "special operations company." That last recommendation was followed by the comment that "this notion should be deferred pending receipt of recommendations from the Joint Chiefs of Staff regarding a proposal to establish a guerrilla warfare corps.[10]

JCS and NSC Activities

The JCS proposal referred to was actually a series of studies on guerrilla warfare that culminated on 17 August 1948 in JCS 1807/1, a memorandum forwarded to the Secretary of Defense. Pertinent aspects of that memorandum were as follows:

1. The United States should provide itself with the organization and the means of supporting foreign resistance movements in guerrilla warfare to the advantage of United States national security during peace and war.

2. Guerrilla warfare should be supported under policy direction of NSC.

3. Agencies for conducting guerrilla warfare can be established by adding to the CIA's special operations functions the responsibility for supporting foreign resistance movements and by authorizing the Joint Chiefs of Staff to engage in the conduct of such operations.

4. Primary interest in guerrilla warfare should be that of CIA in peacetime and NME [National Military Establishment] in wartime.

5. *A separate guerrilla warfare school and corps should not be established* [emphasis added]. Instead, NME, in coordination with State Department and CIA, should select personnel, give them necessary training in established Army schools, supplemented by courses in other military and State Department schools.

6. The trained personnel should not be permanently separated from their original service. They should be available on call for introduction into countries to organize, direct, and lead native guerrillas.[11]

The JCS was clearly backing away from the idea of establishing a "guerrilla warfare corps" within the military services. Why? Because during this same period the CIA was beginning to establish its position in the field of covert activities. Driven by the impetus of the cold war, the National Security Council in December 1947 gave the CIA responsibility for the conduct of covert psychological operations (NSC 4/A), and in May 1948 expanded that charter with NSC 10/2 to include the following:

Any covert activities related to propaganda; preventive direct action, including sabotage, antisabotage, demolition and evacuation measures; subversion against hostile states, including assistance to underground resistance movements, guerrillas and refugee liberation groups, and support of indigenous anti-Communist elements in threatened countries of the free world.[12]

To carry out these activities for the CIA, the Special Procedures Group was established in December 1947. After NSC 10/2 was issued, it was replaced by the Office of Special Projects, which was soon renamed the Office of Policy Coordination.[13] Apparent in all of these JCS and NSC actions during the late 1947-early 1948 period was a shifting of responsibility for covert activities to the CIA.

The Army Staff's reaction to this shift was cold war enthusiasm mixed with caution about jurisdictional prerogatives. For example, in a May 1948 memorandum to the Secretary of the Army about NSC 10, Plans and Operations Division (P&O) made these comments:

P&O considers that there is an urgent need for a Director of Special Studies [eventually the Office of Special Projects in NSC 10/1 and NSC 10/2] under NSC who has a directive to strengthen and extend covert operations with the objective of defeating communism in the present "cold war." A coordinated national effort can win the "war of words" by proving that our American way of life is approaching that ideal desired by all mankind. However, it is believed that the authority of this Director should not infringe on the wartime prerogatives of the Joint Chiefs of Staff concerning plans for the conduct of a war.[14]

And in a 2 June memorandum to the Secretary, P&O suggested changes to a CIA report on NSC 10 to correct portions "which appear to infringe upon the JCS responsibilities concerning training and war plans," as well as to correct "the implication that similarity in operational methods in covert intelligence activities and covert operations makes the CIA the sole agency to conduct such operations."[15] This latter point reveals a touch of resentment concerning the CIA's movement into the covert operations field.

Secretary of the Army Royall had little doubt on this subject, however. On the following day, he emphatically stated "that despite the recommendations of the Army staff, he did not want a representative of the Army to be a member of the special services group [eventually the CIA's Office of Special Projects], and further that he does not want the Army to get into covert activities or even to know anything about it."[16]

Despite Royall's reluctance, the Army provided an officer, Colonel Ivan D. Yeaton, to represent both the JCS and the Secretary of Defense to the CIA's Office of Special Projects, in accordance with NSC 10/2.1.[17] The new office was to plan and conduct covert operations "in time of peace," under the policy guidance of an operations advisory committee composed of representatives from the State and Defense Departments. Such plans and operations would be "coordinated with and acceptable to the Joint Chiefs of Staff for wartime covert operations."[18]

The NSC 10/2 directive had already assigned responsibility for covert operations to the CIA. The military services agreed to this because of their strong desire to "do something" about the perceived threat of communism and because of their reluctance to openly associate with the "dirty tricks" business. At the same time, the services, particularly the Army, sensitive to their institutional prerogatives, resisted any interpretations that would deprive them of a voice in the conduct of wartime covert operations. The planning and preparation responsibilities for such wartime activities, however, were a potential area for ambiguity and discord, as we shall see later.

Creation of the Office of Special Projects did not mean that the military ceased to think about unconventional warfare. In response to a request from the Secretary of Defense to continue examining "unconventional operations," the JCS formed an ad hoc Guerrilla Warfare Subcommittee to prepare a study on guerrilla warfare. (Interestingly, the subcommittee was part of an ad hoc Psychological Warfare Committee.) The subcommittee's study was essentially an exercise to establish those geographical areas of the world where it would be advantageous to have in place resistance movements capable of waging guerrilla warfare. The study established the following priorities: Central Europe, the Middle East, South Europe, West Europe, Scandinavia, and the Far East. The study also concluded that the JCS "should retain strategic and broad policy planning functions of guerrilla warfare" within the National Military Establishment, and that the Army "should be assigned primary responsibility for all other guerrilla warfare functions." The Navy and Air Force should have not primary but "collateral responsibilities" for this activity. Finally, a familiar theme: In time of war, the theater commanders should control guerrilla warfare within their areas.[19]

The Office of Policy Coordination

Without question, the NSC 10/2 directive was perceived as a significant escalation of US interest in the covert side of the cold war. As William R. Corson states:

> The intelligence community's reaction to the NSC's apparently unanimous endorsement and support of the "dirty tricks" authorizations was swift. In their view no holds were barred. The NSC 10/2 decision was broadly interpreted to mean that not only the President but *all* the guys on the top had said to put on the brass knuckles and go to work. As word about NSC 10/2 trickled down to the working staffs in the intelligence community, it was translated to mean that a declaration of war had been issued with equal if not more force than if the Congress had so decided.[20]

The principal agent for this increased emphasis on covert activities was to be the CIA's Office of Policy Coordination (OPC), headed by Frank G. Wisner. A lawyer by training, Wisner had served with distinction in OSS, planning and participating in a number of imaginative operations in the Balkans during World War II. At the time of his selection to head OPC, he was serving as Deputy Assistant Secretary of State for Occupied Countries. Although Wisner appeared by background, experience, and temperament to be an excellent candidate for the new post, Army intelligence leaders opposed the choice on the basis that he was "another Donovan who'll run away with the ball." Nonetheless, Secretary of State George Marshall was confident that Wisner was the right man, and Secretary of Defense Forrestal endorsed the choice.[21]

Since the growth of OPC during the years 1948-52 was to greatly influence the Army's development of its own special warfare capability, it is important to understand Wisner's view of his charter. This was outlined in detail in a memorandum dated 1 August 1949 to Colonel Yeaton of the Joint Chiefs of Staff.[22] Wisner explained the mission of OPC in the following terms:

> To plan and to execute special (covert) operations or measures which are designed to reinforce or to accomplish United States foreign policy objectives; in peacetime, to formulate and execute plans to the necessary state of readiness in order that appropriate special (covert) operations may be executed in time of war as considered necessary by competent authority; in wartime, to plan and execute such special (covert) operations or measures as may be appropriate in the discharge of the OPC mission or as directed by competent authority.

Activities of the new organization would set it apart from other governmental agencies principally through an important distinction:

> The techniques and means by which OPC attains its objectives differ from those of the Department of State and the National Military Establishment inasmuch as OPC operations are conducted in a covert or clandestine manner to the end that official United States interest or responsibility is not permitted to appear and if such interest should inadvertently appear, it can be plausibly disclaimed by this government.

Specifically, OPC was responsible for the planning and conduct of the covert and clandestine aspects of these activities:

1. Political warfare including assistance to underground resistance movements and support of indigenous anti-Communist elements in threatened countries of the free world.
2. Psychological warfare including "black" and "gray" propaganda.
3. Economic warfare.
4. Evacuation, including the paramount responsibility for escape and evasion.
5. Guerrilla and partisan-type warfare.
6. Sabotage and countersabotage.
7. Other covert operations (excluding espionage, counterespionage, and cover and deception for military operations).

Having laid out the mission and responsibilities of OPC, Wisner proceeded to argue the necessity for a "process of mutual education, collaboration and understanding" between OPC, the Department of State, and the military services concerning this "new weapon in the United States arsenal." In particular, he felt that the National Military Establishment should "provide guidance and support with respect to such escape and evasion, countersabotage, sabotage and guerrilla warfare activities *as may be undertaken during peacetime or which must be prepared during peacetime to a state of readiness for wartime execution."* [23] [Emphasis added.]

This last point is important to highlight because differences of view developed later between the Army and OPC over who was responsible for what and to what degree in both peacetime and wartime preparation. At this point, however, the field appeared to be open to the CIA/OPC, and Frank Wisner was eager for help from the military services to launch his operation.

Army Assistance to OPC

In mid-1949, Wisner asked the Army's assistance for training person-nel in guerrilla warfare, for certain logistical support, and for the nomi-nation of an Army officer to be chief of the "Guerrilla Warfare Group" of CIA; the last request was subsequently withdrawn. The Secretary of the Army authorized P&O to contact the CIA directly to determine in detail the assistance required. Lieutenant Colonel John R. Deane, Jr., P&O, was designated the Army's representative for such coordination. Later, Lieu-tenant Colonels R. A. Baker and E. E. Baker were designated for direct contact in the areas of logistics and organization and training.[24]

By November 1949, a series of conferences between representatives of the Department of the Army and the CIA had resulted in the selection of Fort Benning as a suitable location for a training course desired by the CIA. One of the CIA/OPC representatives who took part in these confer-ences was an Army lieutenant colonel who had served with Detachment 101 in Burma during World War II.[25]

The officer's former experience in OSS insured him an important role in these Army-CIA conferences. For example, in one meeting a discussion of OSS theater organizations in World War II led to agreement among participants that the most efficient operation was one in which all clandes-tine organizations were brought under one head. While not committing OPC to a position, this former Detachment 101 member said that he felt "reasonably certain" that all of these plans and projects would be done with the knowledge and approval of theater commanders. He further expressed the view that the proposed joint training endeavor would help train some military personnel in covert activities, thus making the transition of such operations to JCS control in case of war a smoother task.

On this last point, Lieutenant Colonel Deane, P&O, expressed the opinion that if the CIA came under JCS control during wartime, there was no need for the Army to organize OSS-like units in peacetime, because Army resistance operations would conflict with those of the CIA. Thus he believed that the National Military Establishment would want to insure JCS jurisdiction over the CIA during wartime; in this way the Army, by assisting the CIA in its peacetime training program, would be laying the groundwork for possible future behind-the-lines support for its tactical ground operations. The notes on these meetings show considerable agreement on these issues between Deane and the OPC representative, as well as the other participants. Indeed, the importance of these early conferences between the CIA and the Army was not only the influence of OSS experience, but also the degree of harmony that existed, harmony that would later disappear in jurisdictional squabbles.[26]

As further evidence of this cooperative attitude, the Army provided two studies on guerrilla warfare to the CIA to assist that group in preparing a training program for covert operations. The studies, prepared by Major Materrazzi and Captain West of P&O, were forwarded with a memorandum stating that the studies represented solely the individual views of the officers who prepared them. Nonetheless, the studies acknowledged the potential value of resistance operations in a future war. They also acknowledged the influence of OSS experience on those officers interested in the subject of covert operations. Further, both papers concluded that the Army should organize and train a unit in peacetime for the support of foreign resistance movements in the event of hostilities. Both studies had been prepared in early 1949, however, and with the growing prominence of the CIA in this field, they were apparently overtaken by events.[27]

The Joint Subsidiary Plans Division

The emergence of the CIA in both psychological warfare and covert operations, as well as the growing interest among the services in these activities because of increasing cold war tensions, led to the establishment of the Joint Subsidiary Plans Division (JSPD) in late 1949. The mission of this new joint agency, under the control of the JCS, was the following:

> [To] coordinate the peacetime development of psychological warfare and covert operations capabilities within the Armed Services, coordinate detailed military plans and other agencies of the government, particularly with Department of State and the Office of Policy Coordination [CIA], and, in wartime, [to] become the means by which the JCS would provide continuous direction and guidance in these specialized fields to commanders under their control.[28]

Rear Admiral Leslie C. Stevens was selected to be the first chief of the JSPD, although he had limited experience in psychological warfare and covert operations. Stevens, assisted by deputies from each of the other services, initially had a small staff of six officers. The Army concurred in his nomination.[29]

Actually, the principal impetus for establishment of the JSPD appears to have come from the CIA. In a memorandum to the Secretary of Defense in May 1949, the Director of Central Intelligence asked that a staff of service representatives be appointed to "consult with and assist CIA officers in the establishment of a para-military training program." Frank Wisner's request for unilateral assistance from the Army was part of this overall move by the CIA. The JCS considered the CIA's request and determined that a need existed for the proposed training program. Their creation of the JSPD in November 1949, they believed, also provided the staff requested by the Director of Central Intelligence, and the Chief, JSPD, was directed to effect the necessary liaison between the CIA and the National Military Establishment.[30]

The Army and Unconventional Warfare Prior to Korea

By early 1950, it was clear that the responsibility for unconventional warfare—primarily as a result of NSC 10/2—was shifting to the CIA. The intelligence agency had agreed to attach liaison officers to the staffs of unified commands to participate in planning for special operations, and the JCS staffed a message to these commands notifying them that such liaison was available if they desired it.[31] Slowly but surely, the "new kid on the block" was becoming more active, and the services appeared willing to accept him.

This is not to say that the services themselves ceased to consider the potential for unconventional warfare in the face of growing US-Soviet tensions. An excellent example of this interest was a letter from Colonel C. H. Gerhardt, G-2, Headquarters, 2d Army, Fort Meade, Maryland, to Lieutenant General Alfred M. Gruenther, Deputy Chief of Staff for Plans and Combat Operations. Gerhardt, who had just attended a conference that included General Gruenther and the Army's Chief of Staff, General Arthur Collins, indicated his concern for both psychological and unconventional warfare in this paragraph:

> Now as to the ideas: About two years back Froggy Reed of the Ordnance was out here and we got talking about new developments. He stated that there appeared to be no new developments planned in sabotage equipment and other material necessary for an underground.

> We then wrote up a short study to fit the then situation as far as doing
> something about equipment was concerned, Europe being concerned
> after being overrun by the Red Army. The stages being: first, psycho-
> logical warfare; second, an organized underground. This underground
> to be planned for now, and particularly development of equipment,
> new and streamlined explosives, radios, kits of various kinds, etc., that
> could be stockpiled—some here and some in the countries involved,
> and an organization put into being that would blossom into a re-
> sistance movement in case of invasion.[32]

When General Collins saw Gerhardt's letter, he wrote beside the cited
paragraph: "I agree that something definite should be done on a plan and
an organization." Both the Director of Logistics and the Director of Intelligence were asked to "investigate the present status of planning on the
matter and submit appropriate recommendations." The resultant status
report on covert operations summed up basically what has been discussed
in this chapter: CIA's responsibility, under NSC 10/2, for planning and
conducting covert operations in peacetime; the establishment of OPC to
implement NSC 10/2; the work of two ad hoc JCS committees to prepare
guidance to OPC in the fields of guerrilla warfare and escape and evasion;
the creation of the JSPD to insure "the effective discharge of the responsibilities of the Joint Chiefs of Staff for psychological warfare and
covert operations"; and the Secretary of the Army's approval on 28 July
1949 of the provision of unilateral assistance to OPC in the field of guerrilla
warfare.[33]

The draft reply to Gerhardt's letter left out much of the sensitive
material contained in the status reports prepared by the Army Staff. Nonetheless, the paragraph dealing with covert operations was significant:

> We have been active on the Joint and Service levels for sometime now
> in the field of resistance movements and other allied covert operations.
> We are convinced that the utilization of indigenous manpower in
> covert operations is an important and very necessary adjunct to con-
> ventional type operations. We feel that we are making progress in
> these matters but, of course, we must proceed with considerable
> caution.[34]

That statement typifies the Army's attitude toward unconventional
warfare during the interwar years. Prompted by Secretary of War Robert
Patterson, the Army began considering the possibilities for a covert operations capability patterned after OSS units as early as 1946, prior to the
establishment of the CIA and OPC. This interest was fueled by a growing
suspicion of Soviet intentions, but constrained by recognition of the politi-

cal sensitivity of such a capability during peacetime. Thus it was almost with a sense of relief that the services, and particularly the Army, welcomed the emergence of CIA/OPC to take the primary responsibility for covert operations. During a period of personnel and fiscal constraints, this allowed the Army to concentrate on the "conventional type operations" with which it was more comfortable. Nonetheless, the Army could not entirely evade some responsibility for the embryonic development of an unconventional warfare capability. Thus it agreed to assist OPC in its initial organization and training efforts. In fact, the evidence suggests that some Army leaders saw limited cooperation with CIA/OPC as in their enlightened self-interests; that is, an opportunity to preserve some influence during a period when institutional prerogatives and jurisdictional boundaries in a new field were in a process of flux. At any rate, the Army's attitude toward unconventional warfare during the interwar years was ambivalent. Limited though it was, however, the Army's activity in this field—particularly the doctrinal confusion that marked its tentative thinking on unconventional warfare and its early interaction with the CIA/OPC—is important for a full understanding of the subsequent developments that contributed to the creation of Special Forces. The first of these developments was the outbreak of war in Korea.

VI

KOREA AND THE OFFICE
OF THE CHIEF
OF PSYCHOLOGICAL WARFARE

A little over 2 years after North Korean armed forces crossed the 38th parallel, the US Army in May 1952 established the Psychological Warfare Center at Fort Bragg, North Carolina. This institution encompassed a school for both psychological operations and Special Forces training, operational psychological warfare units, and the first formal unconventional warfare force in Army history—the 10th Special Forces Group. We have seen that while basic planning took place during the post-World War II years, the Army's capability to conduct overt psychological warfare was minimal in June 1950. Similarly, while embryonic thinking on unconventional warfare took place within the Army during the interwar years, at the time of the outbreak of war in Korea primary responsibility for that activity had shifted to the CIA/OPC, or so it appeared. Thus, an examination of the period between June 1950 and May 1952 is crucial to understanding the Army's unprecedented decision to establish a center in which capabilities for both psychological and unconventional warfare would be combined at Fort Bragg. This chapter examines the impact of the Korean war on those decisions.

Impetus for a Psywar Division at Department of the Army

When the North Korean invasion began on 22 June 1950, a small Special Projects Branch existed in the G-2 Division of Headquarters (HQ), Far East Command (FECOM), that was charged with the responsibility for developing strategic and tactical warfare plans. This branch, headed by a civilian, J. Woodall Greene (who had been in the Far East since 1943), was initially confined to radio broadcasting from Japan and to leaflet airdrops, both of which began by 29 June. Its personnel shortages were partially overcome by augmentation from local State Department Information Service personnel. The Department of the Army, of course, was unable to furnish adequate support, due to shortages in trained personnel, units, and suitable equipment.[1]

The situation was such that by 5 June, Secretary of the Army Frank Pace, Jr.—who, it will be remembered, had been prodding the Army Staff to get its psychological warfare house in order—showed his concern with a memorandum for the Chief of Staff:

> Events of the current Korean situation further confirm my views on the need for a Psychological Warfare organization in the Department of the Army. Please let me have a report on this matter showing action taken or being taken and, as well, such recommendations as you deem appropriate at this time.[2]

The Secretary was told that action had been taken to activate a branch of 10 officers within the G-3 Division on 31 July 1950 to provide General Staff supervision of all psychological warfare and special operations activities. Additionally, a study to determine how to provide for a nucleus of personnel trained in psychological warfare was in progress.[3] It is interesting that the Army planned to combine psychological warfare and special operations activities in the proposed branch. Even with the CIA/OPC's growing prominence in special operations, the Army apparently wanted to at least keep its hand in the game.

Understandably, Secretary Pace was becoming impatient with the glacier-like movement of the Army bureaucracy on a subject of personal concern to him. Perhaps the most candid analysis of the Army's sluggishness was made in mid-July 1950 by a young staff officer in the G-3 Division:

> With the transfer of primary responsibility of Psychological Warfare from G-2 to G-3 in January 1947, the activity reverted basically to a planning function insofar as the Department of the Army was concerned. Being largely a planning function, the activity consisted mainly of actions on highly classified matters which seldom came to the attention of other General Staff Divisions and the Technical Services. Consequently, because of the relative newness of the activity and because of the high classification placed upon it, a general lack of information gradually developed outside of G-3 (P&O) concerning

Psychological Warfare. The low priority placed on this activity within G-3 in 1948, plus the return to inactive duty of most experienced Psychological Warfare officers, tended to accelerate this condition.[4]

The officer went on to state that with the outbreak of war in Korea, the Army again had an interest in psychological warfare operations. He thus recommended that the responsibilities for that field be more clearly delineated among the General Staff, the Technical Services, and the Chief of Army Field Forces.[5]

Within a month of this assessment, that old World War II psychological warrior, Brigadier General Robert McClure, reentered the scene. In a "Dear Al" letter to Lieutenant General Albert Wedemeyer (who had recently moved from his Pentagon assignment to become Commanding General of the 6th Army, with headquarters in San Francisco), Major General Charles Bolte, the G-3, wrote that the Army's program for psychological warfare was under review to determine "the further organizational steps necessary to meet the operational requirements of the Korean situation or of a general war." He further indicated that the Army's responsibilities in this field were such that the possibility of a permanent staff agency, "preferably in the form of a Special Staff Division," should be considered for the Department of the Army. To develop specific recommendations on psychological warfare organization for the Chief of Staff, Bolte requested the presence of McClure (who was assigned to General Wedemeyer) for a few days because "I know of no one better qualified to assist us in that respect."[6] In less than 2 weeks, Bolte received this message from McClure: "Will report to you for TDY 29 August."[7] Help was on the way.

Despite these steps, by the end of August the Secretary of the Army's patience with the apparent lack of progress in psychological warfare organization came to an end. His displeasure, plainly evident in a memorandum to the Chief of Staff, General Collins, is quoted in its entirety:

1. I have been following the progress of the development of a psychological warfare program within the Department of the Army with considerable concern. I am not at all satisfied that we are giving this matter attention and support commensurate with the capabilities of psychological warfare as a military weapon and an instrument of national policy.

2. The discussion of the Army Policy Council meetings of 15 and 16 August and my own review of the Army's effort in this field have indicated that the principal difficulty for well over a year has been

organization and manpower. Although I am aware of the high caliber of work which has been performed, it is of particular concern to me that a psychological warfare organization which Mr. Gray approved in July 1949 has through delay in its establishment cost the Army the services of these spaces which for the past year could have been utilized in developing the Army program to a more comprehensive degree. Nor do I believe that with the establishment of a psychological warfare branch as of 1 August we have in fact assured ourselves of accomplishing desired results, if in so doing we are forced to rely on the Korean crisis to secure temporary spaces to meet personnel requirements for a unit which was not designed or intended to operate under wartime conditions.

3. The establishment of a psychological warfare organization within the Department of the Army indicates recognition of the importance of this activity in military science. Adequate allowance should therefore be made in the appropriate personnel ceilings to afford this field the permanent spaces it requires. I do not believe an organization which has necessitated so many studies and taken so long to set up should owe its final establishment and complement of personnel to an emergency which may well warrant an entirely different type staff unit.

4. I therefore desire that such spaces as have been allocated to psychological warfare on a temporary basis be established on a permanent basis and that the nomination of suitable personnel to bring the recently established psychological warfare branch to required strength be expedited.

5. I have asked Assistant Secretary Earl Johnson to give this matter of manpower for psychological warfare his personal attention.[8]

This letter is important in several respects, First, the blunt tone of Pace's memorandum—unusually so for correspondence between a Secretary of the Army and the Chief of Staff—vividly demonstrates his exasperation with what he saw as footdragging by the Army on a subject he considered vitally important. Second, the memorandum reveals Pace's desire to have the necessary permanent organization in place during peacetime, rather than rely on a crisis-imposed response to the problem. Finally, the memorandum is further evidence of a theme that we have seen throughout this study—the pressure brought to bear by civilian leaders on an Army somewhat reluctant to grapple with activities of an "unconventional" nature.

What Secretary Pace, and his predecessors, were perhaps less sensitive to, however, were the genuine difficulties that personnel and fiscal constraints posed for Army leaders. Most were men who had advanced in a system that gave highest priority to the "conventional," or "regular" units—in infantry, armor, and artillery—associated with combat arms. Even those senior officers who displayed interest in psychological and unconventional warfare capabilities found it natural, with the exception of a few like General McClure, to give lower priority to those activities when faced with the necessity of making choices.

In any event, the Army Staff, as a result of Secretary Pace's prodding and other current actions, struggled in the face of a deteriorating combat situation in Korea to improve its psychological warfare organization. Ironically, on the same day that Pace's blistering memorandum was signed, General Bolte, the G-3, reported in a meeting in the Army's General Council that McClure had arrived in Washington to advise and assist in preparation of recommendations to the Chief of Staff on several important aspects of psychological warfare, including the possibility of a special staff division at the Department of the Army, operations in FECOM, and adequate preparatory measures in the European command (EUCOM).[9]

On the following day, 31 August, General Bolte forwarded a recommendation to the Chief of Staff for immediate activation of the Psychological Warfare Division, Special Staff, stating that "a review of present organizational arrangements indicates that the Army is not prepared to meet its Psychological Warfare obligations," which had greatly increased because of growing cold war tensions and the Korean conflict. The organizational concept and proposed strength of 102 personnel for the new division were quickly approved by the Vice Chief of Staff on 1 September 1950.[10]

McClure obviously had a hand in these moves, because during the period 28 August to 3 September he held conferences with all the Deputy Chiefs of Staff; the Vice Chief of Staff; Secretary Pace; the Assistant Secretary of State, Public Affairs; and members of the Joint Staff. At the 13 September meeting of the General Council, General Bolte reported that General McClure fully supported his proposal to establish a psychological warfare division, and that approval for it had been obtained. To effect an orderly transition, the Subsidiary Plans Branch of G-3 would be expanded to take care of psychological warfare planning. Later the activity would be transferred from G-3 to the new division, after final approval about its functions and acquisition of sufficient personnel.[11]

Creation of the Office of the Chief of Psychological Warfare

Despite the sense of urgency, creation of the new division did not occur overnight. First, there was the problem of getting authorization for the permanent allocation of the additional personnel needed. A more serious difficulty was procuring the necessary personnel trained in the specialized skills of psychological warfare. Since there was no basic course in psychological warfare available within the Army—indeed, within any of the services—the G–3 requested that a minimum of 6 officers attend a 13-week course on the subject proposed by Georgetown University and scheduled to begin on 2 October. Admittedly, this was a stopgap measure that would not adequately meet the Army's overall requirement for trained officers.[12]

There were, in fact, only seven officers qualified in psychological warfare on active duty in 1950. One of these, Lieutenant Colonel John O. Weaver, was recruited by the Chief, AFF, to become chief of a proposed psychological warfare department in the Army General School at Fort Riley, Kansas. Weaver had served as commanding officer of the combat propaganda team of the 5th Army in Italy during World War II and was a graduate of the British psychological warfare school in Cairo. Brigadier General Robert McClure, in his new position as Chief, Psychological Warfare Division (an obvious choice!), forwarded the request for Weaver's assignment to the Adjutant General. Weaver was ordered to report to Fort Riley by December 1950.[13]

On 31 October, General McClure held his first weekly staff meeting with personnel of his embryonic division. The minutes from this meeting give us valuable insights into McClure's philosophy about psychological warfare and unconventional warfare. First, he stated that he had "backing from the top down" for psychological warfare, and that the division would be granted a considerable number of personnel. But then he issued a warning: "As a general policy, all officers assigned to this work should watch their step as there is an opinion prevalent among individuals not conversant with psychological warfare that anyone connected with the function is a 'long-haired, starry-eyed' individual." Such a pessimistic note at the outset must have been disquieting to the assembled officers, particularly to those who were ambitious. The statement was a commentary on the Army's attitude toward psychological warfare, or at least its attitude as perceived by a "true believer" like General McClure. He hastened to add however, "I think that there is nothing that is not ninety percent common sense," a rather pragmatic approach, perhaps to quell the apprehensions of his new subordinates.[14]

McClure further stated that General Bolte agreed with him that unconventional warfare did not belong in G–3 and should be transferred to the Psychological Warfare Division. The Division, expanded from the Subsidiary Plans Branch, had not yet formally become a separate Special Staff division and therefore was still under the G–3. McClure felt that his new organization could be entitled "psychological warfare" and contain three subdivisions: psychological warfare, cover and deception, and unconventional warfare.[15] We see here not only evidence of McClure's early feelings about the marriage of psychological and unconventional warfare, but also his tendency to give psychological warfare a relatively higher priority. That attitude on his part undoubtedly would influence the subsequent co-location of psychological and unconventional warfare units at Fort Bragg in 1952, and the selection of the title, Psychological Warfare Center.

Finally, on 15 January 1951, the Office of the Chief of Psychological Warfare (OCPW) became officially recognized—but not without difficulty, as expressed in a letter by McClure to Major General Daniel Noce, Chief of Staff, EUCOM, on that same day:

> Orders have been issued effective today, separating this Division from G–3 and setting it up as a Special Staff division. With most of the stops pulled out, it has still taken us four months to get the administrative responsibility from G–3. Even in time of grave emergency the Pentagon moves slowly.[16]

Secretary of the Army Pace would have agreed with that note of exasperation. Nonetheless, a new organization, the first of its type in Army Staff history, had been born. Psychological warfare had evolved from a small section within a branch of G–3 to an office at Special Staff level with direct access to the Chief of Staff.

By early February, McClure had briefed the General Council on the organization and function of OCPW and explained the need for a rapid organization of unconventional warfare. At this point his views on the organization of his new division were firm. Since the division had been recognized and published in orders, he wanted an amendment authorizing special operations activities, and he envisaged three divisions: propaganda, unconventional warfare, and support.[17]

As stated in the special regulation that later outlined its organization and functions, the mission of OCPW was to "formulate and develop psychological and special operations plans for the Army in consonance with established policy and to recommend policies for and supervise the execution of Department of the Army programs in those fields." To carry out this mission, the office was organized into three major divisions: Psychological Operations, Requirements, and Special Operations. Although the thrust of the organization was on psychological warfare, the words "and special operations" in the preceding mission statement and the existence of the Special Operations Division are highly significant because it was in this division that plans for creation of the Army's first formal unconventional warfare capability were formulated. Both the Psychological Operations and Special Operations Divisions were subdivided into branches for plans, operations, and intelligence and evaluation, while the Requirements Division was primarily concerned with organization, personnel, training, logistics, and research needs to support both psychological and special operations activities.[18]

Clearly, the two major concerns of this unprecedented Army Staff office were psychological and unconventional warfare (or "special operations," as the latter was called at this time). Over the next 16 months—a period of frenetic, diverse activity for General McClure and his staff—plans, policies, and decisions made in the Office of the Chief of Psychological Warfare were instrumental in the Army's decisions to establish the Psychological Warfare Center at Fort Bragg, to create the 10th Special Forces Group, and finally, to co-locate the two capabilities of psychological and unconventional warfare at this new center. To fully understand why these decisions were made, we must examine these two capabilities in Korea, as seen from the perspective of OCPW and particularly from that of General McClure.

OCPW and Psychological Warfare in Korea

Shortly after the formal establishment of OCPW, Secretary of the Army Pace reentered the fray to give McClure's embryonic program a well-timed boost of support. In another of his by now well-known memorandums to the Chief of Staff on psychological warfare, Pace referred to OCPW (one can almost sense a between-the-lines "and it's about time!"), then unequivocally presented his views on the subject:

> I am keenly interested in and concerned over the successful development and progress of the psychological warfare program. Its vital importance to national security and defense in the present emergency must be fully recognized by all responsible commanders and staffs throughout the Army.[19]

McClure could have asked for no better entree in the struggle for recognition and influence that any new organization in a bureaucracy experiences. But the Secretary went even further; he also put in a special word for the special operations part of McClure's office. Referring again to OCPW's organization, he stressed that theater commanders should use it as a model to put their own staffs on a sound basis:

> Such a basis should envisage the supervision of a *combination of propaganda and unconventional warfare activities* by staff organizations that will provide for effective integration of those activities in such a way as to insure full support of combat operations now being conducted or contemplated and planned for the future.[20]

Since Pace heretofore had not mentioned unconventional warfare in his prodding of the Chief of Staff, and since he referred in this same memorandum to a recent discussion with the Chief of Psychological Warfare and members of the Army Policy Council, one could conclude that the Secretary's apparent endorsement of combining psychological and unconventional warfare planning functions was influenced at least in part by General McClure's views. The philosophy expressed by Pace's memorandum is significant, for McClure carried it forward in his relationships with the Far East and European theater commands and his attempts to influence their staff organizations, and with Headquarters, AFF, in the US—culminating in the co-location of psychological and unconventional warfare schooling and capabilities under the Psychological Warfare Center established at Fort Bragg in May 1952.

The "present emergency" that Secretary Pace had referred to in his memorandum was, of course, the war in Korea, which had worsened with heightening cold war tensions with the People's Republic of China and the Soviet Union. But Pace believed that the Korean situation offered an "especial opportunity for highly profitable exploitation" of psychological warfare.[21] Indeed, a key feature of this period was the intense personal interest in the psychological warfare aspects of the conflict shown by the Secretary, an interest that was of great help to General McClure.

Examples of the Secretary's preoccupation with the subject are found in his numerous conversations with General McClure and frequent communications with the Commander in Chief, Far East Command (CINCFE), General Matthew B. Ridgeway. In early May 1951, Pace called McClure into his office, reiterated his "keen interest" in psychological warfare, and said that "quality rather than quantity" should be the measure of success in using this tool. He told McClure that he had discussed psychological warfare with General Ridgeway and expressed his wish for an all out-effort in the field. Pace offered to help McClure with his attempts to get the Air Force to furnish a special squadron of aircraft for psychological and unconventional warfare purposes, and concluded the conference by asking the General to keep him informed of activities in the field and to seek his assistance if any problem developed.[22] Later the same month, the Secretary called McClure to ask whether the Army was prepared for psychological warfare activities "should the military success of the U.N. [United Nations] forces result in routing of the Reds." He also wanted to know if McClure was satisfied with FECOM's performance in psychological warfare, and restated his interest in quality rather than quantity concerning production of leaflets and radio broadcasts.[23] By the end of May, Pace was convinced that the time had come for the maximum use of psychological warfare in Korea, and conveyed his "great personal interest in the matter" to General Ridgeway.[24]

Ridgeway's reply to Pace captures the state of psychological warfare activities in Korea at that time. He stated his plan to materially expand the psychological warfare effort in support of military operations, and indicated that current leaflet operations gave priority to tactical leaflets, "whose themes can be varied on short notice to adjust propaganda emphasis to fit different battle situations." The broad themes used for the tactical operations included good treatment of prisoners, U.N. materiel superiority, and mounting enemy casualty figures. Strategic propaganda efforts included newssheets, troop leaflets designed to depress morale and increase susceptibility to forthcoming tactical propaganda, and civilian leaflets designed to arouse anti-Chinese and anti-Soviet feeling. Plans were underway to double the weekly leaflet effort of approximately 13 million leaflets. Radio broadcasts, totaling 13 hours daily in the Korean language, would be augmented by shortwave broadcasts in Chinese to reach Chinese troops in Korea as well as Chinese civilians and troops in Manchuria. While it was too early to determine how influential psychological warfare had been in the recent heavy increase in the number of enemy prisoners taken, "preliminary interrogations indicate considerable effectiveness, both by leaflets and by loudspeakers." Ridgeway concluded by stating his belief that regular psychological warfare guidance from Washington was of "considerable importance," since activities were "an integral part of the worldwide US effort in this field and should be closely geared to activities in other areas, especially in the Far East."[25]

Pace seized upon Ridgeway's last point. During meetings with members of the Army Staff, he frequently stressed his endorsement of psychological warfare and urged the members to give it their full support. He believed that it was not receiving sufficient attention, and considered it the "cheapest form of warfare." He emphasized that psychological warfare had to be conducted within the framework of national policy and that the situation during negotiations in Korea illustrated that point. Explaining that he felt a responsibility to "do something" to insure that necessary high-level Government policy views on the subject were prepared and properly coordinated with field psychological warfare, he directed General McClure to prepare a memorandum stating "what he as Secretary of the Army should do" in this matter.[26]

General Ridgeway followed up his desire for "more positive and definitive policy guidance" on psychological warfare in a cable to Pace in August 1951. He also asked for help in providing a few qualified personnel for a psychological warfare planning group in FECOM, adding an interesting note concerning the qualities he most desired in those personnel: "I personally rate integrity and intellectual capacity above experience, for the latter without both of the former is a liability, not an assest."[27]

Pace's "Personal for Ridgeway" reply again demonstrated his interest in this specialized field: "Psychological warfare can and must become one of our most effective weapons in combatting communism. I am anxious to take whatever steps I can to achieve this end." Pace indicated that the recently established Psychological Strategy Board (PSB), headed by Gordon Gray, should be able to provide the national policy guidance needed, and that "every effort is being exerted to make the board fully operational at the earliest possible date."[28] As directed by President Truman, the PSB was created to provide more effective planning of psychological operations within the framework of approved national policies, and to coordinate the psychological operations of all governmental departments and agencies.

The Secretary's attempts to influence the situation in Korea went beyond these communications with FECOM. He sent a copy of Ridgeway's cable to Gordon Gray, together with his reply. McClure also forwarded copies of the same message to the JCS, urging them to emphasize to the PSB that General Ridgeway's request for high-level policy guidance be included "among the foremost of the Board's priority operational matters."[29]

Secretary Pace's intense interest in psychological warfare influenced the attitudes and decisions of key decisionmakers in the Far East Command. Moreover, his enthusiasm for the subject aided General McClure in his endeavors to carve out a niche for OCPW within the Washington bureaucracy. McClure was to make valuable use of the Secretary's sponsorship of psychological warfare, particularly in his relations with FECOM.

General McClure's attitude toward the Far East Command's conduct of psychological warfare activities was mixed. On the one hand, he often expressed satisfaction with FECOM's progress in this area, publicly complimented its efforts, and enthusiastically attempted to give it assistance. On the other hand, he was privately critical of psychological warfare operations in the Far East and felt that FECOM was not willing to accept the help offered. Undeterred, however, he intended "to put pressure on them to let us help them."[30]

McClure's primary concern was with FECOM's organization for psychological warfare. Initially, the responsibility for psychological warfare resided in the G-2 Division of Headquarters, FECOM. Reflecting his own World War II experience in establishing PWD/SHAEF and, more recently, OCPW, McClure believed that a special staff division combining both psychological and unconventional warfare functions would enhance its stature and facilitate operations. Thus, he urged in letters, reports, and visits that this step be taken. He also recommended that the 1st Radio Broadcasting and Leaflet (RB&L) Group become the theater operating agency for psychological warfare when it arrived from the United States later in 1951.[31] At this point, in early 1951, the only US psychological warfare unit that the Department of the Army had been able to provide to FECOM was the Tactical Information Detachment, a small unit of a little over 20 personnel.

When the North Koreans attacked South Korea in June 1950, the Tactical Information Detachment—organized at Fort Riley, Kansas, in 1947—was the only operational psychological warfare troop unit in the U.S. Army. Sent to Korea in the fall of 1950, it was reorganized as the 1st Loudspeaker and Leaflet (L&L) Company, and served as the 8th Army's tactical propaganda unit throughout the conflict.[32] Tactical propaganda, sometimes called combat propaganda, was directed at a specific audience in the forward battle areas and in support of localized operations.[33] Mobile loudspeakers mounted on vehicles and aircraft became a primary means of conducting tactical propaganda in Korea. One noteworthy example was the use of a loudspeaker mounted on a C-47 aircraft that in 1951 circled over 1,800 Chinese Communist troops and induced them to surrender.[34]

As early as 1947, while there was no real military psychological organization in being, a small planning staff—a Psychological Warfare Section (PWS)—had been created in the General Headquarters (GHQ) of FECOM. Although PWS had no field operating units, with hasty augmentation it did begin using leaflets and radio 2 days after the invasion. Obviously, PWS could not efficiently support full-scale strategic operations, so the 1st Radio Broadcasting and Leaflet (RB&L) Group was organized at Fort Riley and shipped to Korea in July 1951.

The 1st RB&L Group was specifically designed to conduct strategic propaganda in direct support of military operations.[35] Strategic propaganda was intended to further long-term strategic aims, and was directed at enemy forces, populations, or enemy-occupied areas.[36] To accomplish these tasks the 1st RB&L Group had the equipment and capability to produce newspapers and leaflets, and to augment or replace other means of broadcasting radio propaganda. The group supervised a radio station network known as the Voice of the United Nations, and often produced more than 200 million propaganda leaflets a week that were disseminated by aircraft or by specially designed artillery shells.[37] The leaflets expressed various themes. Some, for example, offered inducements for enemy soldiers to surrender; others were intended to bolster the morale of Korean civilians by proclaiming U.N. support.

Although the RB&L group was a concept accelerated to meet the requirements of the Korean conflict (plans were initiated by G-3, Department of the Army, in early 1950), it performed functions similar to those deemed necessary to the conduct of psychological warfare in World War II. Its Mobile Radio Broadcasting (MRB) Company bore a direct ancestral linkage with the mobile radio broadcasting companies formed under PWD/SHAEF to conduct propaganda operations in North Africa and the European theater during 1944-45. In fact, the MRB companies were the basic units organized to perform tactical psychological warfare during World War II, although radio later became an essentially strategic weapon that had no place in a purely tactical psychological unit.[38] Both the strategic propaganda concept embodied in the RB&L group and the tactical propaganda idea expressed by the L&L company were to figure prominently in the psychological warfare capability subsequently formed as part of the Psychological Warfare Center in 1952.

By April 1952, when the military situation was at a stalemate along the 38th parallel, three different kinds of psychological warfare were underway in Korea. "Strategic" psychological warfare was carried out by the Psychological Warfare Section, GHQ FECOM, located in Tokyo, the section having made the transition to a special staff section as recommended by McClure. The 1st RB&L Group, whose headquarters were also in Tokyo, assisted GHQ FECOM in this endeavor. Leaflet operations blanketed North Korea with the exception of a 40-mile zone due north of the military lines; radio operations covered North and South Korea as well as parts of Manchuria and China. "Tactical" psychological warfare was directed by the Psychological Warfare Division, G–3, of HQ 8th Army, eventually located in Seoul. Assisted by the 1st L&L Company, this division directed leaflet and loudspeaker operations within 40 miles of the military line of contact. "Consolidation" propaganda was carried out by the State Department's US Information Service, based in Pusan. Its printed and visual media operations were confined to that part of Korea under the civil administration of the Republic of Korea government. Radio operations in this area were under the control of field teams of the 1st RB&L Group's Mobile Radio Broadcasting Company.[39]

Another concern of General McClure was the failure to use Korea as a profitable testing ground or laboratory. He believed that the campaign there provided great opportunity for both experimentation and testing of methods and equipment, and expressed to the Chief of Staff in August 1951 his disappointment in the results to that point. As an example of what he had in mind, McClure suggested that helicopters be equipped with noise devices for spreading terror.[40]

McClure was particularly critical of the available air support for psychological warfare in Korea and used every means at his disposal to try to improve the situation. In a "Dear Charles" letter to the G–2, GHQ FECOM, Major General Charles A. Willoughby, he unveiled his concerns:

> I only wish that aircraft were assigned for the tactical leafletting and strategic leafletting so that specific targets and timing could be given with an assurance that they would be hit. The New York Times Magazine Section two weeks ago carried a photograph of the interior of a C–47, showing a couple of harassed soldiers attempting to throw out handfuls of loose leaflets which apparently were blowing all over the interior.

Referring to his own experience in World War II, McClure continued:

> I feel that the Air Forces have fallen down badly on us in not using, at the beginning of this trouble, the techniques that we wound up with in 1945, such as: special leaflet squadrons, fibre casings for leaflet bombs (of which there are 80,000 here in the Arsenal), regular operations plans and orders, printing and delivery on call, etc. We are still putting pressures on back here but can do very little unless FEC makes this type of operation a military requirement.[41]

During his visit to FECOM in April 1951, McClure again presented his views on the subject of air support, stating that "unless aircraft demands are made operations requirements, the airdrops will continue on a catch-as-catch-can basis." The C-47, he believed, was inappropriate for leaflet drops; thus, "front line support suffers for lack of delivery by fighter bomber." He recommended that a special squadron be organized for psychological and unconventional warfare purposes.[42]

McClure pursued his basic themes at every opportunity. He told the US Air Force (USAF) Director of Operations in May that "we were using 1918 methods of dropping leaflets over front line troops and that it was both inefficient and expensive," and asked that the special air wings being organized to support CIA activities in Korea be used for psychological warfare. In June, he fired off a memorandum to the JCS recommending that discussions be initiated between the services in order to make maximum use of all tactical aircraft for the support of psychological warfare. He forcefully expressed his views to both the Chief of Staff and the Secretary of the Army, both of whom tried to influence the situation through discussions and correspondence with their counterparts in the Air Force.[43]

Writing to the Chief of Staff, FECOM, on "the question of air support for psychological warfare operations," McClure charged that in actual practice such support was arranged locally, that the theater commander was unable to obtain a specific allocation of aircraft. He observed that the "undesirability of such a haphazard arrangement was apparent in the European theater during World War II and is in great measure borne out by what I saw and covered in my report to General Ridgeway during my recent inspection of psychological warfare operations in Korea." McClure then boldly reiterated his proposal: "The solution we arrived at in Europe, and which I firmly believe is the remedy now, was to place certain specified aircraft under the operational control of the Psychological Warfare Staff of the Senior Commander." But even before doing this, such support "should be determined to be an operational requirement, and this determination should be made now, once and for all." This was rather forceful language to use in addressing a three-star general and smacked of telling the theater commander how to do his job. Perhaps knowing that he had the support of the Secretary of the Army gave McClure a measure of confidence in this matter. At any rate, the point that he was trying to make, McClure believed, was basic to the whole question—psychological warfare must be recognized as *important* by the theater commander. Once that was established, it was "simply a question of the necessity for the theater staff to control its operational tools in order to fulfill its mission efficiently and effectively."[44]

This was vintage McClure. His campaign to improve the air support for psychological warfare in Korea illustrates the strategies and techniques used by this articulate, energetic "true believer" in his attempts to influence events in the theater commands.

Still another example of General McClure's technique was his reaction to "Operation Killer," a phrase used by HQ FECOM in its press releases to describe operations against the North Korean and Chinese forces. The following passage is from a letter written to Major General Willoughby:

> I have personally been disturbed by the comparatively few Chinese prisoners we are taking, either by surrender or by capture. I realize that they are not fighting as the Chinese did in their civil wars in the three-year period that I sat along the Shankiwan Railway line. On the other hand, for two thousand years the Chinese have been induced to change sides, even to that of the Japanese, by considerations of personal gain or creature comforts. Is it possible that the "Operation Killer" and the "Hunter Killer Teams" have been so widely publicized to Chinese forces that they do not believe that they would be allowed to surrender? The wide publicity and constant repetition of the "killer" intent of our operations and the gloating of the press, and apparently even the individuals in the Battle Area, over the numbers killed versus the numbers captured, has led to a good deal of unfavorable international reactions.

Demonstrating that he did indeed understand the perspective of the combat soldier, McClure added:

> I fully recognize that our troops must adopt a tough, hard-boiled killer attitude if they are going to not only survive, but to win these battles. I wonder, however, if that indoctrination, which, I repeat, is very necessary, needs to be widely publicized in the press and broadcast to our enemies.[45]

Willoughby's response to McClure acknowledged that the "unfavorable psychological effects caused by recent publicity of such terms as 'Operational Killer' have been recognized here, and you will note that 8th Army news releases have avoided such phraseology." His reply also indicated that he accepted several of McClure's other suggestions on propaganda themes and techniques.[46] Thus, through personal and official correspondence and discussions with key personnel, adroit use of his relationship with the Secretary of the Army, and visits to the Far East Command—by both himself and members of his staff—McClure kept his finger on the pulse of events in Korea at the same time that he struggled to staff OCPW and establish a niche for his new organization within the Pentagon bureaucracy.

These efforts by OCPW to help were not always appreciated by HQ FECOM. As an example, in January 1952, Lieutenant General Doyle O. Hickey, Chief of Staff, FECOM, wrote to McClure questioning a United Press story entitled, "Psy War Accounts for Third of POW's." Hickey felt that the story was an exaggeration:

> While psychological warfare has unquestionably been one factor in lowering the combat effectiveness of enemy soldiers and in influencing many of them to desert, it seems evident that in almost all cases the action of our ground troops, supported by other combat arms, remains the strongest and most direct reason for the capture of prisoners.[47]

McClure demonstrated considerable tact in his response, telling Hickey, "I share fully your concern over the tendency to overplay the results of psychological warfare operations as evidenced in the United Press dispatch which you brought to my attention in your letter of 13 January." Never losing an opportunity to sell his wares, however, McClure further elaborated:

> On the whole, I believe that we have been successful in our determined effort to keep psychological warfare in a proper context within the "family of weapons." My views on this point are included in the Secretary's report which states: "Psychological warfare has been firmly recognized as an integral member of our family of weapons. While we realize fully that this mode of operation is not decisive by itself, it is also certain that, in combination with the conventional combat weapons, psychological warfare will contribute materially to the winning of wars."[48]

The report that McClure referred to was the Secretary of the Army's semiannual report, which was included in the Semiannual Report of the Secretary of Defense—illustrating again the similarity of views between Secretary Pace and the Chief, OCPW, on the subject of psychological warfare. This exchange of letters, however, also illustrates the tendency of conventional commanders to be sensitive to actions that appear to downgrade the "primary role of the combat role of the combat troops in the field," as Hickey expressed it, and thus to consider psychological warfare as strictly an ancillary, supporting activity. As an infantry officer, McClure recognized this tendency, and his reply to General Hickey reflects an attempt both to placate the conventional commander's view—to take a balanced position, that is—and also to insure that "psywar" received the recognition that he felt it deserved. McClure walked this particular tight-rope often.

The Psychological Warfare Section, FECOM, had other criticisms to make about the support received from the home front. These included a serious shortage of personnel with psychological warfare training or experience, particularly during the first 18 to 24 months of the war; the lack of firm, prompt high-level policy guidance and operational directives; the limitations of current printing, loudspeaker, and dissemination equipment; the serious shortage of linguists; and the lack of understanding of psychological warfare capabilities by commanders and troops at all echelons, which FECOM attributed to an apparently ineffective orientation program in the United States. FECOM finally overcame this last deficiency, it claimed, through high-level emphasis on, and orientation by, the Psychological Warfare Section within the theater; at the end of the conflict, "all divisions and corps commanders were enthusiastic supporters of psywar, demanding psywar support beyond ability of psywar agencies to produce."[49]

In spite of these differences of perspective between FECOM and OCPW, it is apparent that General McClure and his staff genuinely strove both to assist FECOM to influence the organization and conduct of psychological warfare in Korea. In large measure, these efforts were successful, due principally to the personal interest and sponsorship of Secretary Pace, to the provision of psychological warfare personnel and units by OCPW, and to the energetic, dedicated leadership of General McClure. Unconventional warfare activity in Korea, however, was another story.

OCPW and Unconventional Warfare in Korea

General McClure's attitude toward FECOM's conduct of unconventional warfare operations was similar to his views on its psychological warfare efforts, and perhaps even more critical. His criticisms focused on two broad areas: overall organization and planning for unconventional warfare by FECOM, and CIA involvement.

When the Korean war started, the minimal psychological warfare organization that existed in FECOM exceeded the one for unconventional warfare. Operations were initiated in the winter of 1950 by the G-3, 8th Army, when it appeared that the potential existed for the use of disaffected North Korean civilian personnel in behind-the-lines activities. Officers and enlisted personnel—many of them with no previous experience in unconventional warfare—were recruited from within the theater to train and direct these native personnel in guerrilla activities. To control these operations, the G-3 Miscellaneous Group, 8th Army, was formed; later redesignated the Miscellaneous Group, 8086th Army Unit, it finally was called the Far East Command Liaison Detachment (Korea), 8240th Army Unit. According to its Table of Distribution (TD), the mission of the 8086th was the following:

1. To develop and direct partisan warfare by training in sabotage indigenous groups and individuals both within Allied lines and behind enemy lines.
2. To supply partisan groups and agents operating behind enemy lines by means of water and air transportation.[50]

Although tactical conditions dictated that more emphasis be placed at first on operations as opposed to training, by early 1952 the 8240th had three control organizations for guerrilla operations known as LEOPARD, WOLFPACK, AND KIRKLAND; BAKER Section provided air support (C-46's and C-47's). All of the control organizations were based on the islands off the east and west coasts of Korea. While their strengths varied, by late 1952, for example, LEOPARD reported 5,500 combat effectives and WOLFPACK, 6,800. These forces operated as groups from centers within North Korea while others conducted tactical raids, ambushes, and amphibious operations from the U.N.-held offshore islands. Although US personnel often accompanied the tactical operations, they were rarely assigned indefinitely to the guerrilla forces located within mainland North Korea. As an example of their hit-and-run activity, the Far East Command reported a total of 63 raids and 25 patrols launched against Communist forces during the period 15-21 November 1952, resulting in 1,382 enemy casualties, although, as was often the case in such operations, the casualty figures may have been inflated.[51]

WOLFPACK provides an excellent example of the manner in which these unconventional warfare organizations evolved and operated. Established in March 1952, using the standard battalion organization as a guide, the initial force had an aggregate strength of 4,000 North Koreans. At the beginning, the US personnel consisted of four officers—the commander, one officer in WOLFPACK headquarters, and two in subordinate units—and three enlisted men, two of whom were communications specialists. Combat operations were required concurrently with the process of organizing, equipping, and training. Initially, six battalion-type units were organized, each with an operating base on a separate island, and by

June 1952 two more units had been created. By December 1952 the WOLFPACK staff consisted, in US personnel, of a commander, S3, S2, two enlisted radio operators, one operations noncommissioned officer (NCO), and one intelligence NCO. The S3 and S2 were lieutenants without previous unconventional warfare or special operations experience. Only three of the eight subordinate units were commanded by US officers (captains), the others by North Koreans. The captain generally functioned as a commander of a group the size of a battalion. A total of two enlisted men served in these subordinate units as general assistants and, on occasion, as deputies to the captains to whom they were assigned.[52]

The operations conducted by WOLFPACK units were generally divided into three categories: coastal, intermediate, and interior. Coastal operations were planned on a conventional basis with forces of up to 800 men; they often involved the use of air and naval fire support and had as their primary objective the killing and capture of personnel. Intermediate operations further inland were executed by groups of 5 to 10 men over a period of 3 to 5 days, and were generally directed at pinpoint targets such as gun positions, wire lines, and targets vulnerable to sniping and demolitions. Interior operations represented the more classic guerrilla warfare operations; in these operations, a small element made an initial reconnaissance, followed by a larger increment, then by recruiting in the operational area and infiltration of the final group. Planning usually called for these forces to infiltrate in the spring and to remain until November of the same year.[53]

In 1953, a cadre from WOLFPACK and the other organizations subordinate to the Far East Command Liaison Detachment (8240th Army Unit) were used to form what was called the United Nations Partisan Forces in Korea (UNPFK). UNPFK consisted of five partisan infantry regiments and one partisan airborne infantry regiment. It was planned that this "first United Nations Partisan Division" would reach a strength of 20,000 personnel by March 1952. Guidelines to the regimental commanders from the 8240th included the following advice:

> Initiative and aggressiveness tempered by calm judgement will be encouraged. Avoid trying to win the war by yourself; pace the attack in accordance with your advantage; when the advantage has passed, get away to fight another day. Hit and run; these are the guerrilla's tactics. The planning of such an operation should include an escape route and rallying point. Substitute speed and surprise for mass.[54]

Unfortunately, as the organization grew larger and more conventional, according to one participant, the effectiveness of its operations decreased correspondingly.[55]

To oversee these unconventional warfare operations in Korea, HQ FECOM in Tokyo established the Far East Command Liaison Group (FECLG) under the operational control of the G-2. The Documents Research Division, a part of the Special Staff, HQ FECOM (headed by a CIA representative), controlled the CIA's operations. The Joint Advisory Commission Korea (JACK), whose head was a military officer assigned to the CIA, controlled the CIA operations in Korea—both OSO and OPC. Activities of the CIA ran the gamut from covert intelligence to unconventional warfare. The CIA placed agents to collect intelligence and assist downed pilots in escape and evasion. It conducted sabotage and small boat patrols for tactical information on both the east and west coasts. It organized indigenous forces to remain behind for shallow penetration patrolling to augment combat patrolling and gain information for large tactical operations. It conducted some guerrilla warfare. As one might expect, the variety of unconventional warfare activities engaged in by both the CIA and the services resulted in some conflicting and overlapping interests.[56]

In an attempt to eliminate this conflict, an organization for Covert, Clandestine and Related Activities in Korea (CCRAK) was activated in December 1951. Its purpose was to centralize direction of all services and CIA unconventional warfare operations at Headquarters, FECOM, by combining them in one organization to support US forces in Korea. CCRAK was put under the direct command of CINCFE, but continued under the staff supervision of G-2. The Deputy Chief, CCRAK, was an individual designated by the Chief, Documents Research Section, CIA. Colonel Archibald Stuart, US Army, installed as the Chief of CCRAK, soon after was promoted to brigadier general. Essentially, however, the unconventional warfare organization of the services and the CIA in Korea remained unchanged, with continuing lack of coordination between their activities.[57]

It was this apparent lack of coordination of unconventional warfare activities and the relative autonomy enjoyed by the CIA that most concerned General McClure, Chief, OCPW. In early 1951, he had already commented on the "unusual organization" that FECOM had established "whereby responsibility for covert operations and special operations behind the lines is placed in the office of the AC of S [Assistant Chief of Staff], G-2, in addition to its intelligence responsibility." He thought that such operations should be the responsibility of G-3 or, even better, of a special staff division for both psychological warfare and special operations.[58] As we have seen, McClure had recommended to FECOM that such a division be established, and it was, in June 1951. But the new division's responsibilities for special operations apparently existed in name only. In reality those responsibilities resided within the G-2. Calling the G-3's attention to the apparent contravention by FECOM of its own general order that had established a Special Operations Section within the Psychological Warfare Division, McClure recommended that a cable be dispatched to CINCFE requesting clarification of (1) theater command and staff organization for planning and conduct of overt and covert unconventional warfare and psychological warfare, and (2) the relationship of CIA/OPC to that organization.[59]

Two months later, the recommendation was returned to OCPW without action with the comment, "When the psychological warfare organization within FECOM has been established on a firm basis, it is considered that representatives from your office should go to the Far East Command to discuss psychological warfare activities." While this response from G-3 may have been an attempt to keep an overzealous OCPW from appearing to question the prerogatives of a theater commander, it was also indicative of deeper tensions between McClure's office and those of the principal staff agencies, particularly the G-2 and G-3. These tensions were the result of many factors, including the personality conflicts that often develop when strong-willed men disagree over issues. For example, there was "bad feeling" between McClure and the G-2, Major General Bolling, part of which was due to jurisdictional differences over the staff responsiblity for escape and evasion. Perhaps the major factor, however, was the belief of many staff officers that the relatively new fields of psychological and unconventional warfare were "incidental activities" that demanded an unjustified share of attention and resources in terms of their real value to the Army. This attitude extended particularly to the younger field, unconventional warfare. Unfortunately the single-minded dedication with which some of McClure's staff pursued the creation of Special Forces alienated many of those with whom they had to coordinate policies and activities.[60]

Undeterred by the G-3 rebuff, McClure tried other tactics to emphasize his point on staff organization. Writing to the Chief of Staff, FECOM, in October 1951, he observed:

> I understand that in the setup of your new Psywar Division you have not yet reached a firm decision on the placing of the special operations and particularly guerrilla warfare and similar type activities. I

strongly reiterate my comment to you on my visit to your headquarters in April, that Psywar and Special Operations are so interrelated that they should be under the same Staff Division.[61]

With perhaps some exaggeration, he added: "We have found the organization here at the Department of the Army level to be working spendidly and in complete harmony with other Staff Divisions, both General and Special."

McClure's principal concern about placing special operations under G–2 was that it might then be given a lower priority:

> While Special Operations has some aspects of intelligence gathering, that is by no means its principal mission, and if it remains under G–2 risks being subordinated to the intelligence field. All our planning here contemplates the separation of the intelligence field from the Special Operations field. . . . I feel very strongly that the Special Operations is as it states an operation more appropriately monitored by G–3 than G–2.

The recommendation had little effect, so, several months later McClure decided to try another tack. He prepared a comprehensive analysis of FECOM's organization for psychological and special operations for General Mark Clark, who had replaced General Ridgeway as Commander in Chief, Far East, in April 1952. Reviewing his recommendation to Ridgeway in April 1951 to establish an organization to handle psychological and special operations and the subsequent FECOM general order in June 1951 to establish such an office, McClure observed:

> While I have no desire to prescribe or unduly influence the organization which should be adopted by any Theater Commander, I would like to point out the fact that Psychological Warfare Section, GHQ FECOM has to date assumed only those functions pertaining to Psychological Warfare. Special Operations has remained under the Assistant Chief of Staff, G–2.[62]

As a result of a JCS message in August 1951, CIA and Covert Operations in Korea had been placed under CINFE. The activation of CCRAK was an attempt to bring all behind-the-line operations under a single command agency, but CCRAK remained under the general staff supervision of G–2, FECOM, as McClure reminded Clark. Additionally— and this was a particularly crucial point with the Chief, OCPW—CIA, Far East Command, insisted that JACK (CIA, Korea) be maintained as an integral organization and remain under the control of CIA, Far East.

Based on field trip reports by members of his office, their experiences and judgments, plus a comprehensive debriefing of a former member of CCRAK, McClure offered the following conclusions in his analysis for Clark:

1. G-2, FEC, General Staff supervision of CCRAK and all behind-the-line operations have resulted in emphasis on intelligence, rather than adequate developing indigenous forces [guerrilla] in North Korea and in support of 8th Army.

2. To obtain a balance of G-2, G-3 interest, this office is of the opinion that Special Operations functions should be placed in the Psychological Warfare Section, FEC.

3. In order to eliminate duplication of personnel, equipment, and facilities, and to insure efficient coordinated operations, CIA, Korea, should be integrated into a joint task force organization (Army, Navy, Air, and CIA) under the command of CINCFE.

4. The organizational integrity policy advocated by CIA is a basic factor adversely affecting Special Forces operations in Korea.

5. Highly qualified personnel for key positions in Special Operations furnished in accordance with a special FEC requisition are not fully utilized in this field.[63]

These conclusions and their supporting discussion vividly depict the extent of OCPW's disapproval with the autonomous CIA role in Korea. While all behind-the-line operations were ostensibly under the control of CINCFE, in reality, McClure argued, a dual chain of command existed.

The commander of CCRAK took his orders from CINCFE; the Deputy Chief, CCRAK, received his marching orders from Documents Research Division (CIA, Far East), who in turn received its guidance from CIA headquarters in Washington. At the operational level, this meant that JACK (CIA, Korea) did not carry out missions in support of the 8th Army without authority from CIA, Far East. Coordination of the unconventional warfare operations run by CCRAK and the 8th Army was too dependent on the personalities of key individuals, he felt. Ironically, the CIA in Korea integrated military personnel into its organization and often engaged in activities similar to those conducted by the 8th Army, but without proper overall coordination. All in all, McClure argued, CIA's insistence on organizational integrity resulted in an allegedly joint command, CCRAK, that had no authority to exercise command jurisdiction over CIA personnel and efforts, in unnecessary duplication of personnel and activities, and in multiple channels that complicated the coordination and integration of operations. Together with the lack of overall formal planning and training for unconventional warfare by CCRAK or any other agency and the emphasis placed on intelligence as opposed to guerrilla warfare, these problems added up to a situation where the potential for behind-the-lines operations was far from being realized, McClure and his staff believed.[64] As we shall see, OCPW's differences with the CIA were the harbinger of similar frustrations encountered by OCPW in its efforts to create Special Forces and to plan for their use in Europe, and is a major theme in the evolution of the Army's attempt to create its own special warfare capability.

Shortly after his memorandum to General Clark, McClure reiterated his view to G-3: "I believe that the unconventional warfare organization for Korea, including CIA/OPC participation therein, reflects fundamental and serious defects, specifically for the conduct of guerrilla warfare." McClure criticized the conduct of guerrilla warfare in Korea as "essentially minor in consequence and sporadic in nature" and stated the FECOM lacked "an overall, integrated program of Special Forces in Korea." It is interesting to note that OCPW began to use the term "Special Forces Operations," as differentiated from "special operations," to describe US Army participation in guerrilla warfare activities. "Special operations," through long usage in the Army and as outlined in "Field Service Regulations" (Field Manual 100-5), related to "night combat," "jungle operations," "joint amphibious operations," and similar activities.[65]

Actually, few Special Forces personnel were used for unconventional warfare operations in Korea. The 10th Special Forces Group was not officially created until May 1952, at which time it began training and continued recruiting efforts for personnel. Although OCPW urged HQ FECOM in November 1952 and January 1953 to requisition Special Forces staff personnel and detachments, FECOM did not act until the spring of 1953, when it requested deployment of 55 officers and 9 enlisted men from the 10th Special Forces Group. Some of these personnel became disillusioned with their assignments in Korea, believing that their Special Forces and airborne training were not properly utilized. More importantly, however, there were no Special Forces operational detachments, as opposed to individuals, requested and employed by the Far East Command. An excellent opportunity to test unconventional warfare doctrine and organization was lost, or so General McClure thought because he complained of his difficulty in getting experience data from FECOM and of his disappointment in FECOM's failure to conduct "laboratory" tests of guerrilla operations.[66]

Although McClure continued throughout his tenure as Chief, OCPW, to have reservations about the Far East Command's organization and conduct of unconventional warfare, not everyone shared his views. A staff visit to FECOM by a member of the Joint Subsidiary Plans Division in late 1951 not only confirmed that the organization for the "covert" aspects of unconventional warfare did not follow the general lines of command and staff responsibility established by OCPW, but also resulted in the observation that there was little inclination to do so:

> There is nowhere within FEC a desire to organize covert activities under a Psychological Warfare Section as in D/A [Department of the Army]. The organization is suitable to the personalities and operations within the theater. It is sound, workable, and has the unqualified backing of both the military and CIA personnel concerned from top to bottom. Officers within the theater are of the opinion, and rightly so, that the theater should be free to solve its organizational problems in its own way; that what may seem ideal organizationally to far-off Washington is not necessarily the best solution to those more nearly under the guns.[67]

The tone of this report indicates that the JCS had some sympathy with FECOM's posture on this matter. Furthermore, as we have seen, the Department of the Army G-2 and G-3 from time to time resisted OCPW's attempts to influence FECOM's organization and conduct of unconventional warfare. The records of this period reveal instances where G-3 in particular tried to stop or "tone down" OCPW's initiatives and proposed cables. In early 1953, for example, G-3 nonconcurred in a cable from OCPW to FECOM requesting information about the status and role of "partisan forces." Observing tartly that "considering the number of G-2 and PSYWAR officers who have visited FECOM within the past few months for the purpose of examining CCRAK organization and activities, there should be no dearth of information on the subject in D/A," the G-3 response went on to conclude: "While the ostensible purpose of the proposed cable is to obtain information, the overall effect tends towards veiled suspicion that CINCFE is on the 'wrong track.'"[68]

This was, of course, exactly what McClure's office suspected, but OCPW efforts to get FECOM to recognize the errors of its ways in unconventional warfare generally came to naught. Although the Army Chief of Staff, General Collins, shared some of McClure's concerns about lack of a fully integrated joint staff in Korea for unconventional warfare, the Far East commander, General Clark, insisted that the CIA's organizational integrity under CCRAK be maintained. And while Clark also instructed his staff to establish closer liaison with OCPW, this did not result in any significant organizational changes by FECOM in its handling of unconventional warfare.[69]

For all practical purposes, both Far East Command and the CIA went their own ways, uninfluenced by General McClure and his staff.

In summary, with the impetus of the Korean war, the Army moved in late 1950 to create an unprecedented staff organization—the Office of the Chief of Psychological Warfare. The personal interest and persistent pressure that Secretary of the Army Pace brought to bear on senior Army officers, both before and after the outbreak of war, were key factors in this step. With Pace's support, Brigadier General McClure created a staff under which were placed the responsibilities for both psychological and unconventional warfare. While in the process of staffing and organizing this office, McClure energetically turned to the emergency in Korea in an attempt to assist and influence FECOM's organization and conduct of psychological and unconventional warfare—capabilities that the Army had neglected during the interwar years. He was successful with psychological warfare, less so with unconventional. The conflict in Korea, however, is only one part of the story in our quest to determine why the Army decided to establish the Psychological Warfare Center and to create the 10th Special Forces Group. To complete the picture, we must next examine the events that were taking place in the United States and in Europe.

VII

THE ROAD TO FORT BRAGG

Spurred by the war in Korea and the persistent pressure of Secretary of the Army Frank Pace, the Office of the Chief of Psychological Warfare (OCPW) was created in early 1951—a key link in the chain of events leading to establishment of the Psychological Warfare Center at Fort Bragg, N.C. Under the leadership of Brigadier General Robert A. Mc-Clure, OCPW initiated plans that resulted in this unprecedented center and in activation of an equally unprecedented concept and organization, Special Forces. To complete our examination of how and why this occurred—that is, to understand the origins of a "special warfare" capability for the Army—we must look beyond the more obvious stimulus of the Korean emergency to events taking place both in Europe and in the United States.

Psywar in Europe

While the conflict in Korea naturally occupied a major share of OCPW's attention, McClure found soon after arrival in Washington that acquaintances in the European theater would be reminding him of their needs. In December 1950, Major General Daniel Noce, Chief of Staff of Headquarters, European Command (EUCOM) sent him a "Dear Bob" letter:

> I was sorry to hear that you lost your nice billet on the West Coast, but feel that the Army will benefit materially from your assignment as head of the new Psychological Warfare Division in the Department. Certainly, we have no other officer who has the broad experience which you have had in that field.[1]

After this introductory compliment, General Noce got down to business, stating that EUCOM's difficulty in obtaining qualified officers for psychological warfare and special operations had substantially slowed progress in planning for these activities. He outlined his needs for trained officers in both fields, indicating that these needs had been discussed recently with Lieutenant Colonel J. R. Deane, Jr., whom McClure had sent to Europe on a liaison trip. Interestingly, in a comment that reflects some of McClure's organizational philosophy, Noce added:

> The organization of your division works in quite well with the psychological warfare and unconventional warfare organization which we have established in this headquarters, since we have placed both of these activities in one branch of our OPOT (G-3) Division.

McClure's reply on 15 January 1951 reflected his frustration in attempting to restore specialized skills neglected in the immediate post-World War II period:

> I fully appreciate your difficulty in obtaining qualified officers for psychological warfare and unconventional warfare activities. We are encountering the same difficulties here. I am greatly embarrassed that we have been unable so far to furnish you the two officers for psychological warfare planning which you requested in a radio message some time ago.[2]

This is precisely the condition that McClure and a few other farsighted individuals had tried to avoid when, just a few years earlier, they had lamented the dispersal of people with World War II experience and had warned about the lack of attention being paid to maintaining a psychological warfare capability. Now their prophecies had been fulfilled. As one of the few senior officers who grasped the complexities and possibilities of this specialized field, McClure struggled to train personnel in both the US and the overseas theaters.

Unable to provide the planners that General Noce immediately needed, McClure offered in his 15 January letter to do "some little work here along that line as suggestions for you." In this same letter, McClure again discussed the valuable contribution made by civilians in psychological warfare, mentioning specifically the forthcoming visit to Europe of C. D. Jackson, his former deputy throughout World War II. He also provided a lengthy illustration of what he called the "practical side of back stopping" psychological warfare operations, emphasizing:

> It is for this reason of thinking the problem through from the leaflets in the enemy soldier or civilian hands back to the tree from which the pulp is produced, that a man with Jackson's experience will be essen-

tial. God forbid that you go through the growing pains, trial and error, and frustrations that we did in World War II until we finally reached maturity. I can assure you that we will give you all the help possible back here.

And help he did. McClure sent General Noce several guidance materials for psychological warfare planning, including training circulars, program schedules, a draft National Psychological Warfare Plan for General War, the State Department's "Russian Plan," and estimates of logistical requirements for psychological warfare planning.[3] Increased efforts were made to provide the officers EUCOM needed, and by October a small Psychological Warfare Section had been formed in the Special Plans Branch of Headquarters, EUCOM. The 301st Radio Broadcasting and Leaflet (RB&L) Group, a New York City reserve unit, was recalled to active duty, sent to Fort Riley, Kansas, for training, and shipped to Europe in November, together with the 5th Loudspeaker and Leaflet (L&L) Company.[4]

The decision to ship the 301st RB&L Group to Europe was itself fraught with controversy and indicative of the competing requirements that OCPW faced during this hectic period. General Willoughby, G-2, GHQ FECOM, felt that assignment of the 301st to the Far East Command would be the most practical solution to FECOM's urgent needs, and McClure initially agreed with this assignment. A decision by G-3 to honor the corresponding and prior need expressed by the European theater forced McClure to backtrack, however. Instead, the 1st Radio Broadcasting and Leaflet Group, a prototype unit stationed at Fort Riley, was shipped to FECOM.[5]

In addition to providing such help as it could to EUCOM, OCPW was also involved in numerous planning actions for balancing the perceived Soviet threat in Europe. An example of such actions was a meeting called by the Joint Strategic Plans Division (JSPD) of the military services' psychological warfare representatives. The meeting explored sources of discontent within Soviet satellite services (which could be exploited for propaganda to reduce morale), and means by which the services could furnish the State Department with materials for psychological warfare against the U.S.S.R. and its satellite forces. The Acting Chief, JSPD, agreed to await OCPW's submission of an outline plan for overt psychological attack against Soviet and satellite forces—a plan that would confine itself to military psychological vulnerabilities—before taking further action. The Army could make this contribution because McClure had previously alerted his staff to prepare a draft plan, "EEI [Essential Elements of Information], Psychological Vulnerabilities of Soviet Armed Forces in Current Period (Draft)." This particular plan was illustrative of many such actions initiated by McClure during this time and reflected both his ability to anticipate needs and his desire to lead the way in psychological warfare planning among the services.[6]

He was to have some competition on that latter score, and OCPW's running feud with the Air Force was indicative of the interservice rivalry that marked these years. While attending a joint EUCOM-USAFE (US Air Force, Europe) conference in Europe, McClure noted somewhat peevishly that while both the Army and Air Force had exhibits at the conference illustrating psychological warfare objectives, techniques, and historical examples, the Air Force exhibit "was an elaborate and expensive one" that had been on tour in the United States and would visit parts of Europe. Moreover, in his eyes the exhibit was misleading:

> It is unfortunate that the air exhibit fails to indicate any joint participation by other services in the field of Psychological Warfare. A false impression is given that Air Force is unilaterally conducting Psychological Warfare even in Korea today. Korean leaflets used in the exhibit and sample ones given to the audience leave the impression that the Air Force determines the content, prints the leaflet, selects the target, and then makes distribution. Quite the contrary, no leaflet has been designed or printed by the Air Force in the Far East command to date. It is an Army operation except for airlift distribution. This is the same practice as World War II.[7]

McClure had been critical of Air Force support of Army psychological warfare operations in Korea, but this statement reveals an even deeper concern that the Air Force, in its organization and activities, was "going into Psywar in a big way, disturbingly so in some respects," as he remarked to his staff.[8] Apparently the Air Force felt that it had claim to a strategic role in psychological warfare beyond that of simply providing the airplanes for leaflet distribution. Not illogically, it argued that in addition to providing the airlift through its special Aerial Resupply and Communication (ARC) Wings, it should also be able to compose and print leaflets.[9] In its staff organization, research projects and training plans, the Air Force embarked upon a psychological warfare program that resulted in what one disinterested Navy observer characterized as "the clash of two growing organizations, Army and Air Force Psychological Warfare."[10] But McClure believed that the Air Force plans, if implemented, would "result in extravagant duplication of the minimal numbers of personnel and items of equipment envisaged for Army propaganda operations."[11] McClure's suspicions of Air Force intrusions into what he considered Army terrain continued unabated and were intensified by disagreements over responsibilities for unconventional warfare.

Psychological Warfare Activities in the United States

The requirements of the theater commands in both Europe and the Far East, and the concurrent need to develop a training program and supporting structure for psychological warfare in the United States, placed heavy demands upon McClure's office. The immediate need for a qualified Psychological Warfare officer in each Army headquarters was met by sending selected personnel to a 17-week course at Georgetown University, but this stopgap measure only scratched the surface. A letter from one of McClure's staff to the harried commander of the 1st Radio Broadcasting and Leaflet Group, being readied at Fort Riley for deployment to the Far East, vividly depicts the situation:

> In order that you will be better able to appreciate the personnel problems facing us here, I would like to give you a little indication of our immediate requirements for officers. We must find 38 officers for your Group, 24 officers for a student body for the first unit officers' course in the Psychological Warfare School, 14 officers for the Staff and Faculty of the Psychological Warfare School, 5 officers for the 1st Loudspeaker and Leaflet Company, 8 officers for the 5th Loudspeaker and Leaflet Company, which is to be activated in the near future, and approximately 20 additional officers for this office. That totals 109 officers needed in the immediate future and there are additional miscellaneous slots to be filled. To meet this requirement, we have so far requested approximately 100 officers. We are finding that we get only fifty percent of those we request. Those now being requested will not be available at the earliest until late April or May. However, we hope to have enough available by Mid-April to provide a minimum staff for the units at Riley, a minimum staff for the School, and a small student body for the first unit officers' course.[12]

As seen earlier, plans to establish the Psychological Warfare Department as a part of the Army General School at Fort Riley began in the winter of 1950 when General McClure forwarded a request from the Chief, Army Field Forces (AFF), to assign Lieutenant Colonel John O. Weaver as the Department's first Chief. Weaver finally acquired enough of a faculty to establish "the world's first formal school of military propaganda" in the spring of 1951. The purpose of his first endeavor, the psychological warfare officer course, was

> to train selected officers for assignment to psychological warfare staff and operational units; to develop in officers an understanding of the nature and employment of propaganda in combat and to make them knowledgeable of the organization's methods and techniques for the tactical conduct of propaganda in the field.[13]

The courses were designed to provide a general introduction to psychological warfare, strategic intelligence, foreign army organization, intelligence, and psychological operations, and lasted 6 to 7 weeks. Between June 1951 and April 1952, 4 officer and 2 noncommissioned officer classes were graduated—a total of 334 students, including Navy, Marine Corps, and Air Force students, as well as Allied students from Canada, Great Britain, Denmark, Belgium, France, and Italy.[14]

By April 1951, OCPW had requested the activation of five psychological warfare units: the 1st L&L Company with the 8th Army in Korea; the 2d L&L Company at Fort Riley as a prototype unit; the 5th L&L Company at Fort Riley, but scheduled to be sent to Europe; the 1st RB&L Group at Fort Riley, originally a prototype unit but scheduled to be sent to the Far East Command; and the 301st (Reserve) RB&L Group, to be trained at Fort Riley in May, then shipped to Europe. In addition, OCPW developed organizational concepts and functions for these troop units, as well as for OCPW and a Psychological Warfare Division, Special Staff, for theater command use. Army Field Forces received a directive to establish training programs for the general indoctrination of all military personnel in psychological warfare and to prepare detailed programs for both active and reserve psychological warfare units. In accordance with this directive, all Army schools received a request to include general indoctrination instruction in psychological warfare in their curricula. And by the end of May, McClure began sending out the first of a series of informational letters designed to maintain a close contact between OCPW and Psychological Warfare officers in all Army headquarters.[15]

To conduct nonmateriel research in support of the burgeoning psychological warfare effort, the Army relied almost exclusively upon a civilian agency, the Operations Research Office (ORO) operated under contract by the Johns Hopkins University. Studies by ORO included a three-volume basic reference work for psychological warfare, manuals for use by psychological warfare operators in specific countries, an analysis and grouping of sample leaflets from World War II and Korea to develop classification schemes, and a large amount of field operations research in Korea. McClure's staff was not entirely satisfied with ORO's work, claiming that their projects were "too general in concept" and not suitable for use by the Army's psychological operators. The Johns Hopkins University also began to have misgivings about the contract, believing that it could not properly perform the development research (as opposed to operations research) required by OCPW in support of psychological warfare. Eventually the Human Resources Research Office was formed to supplant ORO and undertake a general program in psychological research for the Army.[16]

McClure was particularly interested in improving the development and procurement of suitable materiel for the conduct of psychological warfare. He felt that "as a result of the 1945–49 hiatus in psychological warfare and special operations planning," the military "entered the Korean conflict with little more than obsolete pieces of World War II equipment." Examples of equipment under development were a mobile reproduction unit for propaganda leaflets, a newly designed lightweight portable loudspeaker for use in frontline operations, and a completely equipped mobile 5,000-watt radio broadcasting station.[17]

As if these myriad competing requirements were not enough to keep it busy, OCPW soon faced the possibility of a reduction in civilian and military personnel strength, a threat that it avoided by invoking Secretary Pace's views in support of the Army's psychological warfare program. McClure had a hard enough time as it was obtaining the qualified people needed for the specialized skills of psychological warfare and special operations. That, coupled with the fact that many officers were reluctant to become involved in an activity considered "out of the mainstream," meant that he often had to "take what he could get," in the words of one of his former staff officers. Many of the officers assigned to OCPW felt "trapped" by the assignment because of McClure's reluctance to release them for other jobs, which apparently caused considerable discontent.[18]

There was also some disgruntlement among his officers concerning McClure's insistence on special staff status for OCPW, rather than remaining under the G-3 as a part of the General Staff, a position, they thought, of greater stature and "clout" within the Army bureaucracy. Certainly there was some basis for these feelings—under normal circumstances the General Staff does carry more "clout" and an aura of greater prestige. But McClure's World War II experience had firmly etched in his mind the overriding advantages of relative autonomy and access to the top decisionmakers that special staff status afforded. As we have seen, this was a theme consistently advocated by him, both in the United States and in his relations with the theater commands. Despite these resentments, however, McClure was both liked and esteemed by those who worked for him. "Robbie" backed his subordinates loyally, evinced tremendous energy and enthusiasm about OCPW's role, and displayed more ability to articulate than did most general officers of his time.[19] And he had vision. This vision extended to the field of unconventional warfare.

The Special Forces Ranger Regiment

At the time of OCPW's creation, General McClure had successfully lobbied to have responsibilities for the unconventional warfare function transferred from G–3 to him. While some thinking on the subject of behind-the-lines activities and special units had taken place in the Army during the interwar years, nothing much had been done to follow through on those initial ideas—particularly since CIA/OPC's assumption of the primary responsibility for covert operations. Under McClure's leadership, this situation was to change, for within a year and a half the plans formulated within his Special Operations Division (later renamed the Special Forces Division) to create a formal unconventional warfare capability for the Army came to fruition. But the path to that goal was not easy, nor did it proceed in a straight line.

McClure realized that his firsthand expertise was basically in the psychological warfare field, so early on he indicated to his staff that he was "fighting for officers with background and experience in special operations."[20] He brought into the Special Operations Division several officers with World War II and Korean war experience in guerrilla warfare or with long-range penetration units: Lieutenant Colonel Melvin Russell Blair and Lieutenant Colonel Marvin Waters, both of whom had served with "Merrill's Marauders"; Colonel Aaron Bank, who had fought with the French Maquis as a member of OSS; Colonel Wendell Fertig, who had commanded the guerrillas on Mindanao after the Japanese occupied the Philippines; and Lieutenant Colonel Russell W. Volckmann, who had organized and conducted guerrilla warfare operations in North Luzon and had planned and directed behind-the-lines operations in North Korea.[21]

Colonel Volckmann remembered that General McClure had approached him in the hospital (he had been evacuated from Korea in December 1951 to Walter Reed Army Medical Center in Washington) with a request to help organize the Special Operations Division, and it was only after being assured that the Department of the Army was interested in organized behind-the-lines operations that he agreed to take the job.[22] Together, the group in OCPW prepared studies, plans, organizational and operational concepts, and training programs for a formal US Army unconventional warfare capability—Special Forces.

These studies and organizational concepts were inevitably based on the personal operational experience of the officers involved, as well as on research of the past major resistance movements. In addition to his World War II guerrilla warfare experience, Colonel Volckmann possessed a considerable amount of information resulting from more than 6 months of research he had undertaken in 1949 at Fort Benning, Georgia, while preparing the draft field manuals for *Organization and Conduct of Guerrilla Warfare* and *Combatting Guerrilla Forces* [23] Colonel Bank, another key figure, had operated as a Jedburgh in southern France, later organized and trained anti-Nazi German prisoners of war for harassing tactics against the Germans in Austria, and still later completed two OSS missions in Indochina.[24]

Bank, who joined OCPW as Chief of the Special Operations Division at the end of March 1951 (to be succeeded by Colonel Fertig in July),[25] gives Volckmann considerable credit for "the development of position, planning, and policy papers that helped sell the establishment of Special Forces units in the active Army." Bank also makes clear that he and Volckmann based their plans for the Army's unconventional warfare capability on their World War II experiences with the Philippine guerrillas and OSS, and that Special Forces units were developed "in the OSS pattern of tiny units with the prime mission of developing, training, and equipping the guerrilla potential deep in enemy territory." To those who would insist on viewing the Army's Ranger units as forerunners of Special Forces, Bank unequivocally states that "actually they [Special Forces] have no connection with ranger-type organizations since their mission and operations are far more complex, time consuming, require much deeper penetration and initially are often of a strategic nature."[26]

The comments of Volckmann and Bank, made in retrospect, may give the impression that a rather clear delineation of roles and missions for Special Forces was clearly understood from the beginning. The evidence suggests otherwise. In actuality, the path that led to the concept for organization and employment of Special Forces was tortuous and marked by controversy. The initial discussions within the Army on this subject, in fact, were reminiscent of the rather confused dialog that took place during the interwar years concerning the "Airborne Reconnaissance units," the

"Ranger Group," and the "Special Operations Company," all of which tended to intermingle OSS and Ranger precepts. The task of clearing up this doctrinal confusion proved to be no easier in 1951 than it had been during the period prior to Korea.

We have seen that in early February 1951, General McClure briefed the Army General Council on the need for a rapid organization of unconventional warfare, and that shortly thereafter Secretary Pace provided strong official support for the combining of psychological and unconventional warfare planning functions. By late March, a few weeks after Volckmann joined OCPW, McClure's new office received a copy of a brief memorandum to the Director, Organization and Training Division, from Major General Maxwell D. Taylor, G-3:

> In consultation with General McClure, please develop the Army responsibility for guerrilla and antiguerrilla warfare within the field of G-3 interests. Having determined what our responsibility is, I should then like to verify that the various elements in the guerrilla mission are clearly assigned to subordinate Army units.[27]

It is interesting to note that Taylor's directive included antiguerrilla warfare. While some lip service was given to this in the studies that followed, it was not considered an important part of Special Forces until the 1960's, when "counterinsurgency" became the third leg of the "special warfare" triad at Fort Bragg.

Up to this point, General McClure had not been able to do much about the unconventional warfare part of his mission. Arrangements had been made for a few officers from Army Field Forces and the various Army headquarters in the United States to attend a staff familiarization course in guerrilla warfare at Fort Benning beginning 5 April 1951. Those attending were generally the same officers who had attended the special psychological warfare course run by Georgetown University.[28] The course in guerrilla warfare was set up after a series of conferences in 1949 between the Army and the CIA had led to the selection of Fort Benning as the site for a training course desired by the CIA. McClure had also requested that his office receive full reports on all behind-the-lines operations in Korea in order to carry out its assigned responsibilities in the field of unconventional warfare.[29] Except for these tentative steps, however, special operations planning in OCPW lagged behind psychological warfare planning, primarily because of a lack of experienced personnel. But when McClure acquired the people he needed, he plunged ahead.

Within 10 days of receiving General Taylor's memorandum, McClure discussed the subject of guerrilla warfare with him and General Bolte, and reported to his staff that both were "very much" in favor of organizing "foreign national units." General Taylor was to do a study on the use of foreign nationals as individuals or in units, while OCPW's Special Operations Division was asked to study the possibility of organizing a Ranger company at Fort Riley with each platoon made up of a different nationality group. One of the purposes of the company would be to work with US aggressor forces in exercises to teach soldiers counterguerrilla tactics. McClure's tentative thinking at this early stage was to propose organization of six Ranger companies of foreign nationals in Europe, each company consisting of a different nationality and attached to a US division. The companies were to be in addition to the "regular" Ranger battalions of US personnel.[30]

Two points need to be noted about this early dialog. First, it was clear that the focus of attention for future possible use of unconventional warfare was Europe, even though the Army was currently engaged in a "hot war" in Korea. The "foreign nationals" referred to were those from Eastern European countries and would be brought into the US Army through the provisions of the Lodge bill (Public Law 597, 81st Congress, 30 June 1950). Second, it was also clear that the principals involved in this dialog, including General McClure, had not sorted out in their minds the type of special unit desired or its primary objective.

Perhaps this was because the Chief of Staff, General Collins, was himself unclear on the subject, as was evident in his visit to the Infantry Center at Fort Benning a few days later. During his conference there, General Collins observed that "the Infantry School should consider the Rangers as well as other troops and indigenous personnel to initiate subversive activities. I personally established the Rangers with the thought that they might serve as the nucleus of expansion in this direction."[31] This statement is particularly revealing when one considers the clear-cut delineation between the roles and missions of Special Forces and Ranger units later insisted on by the Chief of Staff. But such a delineation was neither well understood nor agreed to by key decisionmakers in early 1951.

Lieutenant Colonel Volckmann from OCPW was present at the conference attended by General Collins at Fort Benning, and was asked by the Infantry School to analyze portions of the Chief of Staff's statements. Volckmann's analysis should be examined in some detail, for it is the first evidence within OCPW of the philosophical basis for creation of an Army unconventional warfare capability.

First, Volckmann interpreted General Collins' use of the phrase "subversive activities" to mean what he called "special forces operations." He defined these operations to include those carried on within or behind the enemy's lines, which could encompass the following:

1. Organization and conduct of guerrilla warfare.

2. Sabotage and subversion.

3. Evasion and escape.

4. Ranger and Commando-like operations.

5. Long-range or deep penetration reconnaissance.

6. Psychological warfare (through the above media).[32]

Second, commenting on the Chief of Staff's reference to indigenous personnel, Volckmann offered the following theoretical framework to clarify the overall objective of special forces operations:

> We may visualize the world today as being divided into two major groups or layers of individuals that cover the earth unrestricted by national boundaries. These layers, a red and a blue, are held together by common ideologies. Any future war may well be regarded as an international civil war waged by these opposing layers. The full exploitation of our sympathetic blue layer within the enemy's sphere of influence is basically the mission of special forces operations. It is from the blue layer within the enemy's sphere of influence that we must foster resistance movements, organize guerrilla or indigenous forces on a military basis, conduct sabotage and subversion, effect evasion and escape. We should, through special forces operations, exploit this layer to assist our ranger and commando operations, and as a media for psychological warfare.

Exploitation of the "sympathetic blue layer," stated Volckmann, would enable the West to offset the manpower superiority of Soviet forces in Europe, particularly during the initial stages of their invasion. Similarly, the Allies must be prepared to counter the "red layer" within their friendly sphere of influence, a problem that involved rear-area defense, for the Soviets would exploit their "sympathetic red layer" to the maximum.

To effect the transition from this theoretical framework to reality, at least as far as the Army was concerned, Volckmann advocated concrete measures: "Through actual command, staff, training, and operations we should pull the overall field of special forces operations out of the clouds, out of the discussion stage, and reduce it to organization, training, and operations." To accomplish this he recommended that the Infantry Center be designed as the focal point for doctrine, policy, and technique, and further advocated the activation of a "Special Forces Command" under the center to "explore, develop and conduct training in the field of special forces operations." Under this command should be placed Ranger training and "all other special forces operations."

Two other points should be noted about Volckmann's analysis. He believed that "special forces operations" should be an accepted field of conventional ground warfare; therefore "we should cease to regard special forces operations as irregular or unconventional warfare." Thus, the ultimate objective of special forces operations would be to "organize and support, wherever possible within the enemy's sphere of influence, guerrilla or indigenous forces on a military basis that are capable of efficient and controlled exploitation in conjunction with our land, air, and sea forces."

Having established that point, Volckmann proceeded to present what he envisaged as the Army's role in this activity in relation to the other services as well as to the CIA:

> To me, it is basically sound that the military (the Army, since this field falls within ground operations) has the inherent responsibility *in peace* to prepare and plan for the conduct of special forces operations and in time of war to organize and conduct special forces operations. Further, I feel that it is unsound, dangerous, and unworkable to delegate these responsibilities to a civil agency.[33]

Volckmann's analysis is important because it contains most of the major elements of controversy attendant to the creation of the Army's unconventional warfare capability. It also provides insight into the philosophy of the man who, probably more than any officer in General McClure's employ, shaped the creation of Special Forces.

Certainly, Volckmann's reservations about the CIA's role vis-a-vis the military services—and particularly the Army—was a major theme during these early years of OCPW's existence, as was his view that among the services the Army should have the predominant responsibility in this relatively new field. (The Air Force, in particular, disagreed with this contention.) His attempt to avoid terms like "irregular" or "unconventional" warfare indicated an early recognition of the need to allay the suspicions of conventional military men (although the term "unconventional warfare" remains in use to this day). And his advocacy of a "Special Forces Command" and training center was to come to fruition the following year but not at Fort Benning, and not in the form that he intended. While Volckmann clearly advocated the use of indigenous personnel in guerrilla warfare, he apparently intended that a Ranger unit would support and direct these personnel and not the OSS-type of Special Forces organization that he ultimately played such an instrumental role in creating. His use of the words "special forces operations," then, was synonymous with OCPW's understanding of "special operations;" that is, all types of behind-the-lines activities conducted for a military purpose, not just guerrilla warfare.[34] Later he would be more specific in differentiating between Ranger and Commando missions and those involving the organization and support of indigenous personnel in guerrilla warfare.

Another interesting aspect of Volckmann's memorandum was the bureaucratic tactic used to bring it to the attention of decisionmakers. After Volckmann returned from the Fort Benning conference, his memorandum was sent to the Chief of Staff, General Collins, with a request that "the interpretation that has been placed on these statements of General Collins be confirmed or commented on in order that appropriate action may be initiated by the Assistant Chief of Staff, G-3, to initiate the directives necessary to accomplish the desires of the Chief of Staff."[35] This proved the impetus for a series of foundational studies by OCPW, including the first one, "Army Responsibilities in Respect to Special (Forces) Operations," written principally by Volckmann and later approved by the Chief of Staff, a classic illustration of the manner in which one achieves "visibility" for a pet project in the Pentagon bureaucracy.[36]

By the end of May, the thinking in G-3 and OCPW had begun to crystallize concerning the utilization of the Eastern European recruits who would be brought into the Army via the Lodge bill. Standards of selection were established, and a goal of 800 set for persons who would volunteer for airborne training and who also possessed specialties related to the conduct of guerrilla warfare. The mission of these aliens would be to organize guerrilla bands in Eastern Europe after war began and attack the Soviet lines of communication, their purpose being to slow, or "retard," the Soviet advance into Western Europe. Plans were under development to train these personnel in increments of 100 in a cycle that included basic combat training, completion of the Ranger course at Fort Benning, and then further specialized instruction in guerrilla warfare, sabotage, clandestine communications, and related subjects.[37]

At the end of this training cycle, the aliens were to be sent to the European theater command. It was here that the planning was less precise. One alternative was the formation of additional "(Special Forces) Ranger Companies" to which could be assigned those Americans and Eastern European aliens trained for behind-the-lines operations, and which would be available to the theater command for commitment on D-day. Another alternative was to move the aliens to Europe for organization into provisional units, so as to be available for such operations upon the outbreak of hostilities.[38] These options evidence McClure's initial ruminations on the subject, but it was clear that nothing definite had been settled.

Approximately a month later, OCPW's thinking on the Lodge bill recruits began to show more specificity. The formation of a "Special Forces Regiment" of 3 battalions, a total of 2,481 personnel, was proposed. Approximately 1,300 of the 2,097 enlisted personnel would be Lodge bill recruits. The force could be trained and deployed to Europe in company-size increments to implement the unconventional warfare section of current war plans and "exploit the estimated 370,000 man potential within the U.S.S.R. and its satellites."[39] That last statement is particularly prophetic because, as we shall see, the subject of resistance potential in Europe was to become a point of contention between the Army and the CIA. Also noteworthy during this period were discussions by OCPW that included the idea that approximately 4,415 personnel organized into appropriate "operational groups" (an OSS term) would be needed in peacetime for commitment in the event of war. The object of this peacetime commitment would be to avoid the mistakes made during World War II: "We must not scatter arms, ammunition and supplies like so much grass seed and hope that they will fall on fertile soil and in turn prove of some assistance to our aims." To direct the forces in Europe, a "Theater Special Forces Training Command" in the United States was proposed, and the basic frame of reference was the Special Forces Ranger unit.[40]

This frame of reference took on a different perspective when the Commander in Chief, Far East Command, deactivated his Ranger companies in July 1951. The Rangers had been reactivated during the Korean conflict as separate companies and attached to infantry divisions. The 8213th Army Unit, known informally as the 8th Ranger Company, was the first to be created. It was formed at Camp Drake, Japan, in August 1950, with volunteers from US forces in the Far East. It was attached to the 25th Infantry Division, took part in the drive to the Yalu, and was deactivated in March 1951. Between September 1950 and September 1951, the Ranger Command at Fort Benning formed and trained 14 Airborne Ranger companies. The 1st, 2d, 3d, 4th, 5th, and 8th Companies were assigned to divisions throughout the 8th Army in Korea and were used primarily to perform long-range patrols for specialized missions and to spearhead attacks. The 2d and 4th were also attached to the 187th Regimental Combat Team for the combat jump at Munson-ni. After suffering more than 50-percent casualties, the Ranger companies were inactivated and the remaining personnel assigned throughout the divisions.[41]

At the time of CINCFE's action, the Commander in Chief, Europe (CINCEUR), indicated that he saw no need for Ranger companies in Europe, although he believed that there might be a need for Ranger units of battalion size under certain circumstances. One of CINCEUR's primary reasons for that position was the feeling that "Rangers, as a whole, drain first class soldiers from infantry organizations," a common complaint leveled against elite units, and one that Special Forces would have to contend with.[42] More pertinent to the advocates of "Special Forces Operations," however, were the views of both CINCFE and CINCEUR that the Rangers were not capable of conducting guerrilla warfare missions in their theaters because of racial and language barriers. Instead, they believed, such missions should be conducted by indigenous personnel who were in turn trained, supplied, and controlled by American military personnel.[43]

Voicing a related concern, Army, Field Forces (AFF)—commenting on OCPW's staff study, "Special Forces Ranger Units"— forwarded the view that any reference to Rangers should be deleted because "envisioned Special Forces will in all probability be involved in subversive activities." AFF believed that the concept of Special Forces should focus on the use of indigenous guerrilla groups behind enemy lines rather than American-staffed Ranger units; therefore, Rangers and Special Forces should be kept as separate and distinct organizations.[44]

The result of all this was a meeting on 23 August 1951, presided over by the G-3, General Taylor, from which came a decision to deactivate all Ranger units and convert the Ranger Training Command into a Department of the Infantry School. This department would conduct Ranger training for selected officers and enlisted men who on completion of the course would return to their parent units (a pattern that has continued until the present day). During the meeting the question arose concerning what agency would be capable of conducting "deep penetration activities," at which point, according to Colonel Aaron Bank's memorandum, "General Taylor was thoroughly briefed on the mission and capabilities of a Special Forces organization."[45]

This was perhaps the perfect illustration of the adage, "being at the right place at the right time," because the personnel spaces needed to create the 10th Special Forces Group ultimately became available as a result of the deactivation of the Ranger units. Henceforth there was to be little use of "Ranger" terminology by OCPW in its efforts to sell the concept of Special Forces or in its proposals for the organization to carry out guerrilla warfare. Its initial draft Table of Organization and Equipment (TO&E) for the "Special Forces Group," for example, presented as the group's mission the following: "To infiltrate its component *operational groups* [emphasis added] to designated areas within the enemy's sphere of influence and organize the indigenous guerrilla potential on a military basis for tactical and strategic exploitation in conjunction with our land, sea, and air forces."[46] The organization and functions of the group and its subordinate operational elements clearly depicted the influence of OSS concepts— particularly the Operational Group command—rather than those of the Rangers.

Ironically, a year later OCPW found it necessary to point out to Army Field Forces that use of the subordinate units of the Special Forces Group on independent Commando- or Ranger-like missions, "while a capability," was "to be discouraged as being highly wasteful of the highly developed skills wrapped up in the operational teams."[47] This was in the fall of 1952, when the 10th Special Forces Group was recruiting and training at Fort Bragg for deployment to Europe.

But Army Field Forces was not the only command in late 1952 whose ideas on the use of Special Forces elements differed from those of OCPW. In his preliminary planning for the utilization of the 10th Special Forces Group, Brigadier General Willard K. Liebel of the European Command envisaged the D-day employment of small groups to strike at close-in targets within a 50-mile zone immediately in front of US tactical divisions. McClure objected strenuously on this question of "basic Special Forces doctrine," telling Liebel that such an activity was a Ranger- or Commando-like action, normally of short duration, that did not require highly trained Special Forces personnel, and that this "was not in consonance with the concept underlying the creation of the 10th Special Forces Group." That concept was clear, thought McClure: "We continue to maintain that Special Forces Operational Detachments have the mission and capability of developing indigenous guerrilla forces, conducting operations behind the enemy lines, and of sustaining these operations for an indefinitely long time." To buttress his case, McClure told Liebel that "the Chief of Staff has insisted that Special Forces shall not duplicate the training and doctrine of ranger and commando units." [48] This was the same Chief of Staff, General Collins, who in April 1951 stated that he had "personally established the Rangers with the thought that they might serve as the nucleus for expansion in this direction [to initiate subversive activities]."

This apparent turnabout in the Chief of Staff's philosophy illustrates the confusion and difficulties that often accompany the emergence of a new concept within the military bureaucracy, particularly if that concept involves the creation of an "elite" unit. One of the principal requirements for "eliteness" is the possession of a specialized function, one that does not fall within the province of other military organizations. It is difficult to justify the existence of elite units if there appears to be unnecessary overlapping or redundancy of their functions and capabilities with those of other units. This is particularly so during periods of acute manpower shortages. In order to survive, the definition of an elite unit's special mission (and the acceptance of that mission by the bureaucracy) is a crucially important task. [49]

McClure and his staff came to recognize this necessity. With the deactivation of the Rangers, OCPW expended more and more effort to specify guerrilla warfare as the primary mission of the Special Forces organization that they proposed. Part of the confusion that marked this effort was of their own making, however. Their concept of "Special Forces Operations," for instance, was in actuality an all-encompassing heading under which were grouped the many kinds of operations—of which guerrilla warfare was one—whose only common denominator was that they were conducted within or behind enemy lines. One would have thought, obviously, that a Special Forces unit should conduct "Special Forces Operations" that included, by OCPW's definition, Ranger and Commando activities. But as time went on, the architects of Special Forces found it necessary to point out the error, as they saw it, of linking the Special Forces group and its component unit missions with the term "Special Forces Operations," on the assumption that the Special Forces Group was a TO&E unit designed to conduct all such operations. Needless to say, this rather subtle distinction was lost on many. This blurring of roles and missions was not aided, either, by OCPW's initial moves to graft the guerrilla warfare concept onto the Ranger organization, followed by its rather vigorous efforts to dissociate Special Forces from the Rangers.

Eventually, OCPW did answer General Taylor's initial directive to develop the Army responsibility for guerrilla warfare and then to assign that responsibility to subordinate Army units. The unit that evolved at Fort Bragg in 1952 was the Special Forces Group and its organization was based on OSS concepts, not Ranger. Perhaps Volckmann and his colleagues had OSS organizational principles clearly in mind from the beginning but found it more opportune to gain initial acceptance for their ideas by tagging them onto the Rangers, whose history in the Army was known—particularly since the Chief of Staff initially seemed to favor using the Rangers in a guerrilla warfare role. Or perhaps it was simply that the officers involved were grappling with new ideas and experimenting with the organizational machinery to implement those ideas. In all probability, the answer is that a combination of the two motives was at work during this conceptual period, and the deactivation of the Rangers helped to clarify the situation.

The Road to Fort Bragg

Concurrent with the deactivation of the Rangers, General McClure began to take an interest in establishing a training facility for both psychological warfare and unconventional warfare. To be sure, Colonel Volckmann had campaigned since April for a training command or center that would fully develop the doctrine, techniques, and logistics of special forces operations. And there had been some discussion between the G-3 Division and Army Field Forces in early 1950, before the creation of OCPW, about the need for a "school center" for psychological warfare. That discussion had resulted in establishment of the Psychological Warfare Department at Fort Riley, just then producing its first graduates. But now McClure began to entertain the idea of centralizing the functions of "the whole field of OCPW" at a post other than Fort Riley.[50]

McClure and Colonel Bank visited Army Field Forces in mid-August to outline the Army's responsibilities for unconventional warfare and to stress the lack of organization, training, and planning in that field as compared with the progress made in psychological warfare. The possibility was raised of establishing a "Guerrilla Training Command" at Fort Benning or perhaps Fort Campbell and moving the Psychological Warfare Department from Fort Riley to this new center.[51] Thus began the search for a training center, a search that would end with the selection of Fort Bragg.

It was not an easy journey. First, there was the matter of the CIA. As we have seen, the Army basically welcomed the emergence of CIA/OPC during the interwar years, and in 1949 agreed to provide it unilateral assistance in the field of guerrilla warfare, which included help in setting up a training course at Fort Benning. After the outbreak of war in Korea, the Army also provided some personnel to the CIA for its activities in that theater.

But then General McClure and his OCPW appeared on the scene. By the spring of 1951, McClure had already expressed his reservations about the relatively autonomous role of OPC in Korea. In subsequent months, the frustration of his unsuccessful attempts to influence the situation in Korea, plus his battle to bring Special Forces into being and plan for its use in Europe, transformed McClure's reservations into outright suspicions about the CIA's motives.

The CIA reciprocated those suspicions. For example, in mid-1951, both CIA/OPC and OCPW entered into a series of conferences to determine means of further collaboration in guerrilla warfare training programs. Even though the study that resulted indicated that the CIA would benefit by sending some of its personnel to the center being proposed by OCPW, the forwarding memorandum sent General McClure stated that "Mr. Wisner [head of OPC] would like it to be clearly understood that this understanding is reached on the assumption that the Army is creating a Special Forces Training Command for its own purposes and not at the request of CIA."[52] The caveat expressed by Frank Wisner was obvious: The CIA was not going to place itself in the position of giving the Army an excuse to justify the creation of its own unconventional warfare capability. Perhaps it was inevitable that two strong-willed men like Wisner and McClure, both eyeing the same "turf" in a relatively new field, would come into conflict in attempting to establish the boundaries within which each would operate.

Not that there were no attempts to define those boundaries and to cooperate with each other. There were. Both men entered into an initial, tentative agreement in July 1951 concerning their understanding of the respective roles of CIA/OPC and OCPW in the field of unconventional warfare. The aforementioned conferences on training programs followed, and in April 1952 the two agencies agreed to an official liaison arrangement to coordinate materiel research activities.[53]

There is also evidence that despite his early reservations about OPC's activities in Korea, McClure took a considerably more broadminded view of the CIA's role in unconventional warfare than did certain members of his staff. After returning from a visit to Europe in August and September

1952, where he had discussed unconventional warfare planning for that theater, McClure chided his staff:

> Putnam [a JCS officer] and I talked at length reference the philosophies I expressed—as I have repeated over and over with you people. Putnam says they are not being reflected by you people at the JSPD level. I believe the Army should be the Executive Agent for guerrilla activities. I am not going to fight with CIA as to their responsibilities in those fields.

> Another is the fact that I am fully in accord with supporting the CIA in their peacetime activities in getting ready for war to the maximum extent I can and in wartime will welcome any of their resources to the maximum of their capability.[54]

This was the pragmatic McClure of World War II who, as Chief, PWD/SHAEF, had brought together a number of disparate agencies and nationality groups, civilian as well as military, in order to get the job done. He had learned well from that master of compromise and cooperation, Dwight D. Eisenhower. But as the months and years went by, McClure became less tolerant, gradually adopting in his condemnation of the CIA the phrases of the most virulent critics on his staff. At the end of his tenure as Chief, OCPW, the subject preoccupied him.

What caused this turnabout? Perhaps the most succinct explanation of McClure's change of attitude is found in one of the last letters he wrote before leaving OCPW in early 1953. Writing to his old friend General Bolte, then Commander in Chief, Europe, McClure explained:

> Unfortunately I will not go through Germany on my way to Iran else I would take the opportunity to bring you up to date on the Army/CIA relationship. I feel that the latest paper on command relationship has so much fine print in it that we have committed ourselves to the creation of a fourth service which will effectively tie the hands of the military and require the Theater Commander to lean on and support CIA for all Unconventional Warfare. In recent conferences at CIA, I have heard the statement made repeatedly that, "Since we are now a fourth service many of the activities for which the Army was planning should be transferred to CIA, including the command of military forces designed for guerrilla warfare in time of war." Needless to say I am very unhappy about it both because I question the ability of CIA and second, because I have never believed the Joint Chiefs intended to abrogate their responsibilities for the active command of military operations in time of war.[55]

Here, then, were McClure's key grievances. Aside from the perennial question during these early years of the precise delineation of peacetime and wartime responsibilities for unconventional warfare between the CIA and the Department of Defense, McClure had simply come to believe that the CIA was not capable of holding up its end of the bargain, however it was defined. Imbued with the urgency of preparing the Nation and the Army for a possible war in Europe, McClure was dissatisfied with the CIA's apparent lack of progress in preparation for guerrilla warfare. He reported to the Chief of Staff in early September 1951 that the "CIA has only now initiated planning for the execution of preparatory measures to aid in the retardation of a Soviet advance."[56] He believed, therefore, that the military—and particularly the Army—needed to have unconventional warfare forces in being, and that necessary planning, organization, and training had to be carried out before D-day. In his view, the military services could not leave these preparations to chance or in the hands of a civilian agency. Nor should the JCS allow a situation to develop where the theater commander in an active theater of war lacked full control over all military operations in his area of responsibility, as had happened in Korea, McClure believed.

Underlying McClure's doubts about the CIA's capability to perform the unconventional warfare mission, however, was a difference of philosophy between OCPW and the CIA concerning the nature of resistance potential in Europe. The CIA position on this subject was perhaps most eloquently stated by its Director, General Walter B. Smith, in a letter written to the Army G-2 in March 1952. Smith opened his letter by referring to McClure as follows:

> At certain times in the past we have been importuned by General McClure's people to provide them with detailed information concerning guerrilla groups of which we may have some knowledge. We have consistently declined to furnish this information to General McClure because the information requested impinges directly upon secret operations in which we are currently engaged and for which, at this time, we are solely responsible.[57]

Here was a real source of irritation. The CIA, understandably, was reluctant to share information about its operations that could compromise important intelligence assets and perhaps undermine by premature disclosure the very resistance potential that would be counted upon in wartime. McClure's office—also understandably—was frustrated by its inability to receive the information it believed necessary for proper prewar planning, and the extreme secrecy involved only heightened OCPW's suspicions about the CIA's lack of preparedness. It was to be a persistent topic of discord between the two agencies.

In his March letter to the Army G-2, the Director of the CIA also questioned "the validity of General McClure's proposal for retardation by guerrilla forces." Expressing both the views of his agency and those of "the leading British experts in this field," Smith explained:

> It is highly doubtful that general resistance forces will develop any substantial offensive capability until at least D plus six months. Enemy controls and reprisals will be extremely severe upon the outbreak of war. Certain underground organizations have even indicated that they will hesitate to go into action until the Allied battle line is stabilized on the continent and the tide is turning our way.

After enlarging upon this theme for several paragraphs, Smith then summarized his position:

> For the reasons outlined above, any program which contemplates that large scale resistance organizations, developed prior to D-day and held in readiness for an indefinite period of time would be willing and capable to deliver major offensive blows within the first few weeks after the commencement of hostilities is considered by us to be unrealistic and infeasible.[58]

McClure had, of course, considered the pros and cons of what he termed the "two different schools of thought on the timing of the commitment of unconventional forces." One school held that the first few days of a Soviet attack were critical, and that even a few hours of delay produced by unconventional warfare forces would be significant. The other school (the "British view") held that guerrilla forces should not dissipate their efforts prematurely and thus did not favor any uprising until regular Allied military forces were in a position to support them. McClure presented his own analysis to the Chief of Staff September 1951:

> To accept the latter view would mean nothing would happen on D-day and not until we were in a position to start liberating over-run countries. To accept the former view would mean attrition might completely dissolve that work and organization which has been created. My personal view is that even with the attrition we have more to gain than to lose, and that if the British can organize after D-day for a future use, such guerrilla forces as desired, obviously we could reorganize in those areas where attrition had taken its toll.[59]

In addition to disagreeing with OCPW about how the resistance should be generated and when it should be committed, the CIA also took exception with OCPW's estimates of resistance potential in Eastern Europe; it called the projected indigenous strength estimates in OCPW's Special Forces Operations Plan for Europe "unrealistic and unattainable." These and other views advanced by the CIA apparently formed the basis for initial JCS disapproval of the plan in late 1952.[60]

These were fundamental differences. McClure's deepest concern, however, was best illustrated by the remark in his letter to Bolte about CIA ambitions to become a "fourth service." He was genuinely apprehensive of allowing too much latitude to the CIA because it could lead to an undue reliance by the military on CIA/OPC for unconventional warfare activities. If that happened, he feared that unconventional warfare might "become regarded among military commanders and planners as a limited, special 'cloak and dagger' function rather than as a basically important, possibly essential military responsibility."[61]

Here again is a reminder of the problem with image as perceived by McClure and his staff—the constant battle to achieve legitimacy for unconventional warfare among "conventional" military officers. If too much responsibility for unconventional warfare was passed to the CIA, it could reinforce the reservations that many officers already harbored concerning the Army's role in unconventional warfare. In a period of budgetary and manpower shortages, such reservations could quickly lead to the conclusion that the Army could not and should not attempt to duplicate the functions of a civilian agency. In short, McClure's primary concern, while well intentioned, was bureaucratic in nature and aimed at the establishment and preservation of an unconventional warfare capability for the Army.

Another threat to McClure's attempts to establish a strong Army role in unconventional warfare was the opposition of the Air Force. We have already seen that he was critical of the Air Force support of Army psychological warfare activities in Korea and was concerned about what he considered the unnecessary duplication of propaganda equipment and personnel in their Aerial Resupply and Communication (ARC) wings. By their support of CIA operations in Korea, these same wings also gave the Air Force claim to a leading role in unconventional warfare. The Air Force list of wartime missions for these ARC wings included introduction and evacuation of agents behind enemy lines, aerial resupply of guerrillas, support of commando-type operations and isolated Army units, printing and packaging of leaflets, and providing trained personnel capable of conducting psychological warfare through other media. In short, the Air Force claimed the ARC wings gave them the capability to support CIA activities during peacetime or wartime, to conduct overt psychological warfare, and to direct, coordinate, and support unconventional warfare operations.[62]

This close peacetime association with the CIA caused the Air Force, in the eyes of OCPW, to champion CIA/OPC as the agency responsible for planning and preparing the conduct of unconventional warfare, thus taking issue with the concept that the Army had a major responsibility and principal function in this field as part of land warfare. Similarly, the Air Force used this association with CIA/OPC, thought OCPW, to seek a unilateral, preeminent position among the military services for control and direction of wartime unconventional warfare activities.[63]

As one might have expected, General McClure disagreed with the contentions of the Air Force. In his view, the Air Force was essentially a "supply agency" for unconventional warfare activities, "with transportation capable of doing certain things that the Ground Forces are going to require and going to command." He favored Air Force development of special wings to support psychological and unconventional warfare activities, but not to duplicate the Army's capabilities, and certainly not to be used as a license to claim a dominant role in those fields.[64] McClure was particularly disturbed by the lack of joint unconventional warfare planning that he found when he visited Europe in the fall of 1951, and told the Chief of Staff that the Air Force not only disagreed with the Army view on retardation but also "felt they had a major responsibility in the field of unconventional warfare which did not exclude the actual command of guerrillas." Because of the unilateral efforts of the services and what he saw as unnecessary duplication and confusion among them and in their relationship with the CIA, McClure believed that one service should be designated as the executive agency for guerrilla warfare, and that service, of course, should be the Army.[65]

Valuable support for McClure's view of a dominant role for the Army in unconventional warfare came from General Eisenhower, the Supreme Allied Commander in Europe. During another visit to Europe in November 1951, McClure briefed Eisenhower on the command and coordination difficulties that had arisen with respect to unconventional warfare planning for Europe. Eisenhower was "keenly alert" to the potential that unconventional warfare offered, stated McClure in his trip report to the Chief of Staff, and gave McClure permission to quote him on the following views:

One Service must not only have a paramount interest in this field but also be the controlling authority.

In my opinion this field is an Army one and . . . in my theater it will be.

All facilities must be put under the Army. The Navy and Air Force will have to support the Army. Air support is essential but in this field the Air Force is only a transport outfit.[66]

Eisenhower went on to speak strongly against extravagance resulting from duplication or individual service jealousies. It was a strong endorsement of McClure's views, but the interservice rivalry in unconventional warfare continued, particularly with respect to planning and command responsibilities in Europe. OCPW eventually did obtain recognition for the Army as having primary responsibility among the services for this new field.[67] But the conflict between the Air Force and Army that marked this process—along with the conflict between the Army and the CIA—was a key feature in the backdrop of McClure's efforts to create Special Forces and establish the Psychological Warfare Center.

In addition to the interagency and interservice rivalry that OCPW had to contend with, there was the not inconsiderable challenge of selling the Army on the concept of Special Forces and the idea of a centralized training command for both psychological and unconventional warfare. In June 1951 General Collins, the Chief of Staff, approved the conclusions of Volckmann's initial study "Army Responsibilities for Special Forces Operations" and forwarded it to the JCS, indicating that until the JCS delineated service responsibilities for unconventional warfare, the Army would use this study as a basis for planning.[68] Although an important first step, this general endorsement by Collins to proceed with investigation and planning on the subject did not provide OCPW with the specific authorization needed.

That came only after the initial discussion by McClure and Colonel Bank with Army Field Forces in August 1951; in mid-September the G-3 concurred with the recommendation of the Army Field Forces that a training center should be established for psychological warfare and special operations. Indicating to OCPW that this center should be established "on an austere basis," the G-3 also directed action "to establish the extent to which the resources of the Army are to be allocated to Special (Forces) Operations." But the following caution was pointedly added:

In view of the acute manpower situation and the known reluctance of overseas commanders to accept special units within their troop ceiling, in preference to established units, the basic policy in regard to Special

(Forces) Operations should be the maximum utilization of indigenous personnel for such operations and the minimum use of American personnel.[69]

Following on the heels of the deactivation of the Ranger units, this statement clearly indicates the wariness with which conventional commanders and staffs regarded "elite" and "special" units, particularly during periods of budgetary and manpower shortages.

The opening, albeit narrow, provided by G-3, allowed OCPW to act. A cascade of actions poured from McClure's staff: representatives met with the staff of Army Field Forces to develop an agreed Table of Distribution for a Psychological Warfare Center; Tables of Organization and Equipment for the units of a Special Forces Group (no longer called a Special Forces Ranger Regiment) were developed for staffing; a proposed training circular describing the mission, capabilities, organization, concept of employment, and training of a Special Forces Group was written; a requirement for 3,700 personnel spaces, including 300 spaces for the proposed training center, was submitted; a proposed directive to the Chief of Army Field Forces outlining his responsibilities in psychological warfare and Special Forces Operations, as well as a suggested Army Field Forces training program for these areas, was prepared; and Fort Campbell, Kentucky, was recommended as the site for the new center, with a suggested activation date of 1 December 1951. These actions were reported to G-3 on 5 October, scarcely 3 weeks after OCPW had received the go-ahead from them.[70] McClure wanted to move fast.

Army Field Forces had recommended that the proposed training center be established at either Fort Campbell or Camp Pickett, Virginia. OCPW favored Fort Campbell because it had airborne and parachute maintenance facilities, but recommended to G-3 that a final decision on the location be withheld until a survey of installations was conducted.[71] In the end, though, the personnel spaces requested for Special Forces and the center, the target date for activation, and the tentative location all proved inaccurate. But McClure was making rapid progress toward his goal.

Both McClure and his chief architect for Special Forces, Volckmann, were aware of the suspicions engendered among many officers by these efforts to introduce into the Army new ideas and a new organization to carry out those ideas. Both men took steps to dispel those suspicions. In a paper written in late October 1951, Volckmann analyzed the problem this way:

> The question of assets, capabilities and support that must be diverted to behind-the-lines operations brings us to a final major problem. So many strictly conventional military minds "flash-red" at the mention of anything "special" or at the diversion of personnel and equipment to any channel other than conventional regular forces. In a way, they are justified in safeguarding the diversion of personnel, equipment and support that will in any way tend to weaken the capabilities of our regular forces. For the most part, however, their fears are without foundation. If they will but take time to view the problem of any future war as a whole, their initial reactions should be modified and their fears dispelled.[72]

Volckmann believed that World War II behind-the-lines operations had fallen far short of their potential. He blamed this on the failure by the military to regard these activities as an integral part of conventional warfare. Proper emphasis, in other words, had been lacking at both staff and operating levels. The result, in his view, was guerrilla warfare conducted as a "sideshow" on a "shoestring," uncoordinated with the operations of conventional forces. To prevent this from happening again, and to convince military men of the importance of behind-the-lines operations in modern warfare, he advocated general indoctrination on the subject in service schools and specialized training in appropriate centers, such as the one for "special forces operations" that he had advocated 6 months earlier.[73]

Similarly, in a briefing prepared for the Secretary of Defense in early November 1951, General McClure voiced his concerns about the adverse image that unconventional warfare had among some military men:

> I have been told that the dynamic manner in which my office developed led to apprehension on the part of some that the Army was seeking to enter fields not properly a part of ground warfare. This is furthest from our intent. We have sought and will continue to seek to prepare ourselves and the Army to discharge those responsibilities which are proper and appropriate Army functions. . . . This broad field of unconventional warfare must be planned and conducted on a Joint and National basis. No one Service can "go it alone."[74]

While he was proud of what his office had accomplished, McClure told those present at this briefing that he was also "deeply apprehensive over the future." Typifying the cold war fears that imbued so many senior officers with a sense of urgency, he stated that "none of us in this room today knows how much time we will have" because "we face an enemy who is prepared to take the field tomorrow morning." His summation: "In Psychological

Operations we are fast approaching a state of readiness," but in Special Operations, "we are years behind."[75]

An ironic footnote concerning the term "special operations" should be mentioned. It was about this time—the fall of 1951—that the Army began to use the term "special forces operations" as opposed to "special operations," the reason being that the latter term was defined through long usage in the Army and as set forth in Field Manual 100-5 as relating to such activities as "night combat," "jungle operations," and "joint amphibious operations." OCPW argued that to adopt some other term for those operations "would only lead to confusion or result in costly expenditure of funds . . . to modify existing literature and doctrine already published."[76] Later, the term "special forces operations" itself would be dropped by the Army, and replaced by "unconventional warfare" (which encompassed guerrilla warfare, evasion and escape, subversion and sabotage) as the primary mission for Special Forces units. The irony is that during the 1970's, Special Forces would again adopt a version of "special operations" (with the official definition still relatively unchanged in JCS and Army literature) as one of their primary missions, a move that contributed to the perception that they were duplicating functions and capabilities of Ranger units.[77]

A few days after McClure's briefing for the Secretary of Defense, a discussion took place during McClure's weekly staff meeting on the forthcoming survey of Army posts to select a site for the Psychological Warfare Center. Of the posts to be visited—Fort Benning, Fort Campbell, and Fort Bragg—McClure had a definite preference. He stated to Colonel Bank: "Make it Bragg if you can."[78]

And Fort Bragg it was, but not without difficulty. The surveys conducted in November by representatives of OCPW, Army Field Forces, and the 3rd Army, revealed some resistance to that site. The Infantry Center at Fort Benning did not want to allocate space and facilities to any activity not directly related to its mission, an ironic position in view of the direct support being provided to infantry divisions in Korea by psychological warfare teams; and there were other objections as well. The 3rd Army opposed establishing the center at Fort Bragg on the grounds that other conventional combat units scheduled for activation there would have to be organized at a less desirable post. They suggested Camp Rucker, Alabama, as an alternative, but that site offered little for airborne and amphibious training and had no housing for dependents—a potential morale problem. Of the sites considered, the representatives from OCPW and Army Field

Forces clearly favored Fort Bragg: the necessary personnel spaces could be accommodated; buildings, with some modification, were available; and it offered superior training advantages and facilities for both psychological warfare and Special Forces units.[79] But first the impasse had to be broken.

This was accomplished by Colonel Glavin, the Army Field Forces representative recently transferred from OCPW, who arranged a conference between General Leonard, General Bradford, and General Hodge in an attempt to break the deadlock. Colonel Fertig, Chief of OCPW's Special Operations Division, urged McClure to personally brief General Hodge on the desirability of Fort Bragg, which he apparently did because on 4 December Glavin obtained approval for the North Carolina post.[80]

Still to be obtained were the exact facilities needed at Fort Bragg, so another survey trip was planned for this purpose. General McClure's guidance was clear: "I want these requirements to be modest. We have to go on a very austere basis at first."[81] He was very aware of the precarious position of these new ideas during a period of budget cutting and did not want to jeopardize their chances of survival by appearing to be too greedy in his demands.

The minutes of the OCPW staff meeting for October-December 1951 also depict continuing efforts to identify personnel on active duty with experience in behind-the-lines activities. OCPW requested the Adjutant General to prepare a roster of officers with OSS, Commando, Ranger, and guerrilla backgrounds, and sent an officer to visit General Donovan, then practicing law in New York, to examine his personal files in an attempt to obtain a list of Army officers who had served in OSS. This last effort resulted in a roster of 3,900 names, which were then screened to identify those still on active duty.[82] Certainly this is still another indicator of the pervasive influence OSS had on the thinking of the architects of Special Forces during this crucial formative period.

The survey team that returned to Fort Bragg to select the exact location decided upon an area known as Smoke Bomb Hill. Its buildings, left over from World War II mobilization, were suitable for barracks, mess halls, administration halls, classrooms, and a library. Estimated cost for rehabilitation of the facilities was $151,000, an exceedingly modest sum. Even this minimal estimate, however, caused some agitation; the 3rd Army representative stated unofficially that his headquarters had no funds available; thus Army Field Forces would have to allocate the necessary monies in order to get the project under way. Despite this minor maneuvering between headquarters to fix fiscal responsibilities, Lieutenant Colonel Melvin Blair from OCPW reported to McClure that "in general, the area is exactly what we wanted."[83] At the end of 1951, only two major tasks remained—to obtain the necessary personnel spaces for activation of both the center and Special Forces, and to get the Chief of Staff's blessing for the whole project.

General McClure personally involved himself in these tasks. After a busy January—during which he made a major presentation before the Psychological Strategy Board on the Army's activity in psychological warfare and guerrilla warfare, pursued the question of funds for his proposed center, and investigated a security breach concerning the activation of Special Forces[84]—he continued the campaign to bring his goals to fruition. In an early February 1952 memorandum to the G-3, McClure urged that the activation of new psychological warfare and Special Forces units "be expedited by every feasible method." His rationale was convincing: no Radio Broadcasting and Leaflet Group existed in the United States to function as school troops, to train replacement personnel for similar units in Europe and the Far East, or to meet emergency requirements; and units of the proposed "Special Forces Group (Guerrilla Warfare)" were needed for planned D-day actions in Europe. Clearly establishing that, in his view, the activation of psychological warfare and Special Forces units was closely intertwined with the concurrent action to approve and authorize spaces for the Psychological Warfare Center, McClure also asked that the latter project be expedited. Recognizing the vulnerability of his plans in the hands of budget cutters, McClure made an eloquent plea:

> At times when the Army as a whole is faced with a reduction in the number of authorized spaces, it becomes necessary to determine areas which can absorb "cuts" without unduly impairing overall efficiency. A new activity faced with an across-the-board cut, or with a "cut" made on a fixed percentage basis, can be crippled to the point where its existence is seriously threatened. This is particularly true in the case of Psychological Warfare and Special Operations activities which are already on an austere basis. I recommend that these factors be considered when an Army-wide reduction in space authorization is contemplated.[85]

The G-3's response to this plea was terse. McClure's request for early activation of the psychological warfare and Special Forces units desired would be acted on after the "implications of the reduced FY [fiscal year] 1953 budget have been fully weighed." On a brighter note, the G-3 did indicate that it was preparing a summary sheet for the Chief of Staff recommending approval of the Psychological Warfare Center.[86]

Sure enough, on 3 March 1952, the promised summary sheet was sent to General Collins. The sheet stated that implementation of the conclusions reached in the study "Army Responsibilities in Respect to Special Forces Operations," previously approved by Collins, required a "Psychological Warfare and Special Forces Center" in peacetime to train individuals and units to support theater Special Forces operations. (Again we see the importance of Volckmann's initial study as the underlying rationale for this concept.) The memorandum also indicated that the proposed center would consolidate psychological warfare and Special Forces training activities at a single installation. Three weeks later, on 27 March 1952, the Chief of Staff gave his approval that such a center be established.[87]

Within 10 days, General McClure proudly provided the details of the Chief of Staff's decision to the JCS. A Psychological Warfare Center would be activated on or about 1 May 1952, at Fort Bragg, North Carolina. The administrative staff and faculty for Psychological Warfare and Special Forces Departments and a Research and Development Board would total 173 personnel on an austere basis and increase to a full strength of 362 officers and men. The Psychological Warfare School and units at Fort Riley, Kansas, would move to Fort Bragg once the new center was activated. A total of 2,220 spaces had been authorized for activation of Psychological Warfare and Special Forces units for fiscal year 1953-54.

A Special Forces Group would be activated at Fort Bragg in 3 increments of approximately 600 men and officers each, commencing about 1 May 1952.[88] General McClure's dream of centralizing the functions of "the whole field of OCPW" was near reality. The long journey to Fort Bragg was soon to end.

VIII

THE PSYCHOLOGICAL WARFARE CENTER AND THE ORIGINS OF SPECIAL WARFARE

After receiving the Chief of Staff's formal approval in late March 1952, the Office of the Chief of Psychological Warfare moved quickly to get the Psychological Warfare Center on its feet. The formal order establishing the center at Fort Bragg, under the jurisdiction of the Commanding General, 3rd Army, was published on 14 April 1952. Copies of the Table of Distribution (TD) for the center were hand-carried by General McClure's staff to 3rd Army, Army Field Forces, and Fort Bragg during the period 16–18 April. The mission of this unprecedented center, as explained by the TD, was:

> To conduct individual training and supervise unit training in Psychological Warfare and Special Forces Operations; to develop and test Psychological Warfare and Special Forces doctrine, procedures, tactics, and techniques; to test and evaluate equipment employed in Psychological Warfare and Special Forces Operations.[1]

Movement of equipment and personnel from Fort Riley to Fort Bragg began by late April, and on 29 May 1952 the Chief of Army Field Forces at Fort Monroe, Virginia, formally announced the activation of the Psychological Warfare Center at Fort Bragg. The same order officially transferred responsibilities for the development and teaching of psychological warfare doctrine from the Army General School at Fort Riley to the newly formed Psychological Warfare Center.[2]

Organization of the Center

As originally established, the Psychological Warfare Center consisted of a provisional Psychological Warfare School, the 6th Radio Broadcasting and Leaflet Group, a Psychological Warfare Board, and the 10th Special Forces Group.[3] Colonel Charles N. Karlstad, former Chief of Staff of the Infantry Center, Fort Benning, Georgia, was selected as the first Commander of the center and Commandant of the Psychological Warfare School.[4] In the foreword to an administrative booklet prepared for visitors participating in a psychological warfare seminar during 1952, Colonel Karlstad offered some thoughts on the role of his new command:

> The PsyWar Center represents an effort unique to the military history of the United States. For the first time, the techniques of attacking both the minds and the bodies of our enemies have been coordinated in a single training operation. The Psychological Warfare and Special Forces Departments [of the Psychological Warfare School], closely linked, instruct in the unconventional weapons and tactics with which our modern army must be equipped to function effectively against enemy forces.[5]

(Karlstad's comments are strikingly reminiscent of General Donovan's all-encompassing concept of psychological warfare when he organized the Coordinator of Information 11 years earlier.)

One may wonder why the Psychological Warfare School was initially given a provisional status. The G–3, Department of the Army, disapproved of its activation as a formally designated Army service school on the basis that such a school was not necessary to the accomplishment of the center's mission and that the establishment of a formal school would require additional funds.[6] This must have been particularly perplexing to the personnel at Fort Bragg; even as an element of the Army General School at Fort Riley, the Psychological Warfare Division had been given service school recognition. Formal service schools enjoyed obvious advantages over the informal schools such as those often set up by divisions and regiments. These advantages included increased prestige, funding, and equipment procurement as well as the opportunity to attract quality faculty personnel. The Psychological Warfare Center, in a letter signed by Colonel Karlstad and addressed to the Chief, Psychological Warfare, Department of the Army, made a strong case for reconsideration of the decision, an appeal that received the strong support of General McClure.[7] Apparently the appeal was effective, for on 22 October 1952 Department of the Army General Order No. 92 officially established the Psychological Warfare School as a service school.

The purpose of the Psychological Warfare School was to "prepare selected individuals of the Army to perform those psychological warfare and special forces duties which they may be called upon to perform in war."[8] The school was organized into a small headquarters staff and two instructional divisions: the Psychological Operations Department and the Special Forces Department. In terms of longevity, the senior element in the school was the Psychological Operations Department; it was a direct descendant of the Army General School's Psychological Warfare Division, which had been transferred and integrated into the Psychological Warfare Center in early 1952.[9]

Lieutenant Colonel Otis E. Hays, Jr., who had been Deputy of the Psychological Warfare Division of the Army General School, became the first director of the Psychological Operations Department. The mission of the department was defined as the following: The instruction and training of selected officers in the duties of psychological warfare operations staffs from Department of the Army to field army and corps levels; the instruction and training of selected individuals, officers, and noncommissioned officers as specialists in propaganda operations and as key persons in psychological warfare operational units; and the preparation and revision of extension course training literature, and field manuals on psychological warfare organization, operations, and doctrine.[10] The importance of the Psychological Operations Department's activities certainly was enhanced by the Army's needs in Korea, as evidenced by this statement from the 1 January–30 June 1953 report of the Secretary of Defense:

> The role of psychological warfare as a support weapon in combat was highlighted by improved psychological warfare operations carried on by the Army during the year, stimulating the development of the program at the Psychological Warfare Center at Fort Bragg. . . . Schools and units have been established there to train officers and enlisted men in all phases of this speciality.[11]

The Secretary's report made no mention of the activities of either the 10th Special Forces Group or its counterpart in the Psychological Warfare School, the Special Forces Department. Nor was there any mention of these two elements—or of the Army's attempts to develop an unconventional warfare capability—in the 1 January–30 June 1952 report of the Secretary, although that report did note the establishment of the Psychological Warfare Center at Fort Bragg "to provide comprehensive courses of instruction in all phases of psychological warfare."[12]

The lack of publicity given to Special Forces was due largely to security considerations. Because the mission of Special Forces was classified, little reference to its organization and activities initially appeared in press releases concerning the Psychological Warfare Center.[13] The center continued this caution with security in its own publications, much to the consternation of the Special Forces enthusiasts among McClure's staff. They complained that the student handbook published by the Psychological Warfare School was "slanted heavily towards Psychological Warfare to the detriment of Special Forces," and feared the result would be "that the Special Forces student, therefore, will look upon himself as a 'country cousin' to the Psychological Warfare Center." Lieutenant Colonel Melvin Blair, who had been on the road attempting to "sell" Special Forces in a recruitment program, was particularly miffed and recommended that OCPW take action "to revise the handbook along more impartial lines."[14] (In later years—particularly during the 1960's, the heyday of the "Green Berets"—psychological warfare would be considered the "country cousin" at the center, an ironic turnabout in perceptions.) While these complaints may appear trivial, they were evidence of a resentment that went beyond the security restrictions on publicity for Special Forces; some of McClure's staff simply did not believe that unconventional warfare units should be associated with psychological warfare, and certainly not in a subordinate role.

In any event, the junior member of the Psychological Warfare School was the Special Forces Department, which, unlike the Psychological Operations Department, had no predecessor in US Army history. With Colonel Filmore K. Mearns as its first director, the missions of this department were outlined as follows: the conduct of regular Special Forces courses for officers and selected enlisted men; the conduct of Special Forces orientation courses for designated personnel; the preparation and revision of literature and lessons for Special Forces extension courses; and the preparation and revision of training literature, field manuals, circulars, and special texts on Special Forces operations.[15] Essentially, the department concentrated on teaching the fundamentals of unconventional warfare, with emphasis on the conduct of guerrilla operations, to personnel being assigned to Special Forces.

Another unique organization created as part of the center was the Psychological Warfare Board, which was to "test, evaluate, and compile reports on materiel, doctrine, procedure, technique, and tactics pertaining to and for Psychological Warfare and Special Forces."[16] By early 1954, the board had completed over 40 projects, among them the operational facets of psychological warfare transmitter and receiving equipment, loudspeaker equipment, mobile reproduction equipment, and different types of leaflet dissemination techniques such as the use of mortar and artillery shells, rockets, light liaison planes, and balloons. It appears that in the early days of 1952-53, the Psychological Warfare Board devoted its activities almost exclusively to the support of units like the 6th Radio Broadcasting and Leaflet (RB&L) Group, rather than to Special Forces.[17]

The nucleus of the 6th Radio Broadcasting and Leaflet Group began on 14 September 1951, with the formation of a provisional Psychological Warfare Detachment at Fort Riley. That unit soon achieved status as a permanent organization, and on 2 May 1952 it became the 6th RB&L Group. The Group consisted at that time of a Headquarters and Headquarters Company, the 7th Reproduction Company, and the 8th Mobile Radio Broadcasting Company. In June 1952, it moved to Fort Bragg to become a part of the Psychological Warfare Center. That month, the 2nd Loudspeaker and Leaflet (L&L) Company was attached to the 6th RB&L Group, and on 27 May 1953 the 12th Consolidation Company was activated and attached to the Group. As previously mentioned, the RB&L organizational concept was first employed in Korea and the Mobile Radio Broadcasting Company's ancestry could be traced to World War II, when several of these companies were used in the European theater. The 6th RB&L Group was designated as a strategic psychological warfare operational unit, and its primary purpose was to assist the national psychological warfare program during wartime within the theater of operation to which it was assigned. In addition to conducting theater-wide strategic propaganda, a further mission of the 6th RB&L was to support tactical operations.[18]

The 10th Special Forces Group

Even before activation of the 10th Special Forces Group, Lieutenant Colonel Blair and Colonel Volckmann from the Special Operations Division, OCPW, began visiting Army installations and schools throughout the continental United States, Alaska, Hawaii, the Far East, and Europe to promote interest in the "new concept" of war. Volunteers had to be at least 21 years old, be airborne qualified or willing to become so, and undergo a series of physical and psychological tests. Enlisted men accepted into Special Forces acquired one or more of five basic occupational specialities: operations and intelligence, engineering, weaponry, communications, and medical aid.[19]

The material used by OCPW for orientation and recruitment specifically drew a distinction between Special Forces and Ranger units:

> Ranger units are designed and trained to conduct shallow penetration or infiltration of enemy lines. They can remain in the objective area for a limited time only. Primarily, they execute missions of a harassing and raiding nature against targets close to friendly front lines. Ranger missions are performed solely by US personnel; they do not utilize indigenous personnel in their objectives. Special Forces units have the capability of conducting long-range penetration deep into the objective area in order to organize, train, equip, and control indigenous guerrilla forces.[20]

Indeed, not only did OCPW make a distinction concerning the missions and capabilities of Special Forces and Rangers, but the term "Special Forces operations" itself underwent a metamorphosis. Volckmann's original definition in early 1951 established that Special Forces operations were behind-the-lines activities that could encompass guerrilla warfare, sabotage and subversion, evasion and escape, Ranger- and Commando-like operations, long-range or deep-penetration reconnaissance, and psychological warfare. From January to late September 1952, OCPW recruiting material used the term to embrace the following: organization and conduct of guerrilla warfare; subversion and sabotage; political, economic, and psychological warfare as it pertains to behind-the-lines activities; infiltration and/or organization of agents within the enemy's sphere of influence in support of actual or projected Special Forces operations; Commando-type operations; escape and evasion, as effected through Special Forces operations; and antiguerrilla warfare in areas overrun by friendly forces.[21] Both "Ranger operations" and "long-range or deep penetration reconnaissance" disappeared during this transformation; only "Commando-type operations" remained as a hint of the earlier conceptual confusion. By November 1952, the focus became even more precise, and potential volunteers for this new elite unit were told that Special Forces operations included guerrilla warfare, sabotage, and "other behind-the-lines missions, which are within the capabilities of guerrilla warfare."[22] The lack of reference to Ranger *or* Commando operations is evident; shortly thereafter, General McClure chastened General Liebel for contemplating using the 10th Special Forces Group for those types of activities in Europe.[23] In effect, "Special Forces operations" were now synonymous with "unconventional warfare."

The Special Forces came to life formally on 19 May 1952 with the establishment of the Headquarters and Headquarters Company, 10th Special Forces Group, constituted and allotted to the Regular Army for activation and organization under the Commanding General, 3rd Army. One hundred and twenty-two officers and men were to perform these activities:

> To furnish command, supply, and organizational maintenance for a Special Forces Group located in rear areas and, when provided with the necessary augmentation in personnel and equipment, for subordinate units committed in the objective area; to furnish administration for a Special Forces Group.[24]

Initially, the Headquarters and Headquarters Company was basically a "paper organization," for when Colonel Aaron Bank left OCPW to join the 10th Group on 19 June 1952 as its first commander, he had a total complement of only 7 enlisted men and 1 warrant officer present for duty.[25]

If Bank expected volunteers to swamp his new unit, he was to be disappointed. By early July he complained that the flow of applications for Special Forces was slow, attributing this to less-than-enthusiastic Army-wide support for the program and to the security classification of Special Forces activities.[26] A month later Colonel Karlstad reported to General McClure that the total assigned enlisted strength of the 10th was 259, of which only 123 were "operational unit" volunteer personnel. The arrival rate of volunteers was, he felt, "wholly unsatisfactory."[27] Another factor inhibiting a rapid buildup was the slow progress in attracting foreign nationals through the Lodge bill. As originally passed, the Lodge bill provided for the enlistment of 2,500 aliens in the US Army. By mid-1951, the Army raised this ceiling to 12,500 but actual recruitment fell far short of expectations. By August 1952, of 5,272 men who had applied for enlistment, only 411 received the necessary security clearances, and of that number only 211 actually enlisted.[28] Concerned, McClure's office reported that "the need to increase Lodge bill enlistments remains a vital problem affecting the accomplishment of missions assigned to OCPW."[29] At the end of November 1952, however, only 22 Lodge bill personnel had been assigned to the 10th Special Forces Group.[30] Despite this disappointing start, by April 1953 the strength of the organization designed to implement a "new concept" had increased to 1,700 officers and enlisted men.[31]

The "new concept" is best illustrated by the training objective proposed for the newly activated 10th Special Forces Group:

> To infiltrate its component operational detachments to designated areas within the enemy's sphere of influence and organize the indigenous guerrilla potential on a quasimilitary or a military basis for tactical and strategic exploitation in conjunction with our land, sea and air forces.[32]

Clearly, Special Forces were designed for unconventional warfare, with emphasis on guerrilla operations. This is significant, because in 1952 little attention was given to counterguerrilla, or counterinsurgency, operations. That portion of the special warfare concept was to come later, in the late 1950's and early 1960's, initiating a doctrinal battle about the proper function of Special Forces. At this early stage of its history, however, Special Forces served unconventional warfare requirements. The framework for the 10th that resulted was a unique blend of Army organizational traditions and conventions with the prominent ideas and principles of guerrilla warfare.

Essentially, the Special Forces Group represented a pool of trained manpower from which units or combinations of units could be drawn to execute specific unconventional warfare missions. The heart of the original group organization was the Operational Detachment, Regiment, a 15-man unit established along the same lines as the OSS Operational Group. Commanded by a captain, with a first lieutenant as executive officer, the Operational Detachment, Regiment, contained 13 enlisted men and was capable of infiltrating behind enemy lines to organize, train, and direct friendly resistance forces in the conduct of unconventional warfare. Depending on the size and makeup of the guerrilla forces in a specific area, the Operational Detachment, District B (commanded by a major), or the Operational Detachment, District A (commanded by a lieutenant colonel) could also be employed, as could be a combination of three types of teams. In other words, these detachments, called "teams," were to be utilized singly or in various combinations, depending on the size and complexities of the specific guerrilla organization involved. The team, in whatever combination necessary, would come under the direct control of the specified theater command for briefing and infiltration into the objective area, then remain in radio communication with the theater headquarters so that the activities of the guerrilla organization could be directed to support operations of friendly conventional forces most effectively. In short, the Special Forces Group was not designed to be employed as a tactical entity—as, for instance, a conventional division or brigade might be—but rather was constructed around a cellular concept in which each area, district, and regimental detachment was viewed as a separate and distinct operating unit.[33]

Colonel Bank had assumed command of a unique organization in June 1952, one that required special training to fulfill the missions envisaged for Special Forces. Based primarily on the wartime experiences of a few former OSS officers in the unit, the 10th Special Forces Group developed a training program that was entirely new to the Army. Early training stressed the individual skills represented in the basic Operational Detachment, Regiment: operations and intelligence, light and heavy weapons, demolitions, radio communications, and medical aid. Each man trained thoroughly in his particular specialty, then participated in "cross-training" to learn the rudiments of the other skills represented in the detachment. The communications and medical aid specialists received the longest training courses since they required the most technical skills. Clandestine operations training in activities such as the formation and operation of intelligence, sabotage, escape and evasion, and security also was stressed, since, as Colonel Bank remarked, "these are easily neglected in favor of the more exciting guerrilla tactics." [34] Detachment training at Camp McKall, North Carolina, followed the individual and cross-training phase. Finally, a lengthy group-level maneuver in the Chattahoochee National Forest, Georgia, completed the initial training cycle for this new organization.

And so blossomed Special Forces, the first formal US Army capability for unconventional warfare, co-located with, but yet a junior partner to, psychological warfare at Fort Bragg. Was this marriage between psychological and unconventional warfare one of choice? Apparently not. Colonel Volckmann remembered:

> Those of us who had worked on these programs were primarily interested in Special Forces and not Psychological Warfare and were very much opposed to have Special Forces associated with and under the Psychological Warfare Center at Fort Bragg. We felt that there was in general a stigma connected with Psychological Warfare, especially among combat men, that we didn't care to have "rub off" on Special Forces. Behind-the-line operations and the "dirty-tricks game" had enough opposition amongst conventional military minds that had to be overcome without adding the additional problems inherent in Psychological Warfare. However, we lost that battle. [35]

Colonel Bank had similar misgivings. Shortly after taking command of the 10th, he differed with the Psychological Warfare School faculty concerning the "position of Special Forces in relation to psychological warfare." He discovered that the concept being taught in the Psychological Operations course was that Special Forces operations were a part of psychological warfare. Bank objected to this interpretation in an early organizational meeting at the Psychological Warfare Center:

> I don't believe that, as far as Special Forces is concerned, that is correct. All the time that I was on the staff of PSYWAR (OCPW) I never saw any paper of any kind that indicates Special Forces operations is a part of psychological warfare. It is our concept that Special Forces operations is a part of unconventional warfare. Just because OCPW is responsible for the monitoring and supervision of planning

and conduct of psychological warfare and special forces operations does not mean that they have to be the same.[36]

Interestingly, at about this same time a Reserve officer doing his annual 2 weeks' training at the Department of the Army took issue with the notion of even combining the two fields within the Office of the Chief of Psychological Warfare. Colonel Oliver Jackson Sands' view was that the kinds of background, education, training, and experience required were inherently different from those necessary for the conduct of special operations; thus "rarely . . . is a person who is suitable for one of these activities qualified for the other." He also argued that the planning, execution, facilities, equipment, and support required for the two operations were "totally different." Because these activities were, in his view, "widely divergent in type and character," he recommended divesting OCPW of the Special Forces function. The latter could then become part of the G–3.[37]

As might have been expected, General McClure did not agree with Sands' analysis, particularly since the special operations function had been moved from G–3 to OCPW at his request. There is evidence, however, that other psychological warfare officers also had misgivings about the Army's organization for psychological and unconventional warfare. Writing in 1954 on tactical psychological warfare during the Korean conflict, Colonel Donald F. Hall expressed this view:

> Many psychological warfare officers experienced in combat propaganda operations have never subscribed to the placement of psychological warfare and special forces under the same controlling staff agencies. Some have felt that a great error was made when the two functions were placed under the same agency at Department of the Army level, and there has been a growing concern about the tendency to combine the two on down through the echelons to the Army in the field.
>
> The doubt as to the justification for this concept has been an honest one although few have had the capacity to question the decision in high places. As a matter of economy in meeting training requirements, most have gone quietly along with the development of the two functions as "twin activities" at the higher levels, and particularly at the center [The Psychological Warfare Center]. But it is difficult to conceive of guerrilla-type operations as true psychological warfare; they seem to be much more closely allied to straight combat operations within the jurisdiction of G–3.[38]

Believing, as did Colonel Sands, that there were few individuals who would have wide experience and capabilities in both psychological and unconventional warfare, Colonel Hall feared that if the two fields were combined under one head, one of them "may suffer as a result of particular emphasis given to the function in which the controlling personnel are especially interested and experienced."[39] This, of course, was part of the anxiety suffered by Special Forces adherents in 1952; at that time the "controlling personnel," both at OCPW and at the Psychological Warfare Center, were those with psychological warfare backgrounds. (In later years, the situation would be reversed, especially at the center.) From early 1951 on, Volckmann and others in the Special Operations Division had spoken primarily in terms of a Special Forces Training Center, not a Psychological Warfare Center in which Special Forces would be relegated to a subordinate role. But, as Volckmann admitted, "We lost that battle."

Indeed they did. But why? Could it have been because there was an even greater "stigma" attached "by conventional military minds" to unconventional warfare than to psychological warfare? Staff representation for psychological warfare had existed at the Department of the Army and in overseas theaters during World War I, World War II, and Korea. In addition, a definite lineage of formal Army units existed from both the Korean war and World War II, when the Army had staff sections and units designed exclusively for the planning and conduct of psychological warfare. To be sure, as Daniel Lerner has shown in his *Sykewar*, psychological warfare in World War II had its share of "characters" who tended to alienate military professionals.[40] But the major point here is that the Army had staff sections and units designed exclusively for the planning and conduct of psychological warfare, an activity that gradually gained respectability in both World War II and Korea. Such was not the case with Special Forces and unconventional warfare in the Army; unconventional warfare's only real ancestry—and that indirectly—was with the civilian-led OSS in World War II, an organization not held in the highest esteem by many senior military leaders.

Viewed from a historical perspective, it seems clear that Special Forces emerged as an unprecedented entity within the Army under the protective wing of an established, ongoing activity—psychological warfare. General McClure's foresight in organizing a Special Operations Division in the Office of the Chief of Psychological Warfare, and his selection of personnel for that division, gave unconventional warfare advocates like Bank and Volckmann the official platform from which to "sell" the Army on the need for Special Forces units. McClure's rationale for including unconventional warfare with psychological warfare can reasonably be linked to his World War II experience with PWD/SHAEF, his knowledge of General Donovan's insistence on the close interrelationship of psychological warfare and special operations, and the fact that the other services—as well as the JCS—had the same organizational philosophy in their staffs.[41] Although it is apparent that key officers in the Special Operations Division wanted to dissociate unconventional and psychological warfare, without McClure's stature and backing as a general officer heading a special staff division at Department of the Army Headquarters, it is improbable that Special Forces would have become a reality at the time that it did. Special Forces and unconventional warfare arrived through the back door of the psychological warfare house. While the marriage of psychological and unconventional warfare was probably a union of convenience (as Colonel Volckmann suggested) rather than choice, it was certainly one of necessity for the Special Forces adherents.

Thus was created the Psychological Warfare Center and the 10th Special Forces Group—the origins of special warfare.

IX

SUMMING UP

Our quest to determine the origins of a special warfare capability for the US Army has led us to investigate the pre-1952 roots of the Psychological Warfare Center at Fort Bragg. In doing so, we have traced the modern historical antecedents of American experience with psychological and unconventional warfare. These two elements had a common point of origin with the establishment of the Coordinator of Information (COI) in 1941; indeed, General William J. Donovan's all-encompassing concept of psychological warfare included all the aspects of what the Army was later to call "special warfare" (with the exception of counterinsurgency). With the dissolution of COI in 1942 and the parallel creation of Office of Strategic Services (OSS) and Office of War Information (OWI), psychological and unconventional warfare took separate paths. They did not formally unite in the Army until the formation of the Office of the Chief of Psychological Warfare (OCPW) in 1951 and the founding of the Psychological Warfare Center in 1952.

Between 1941 and 1952, psychological warfare developed a formal lineage in the Army traceable through units and schools in World War II, the Korean conflict, the Army General School at Fort Riley, and the Psychological Warfare Center at Fort Bragg. Additionally, there had been Department of the Army staff representation for psychological warfare during World War I, and, again, almost continuously since 1941. Psychological warfare, in other words, had a tradition in the Army.

It was a civilian—Assistant Secretary of War, John J. McCloy—who pushed the Army into developing a branch at the War Department for the planning and coordination of psychological warfare activities, initially in June 1941 and again in November 1943. McCloy's interest illustrates a theme seen throughout our investigation of the origins of special warfare:

the initiative demonstrated by influential civilian officials to prod somewhat conservative Army leaders into venturing forth in new and uncertain fields.

Certainly Brigadier General Robert A. McClure was an exception to this theme. The civilian-military team that he headed first in North Africa and then later in PWD/SHAEF, served as the model for successful Army psychological warfare operations. The Mobile Radio Broadcasting companies employed in Europe were the first tactical propaganda units of their kind in Army history and influenced the development of similar units during the Korean war. And McClure himself had a strong hand in urging that the War Department establish a central psychological warfare agency. All in all, General McClure must be considered the most important Army officer to emerge in this new field during World War II.

Contrary to the official lineage of Special Forces, unconventional warfare, in its strictest definition, did not have a traceable formal history in the Army. The Office of Strategic Services, to which the Army contributed personnel in World War II, was the first American agency devoted to the planning, direction, and conduct of unconventional warfare, but it was not a military organization. Nevertheless, it left a legacy of organizational and combat knowledge that, together with a few key officers who had World War II experience in guerrilla warfare, was instrumental in the creation of Special Forces in 1952. This gave the Army a formal unconventional warfare capability for the first time in its history.

During the interwar years, the Army's psychological warfare capability languished, but staff planning activity did not cease entirely (contrary to the claim of one prominent psychological warfare text).[1] This activity was kept alive by growing concerns about Soviet intentions, by the interest of a few senior military officers like General Lemnitzer and General McClure, and by the pressure brought to bear by several Secretaries of the Army. In fact, a great deal of planning went on during that period that carried over to OCPW, more so than was later acknowledged by General McClure even though he substantially contributed to that effort from his posts outside the Army Staff.

Similarly, the impetus for the initiation of covert activities after World War II did not originate in the Central Intelligence Group (forerunner of the CIA); it came from Secretary of War Robert Patterson, whose interest in developing an OSS-type "airborne reconnaissance" unit led the Army to study an organization that combined both OSS and Ranger precepts. Although interest in the subject waned after the growth of the responsibilities of the Central Intelligence Agency/Office of Policy Coordination

(CIA/OPC), the studies and dialog that took place—limited though they were—clearly showed the influence of OSS on Army thinking and presaged similar discussions in the early 1950's prior to formation of the 10th Special Forces Group.

Notwithstanding that more planning activity in both psychological and unconventional warfare took place during 1945-50 than is generally acknowledged, on the eve of the Korean war the Army was ill-prepared in terms of personnel, equipment, and organization to conduct psychological warfare operations; its unconventional warfare capability was nonexistent.

With the impetus of the Korean war, the heightening cold war tensions, and the persistent pressures of Secretary of the Army Frank Pace, Jr., the Army moved in late 1950 to create an unprecedented staff organization—the Office of the Chief of Psychological Warfare. With Pace's support, Brigadier General McClure created a staff with responsibilities for both psychological and unconventional warfare. It was largely as a result of McClure's status and foresight that the Army developed its first capability to conduct unconventional warfare; the inclusion of a Special Operations Division in OCPW and McClure's selection of the key personnel for that office gave officers like Colonel Russell Volckmann and Colonel Aaron Bank the opportunity to form plans for unconventional warfare and the creation of Special Forces. Despite a "hot war" in Korea, the primary influence behind the Army's interest in unconventional warfare was the desire for a guerrilla capability in Europe to help "retard" a Soviet invasion, should it occur. (In fact, the development of Special Forces came too late to play other than a minimal role in the 8th Army's behind-the-line activities.) After some initial experimentation with the organizational machinery to conduct this "new concept" of warfare, the unit that emerged was clearly designed to organize, train, and support indigenous personnel in behind-the-lines resistance activities, and it was based primarily on Donovan's OSS Operational Group concepts—not those of the Rangers or Commandos. In order to provide the necessary training, materiel, and doctrinal support for both Special Forces and psychological warfare units, McClure was able to sell the Army on a separate center at which the functions of the "whole field of OCPW" would be located.

Roughly the same cold war tensions fueled interest in both psychological and unconventional warfare, but there was a crucial difference in the receptivity to each by the Army. Despite some of the "characters" associated with "sykewar," psychological warfare organizations gradually attained increased respectability in the Army during World War II and Korea. On the other hand, the Army continued to view unconventional warfare with a certain distaste. This reluctance to accept Special Forces resulted from the legacy of OSS-military rivalry during World War II, a lack of appreciation for unconventional warfare by officers trained for conventional war, and a continuing suspicion of elite forces by the Army, as well as from the fact that there was no formal precedent in the Army's history for Special Forces units. Most important of all were the constraints of manpower and money in what was, despite the cold war, a peacetime Army. New ideas, particularly those that require an increase in personnel and funds, are understandably difficult to sell to leaders who must make decisions on the basis of essentiality. (In this regard, it is instructive to note that the spaces finally made available for the formation of the 10th Special Forces Group came from the deactivation of the Rangers, another elite concept.)

In the face of resistance, both within the Army and from the Air Force and CIA, Special Forces nonetheless became a reality largely through the support of General McClure and the persistent efforts of Colonel Volckmann and Colonel Bank. But the bargaining position of unconventional warfare advocates was weak in 1951-52; those in OCPW who wanted a separate existence for Special Forces found it necessary to compromise. Because psychological warfare had a formal lineage and a tradition—and unconventional warfare had neither—it was expedient to bring Special Forces into existence under the auspices of, and subordinate to, psychological warfare. This, plus the security restraints placed on the publicizing of Special Forces activities, explains the apparent ascendancy of psychological warfare over unconventional warfare at that time.

General McClure's rationale for combining these two activities within OCPW in 1951 and at the Psychological Warfare Center in 1952 can be partially attributed to the heritage of General William Donovan's organizational philosophy, and to the fact that the other military services and the JCS had the same combination in their staffs. In allowing McClure his way, the Army may simply have found it convenient to lump these two relatively new out-of-the-mainstream (thus "unconventional") activities together while it attempted to sort out both ideas and weapons. The resultant package could well have been called "miscellaneous warfare" instead of the eventual, more glamorous "special warfare."[2] Thus, the combining of psychological and unconventional warfare under the Psychological Warfare Center was a marriage of both convenience and necessity, but one that nevertheless gave the Army the beginnings of a "special warfare" capability.

The person most responsible for achieving this feat was Brigadier General Robert A. McClure, clearly the central figure to emerge in this study. From World War II until early 1953, he alone provided the continuity, expertise, and guidance at the general officer level that was so essential to the ultimate establishment of his dream—the creation of the Office of the Chief of Psychological Warfare, Special Forces, and the Psychological Warfare Center. At every crucial point in the unfolding of events leading to these accomplishments, particularly after World War II, one finds his personal imprint; indeed, the story of the origins of special warfare could almost be told through a biography of this dedicated, energetic visionary. Today his name is recognized by few; the achievements of Volckmann and Bank are more familiar. One searches in vain for McClure's picture on the walls of the Center for Military Assistance or in its museum. But if any one man can be called the father of special warfare, surely that man was Robert A. McClure.

Even after its birth, the Psychological Warfare Center, along with Special Forces, led a precarious existence.[3] And McClure himself left the OCPW in March 1953 an embittered man; the implication was that he had been in a specialized activity too long.[4] But his legacy is clear; the foundation he laid was built upon in the 1960's when special warfare was expanded to encompass counterinsurgency, and to this day Special Forces and psychological warfare units exist, albeit uneasily, under the Center for Military Assistance at Fort Bragg. Ironically, the Office of the Chief of Psychological Warfare has not survived. The manner in which psychological and unconventional warfare evolved from 1941 until their union as a formal Army capability in 1952 suggests a theme that runs throughout the history of special warfare: the story of a hesitant and reluctant Army attempting to cope with concepts and organizations of an unconventional nature.

NOTES

Archival collections cited in notes are abbreviated as follows:

CMH	Center of Military History, Washington, D.C.
National Archives	National Archives, Washington, D.C.
USAJFKCMA	US Army John F. Kennedy Center for Military Assistance, Fort Bragg, N.C.
USAMHI	US Army Military History Institute, Carlisle Barracks, Pa.
WNRC	Washington National Records Center, Suitland, Md.

Some files are designated Top Secret (TS), Secret (S), or Confidential (C).

For other abbreviations and acronyms appearing in the notes, see the glossary.

Chapter I Notes

1. Department of the Army, Office of the Chief of Information, *Special Warfare, US Army: An Army Specialty* (Washington, D.C., 1962), p. 55, USA JFKCMA.

2. Army, *Special Warfare*, pp. 8f.; Joint Chiefs of Staff, *Dictionary of US Military Terms for Joint Usage* (Washington, D.C., August 1968).

3. Army, *Special Warfare*, p. 5.

4. Headquarters, The Psychological Warfare Center, Fort Bragg, N.C., Memorandum No. 14, "Organization and Functions Manual, Headquarters, The Psychological Warfare Center," 12 November 1952, USAJFKCMA.

5. US, Department of Defense, *Semiannual Report of the Secretary of Defense and the Semiannual Reports of the Secretary of the Army, Secretary of the Navy, Secretary of the Air Force, 1 January through 30 June 1952* (Washington, D.C.), p. 92.

Chapter II Notes

1. Kermit Roosevelt, ed., *War Report of the OSS,* 2 vols. (New York: Walker & Co., 1976), 1:5; Propaganda Branch, Intelligence Division, WDGS, The Pentagon, Washington, D.C., "A Syllabus of Psychological Warfare" (October 1946), p. 27, USAJFKCMA; Corey Ford, *Donovan of OSS* (Boston: Little, Brown & Co., 1970), pp. 335f.

2. Ford, *Donovan of OSS,* pp. 91, 106f., 110.

3. Ford, *Donovan of OSS,* p. 108.

4. Ford, *Donovan of OSS,* pp. 110f.; Roosevelt, *War Report of the OSS,* 1:9, 31.

5. William E. Daugherty and Morris Janowitz, *A Psychological Warfare Casebook* (Baltimore: The Johns Hopkins Press, 1958), p. 127.

6. Ford, *Donovan of OSS,* p. 124.

7. Roosevelt, *War Report of the OSS,* 1:16.

8. William R. Corson, *The Armies of Ignorance: The Rise of the American Intelligence Empire* (New York: Dial Press, 1977), pp. 182f.; Roosevelt, *War Report of the OSS,* 1:20.

9. Ford, *Donovan of OSS,* pp. 127f., 337; Roosevelt, *War Report of the OSS,* 1:26f.; Corson, *Armies of Ignorance,* p. 182.

10. Roosevelt, *War Report of the OSS,* 1:26.

11. Edward Hymoff, *The OSS in World War II* (New York: Ballantine Books, 1972), p. 46.

12. Ford, *Donovan of OSS,* p. 176.

13. Hymoff, *OSS in World War II,* p. 70.

14. Ford, *Donovan of OSS,* pp. 124f.; Roosevelt, *War Report of the OSS,* 1:19; Corson, *Armies of Ignorance,* p. 183.

15. Roosevelt, *War Report of the OSS,* 1:26–28; Corson, *Armies of Ignorance,* pp. 184–86.

16. Paul Linebarger, *Psychological Warfare* (New York: Duell, Sloan & Pearce, 1954), p. 93; Hymoff, *OSS in World War II,* p. 70; Daugherty and Janowitz, *Casebook,* p. 128; Propaganda Branch, "Syllabus of Psychological Warfare," p. 2; Ford, *Donovan of OSS,* pp. 126–28.

17. Linebarger, *Psychological Warfare,* p. 93; Daugherty and Janowitz, *Casebook,* p. 128; Corson, *Armies of Ignorance,* p. 185.

18. Daugherty and Janowitz, *Casebook,* p. 129.

19. US, War Department General Staff, Military Intelligence Division G-2, *A History of the Military Intelligence Division, 7 December 1941–2 September 1945* (Washington, D.C., 1946), pp. 289f.

20. Military Intelligence Division, *History,* p. 290.

21. Military Intelligence Division, *History,* pp. 291f.

22. Military Intelligence Division, *History,* pp. 293f.; Linebarger, *Psychological Warfare,* pp. 93f.; Propaganda Branch, "Syllabus of Psychological Warfare," p. 29.

23. Military Intelligence Division, *History*, pp. 305, 309f.; Roosevelt, *War Report of the OSS*, 1:213.

24. Military Intelligence Division, *History*, pp. 310–12.

25. Roosevelt, *War Report of the OSS*, 1:97; Corson, *Armies of Ignorance*, p. 199; Military Intelligence Division, *History*, pp. 312f.

26. Roosevelt, *War Report of the OSS*, 1:99.

27. Corson, *Armies of Ignorance*, pp. 200f.

28. Roosevelt, *War Report of the OSS*, 1:101.

29. Roosevelt, *War Report of the OSS*, 1:105.

30. Military Intelligence Division, *History*, p. 314.

31. Military Intelligence Division, *History*, p. 314.

32. Linebarger, *Psychological Warfare*, p. 97.

33. Psychological Warfare Division, Supreme Headquarters, Allied Expeditionary Force, "An Account of Its Operations in the Western European Campaign, 1944–45" (Bad Homburg, Germany, October 1945), pp. 17–19; Brig. Gen. Robert A. McClure, "Trends in Army Psychological Warfare," *Army Information Digest* 7, no. 2 (February 1952):10.

34. "Records Pertaining to Psychological Warfare in Custody of Historical Records Section," 8 November 1949, p. 5, Historical Records Section, AGO, Reference Aid Number 7, Record Group 319, Plans and Operations Division 091.412 (7 October 1949), FW 25/2, National Archives.

35. Psychological Warfare Division, "Operations in Western European Campaign," p. 13.

36. Psychological Warfare Division, "Operations in Western European Campaign," p. 17.

37. Allied Force Headquarters, Psychological Warfare Branch, Memorandum prepared in Washington, D.C., 26 November 1943, by Maj. Edward A. Caskey, Commander, 1st MRB Company, Research Group 165, MID (G-2), Propaganda Branch Correspondence, 1939–45, POWS, box 333, National Archives.

38. Saul K. Padover and Harold D. Lasswell, "Psychological Warfare," *Headline Series*, no. 86 (20 March 1951), pp. 14f.; Daugherty and Janowitz, *Casebook*, pp. 131f.; Propaganda Branch, "Syllabus of Psychological Warfare," pp. 32–43.

39. Psychological Warfare Division, "Operations in Western European Campaign," pp. 13–17; Daugherty and Janowitz, *Casebook*, p. 131.

40. War Department, Office of the Inspector General, Washington, D.C., Memorandum to the Deputy Chief of Staff from Maj. Gen. Virgil L. Peterson, 17 August 1943, subject: Survey of Organizations, Administration, Supply and Procedures of the North African Theater of Operations, National Archives.

41. Padover and Lasswell, "Psychological Warfare," p. 16.

42. Military Intelligence Division, *History*, p. 316.

43. Roosevelt, *War Report of the OSS*, 1:105–7, 213.

44. Operations and Plans Directorate, WDGS, Washington D.C., Memorandum for Col. O. L. Nelson from Brig. Gen. J. E. Hull, Acting Assistant Chief

of Staff, OPD, subject: Organization for Propaganda Planning, 12 August 1943, Record Group 165, OPD 000.24 (12 July 1943), Section I (Cases 1–39), National Archives.

45. WDGS, The Adjutant General's Office, Washington D.C., Letter to all major commanders, subject: Organization for Propaganda Planning, 20 August 1943, AG 091.412 (16 August 1943), filed with Record Group 165, OPD 000.24, Section I (Cases 1–39), National Archives.

46. WDGS, Office of the Deputy Chief of Staff, Extract from minutes of General Council Meeting, 23 August 1943, Record Group 165, OPD 000.24, Section II (Cases 40–61), National Archives.

47. WDGS, Memorandum to Joint Intelligence Committee with inclosed report by Assistant Chief of Staff, G-2, and Assistant Chief of Staff, OPD, subject: War Department Propaganda Control Agency, 8 September 1943, Record Group 165, OPD 000.24, Section II (Cases 40–61), National Archives.

48 WDGS, Memorandum for the Deputy Chief of Staff, subject: Psychological Warfare/Establishment of Agency for Dealing with Problem of Psychological Warfare, 16 October 1943, Record Group 165, OPD 000.24, Section II (Cases 40–61), National Archives.

49. WDGS, Military Intelligence Division, G-2, Memorandum for Maj. Gen. T. T. Handy from Maj. Gen. George V. Strong, G-2, 6 November 1943, Record Group 165, OPD 000.24, Section II (Cases 40–61), National Archives.

50. WDGS, Operations Division, Memorandum for Maj. Gen. George V. Strong from Maj. Gen. T. T. Handy, subject: War Department, Propaganda Branch, 10 November 1945, Record Group 165, OPD 000.24, Section II (Cases 40–61), National Archives.

51. Military Intelligence Division, *History,* pp. 317f.

52. Military Intelligence Division, *History,* p. 318.

53. WDGS, G-2, Memorandum from Maj. Gen. George V. Strong for Commanding General, Army Air Forces; Assistant Chief of Staff, Operations Division; Chief, Civil Affairs Division; and Director, Bureau of Public Relations, subject: Propaganda Section, MID, 23 November 1943. Memorandum attaches copy of MID memorandum no. 78, 15 November 1943, establishing a Propaganda Branch in the MID, and requests cooperation and coordination of all addressees. Filed with Record Group 165, OPD 000.24, Section II (Cases 40–61), National Archives.

54. JCS, Joint Strategic Survey Committee, Letter from Maj. Gen. L. L. Lemnitzer, US Army, to Lt. Gen. J. E. Hull, Operations Division, War Department, subject: Research and Analysis of PWD Activities in World War II, 22 December 1945, Record Group 165, OPD 000.24, Section III (Cases 62–   ), National Archives.

55. See note 54 above.

56. WDGS, G-2, unsigned letter from individual with Headquarters, Western Task Force, 26 November 1942 (apparently the writer was previously assigned to G-2), Research Group 319, G2 322.001 (1 October 1942), box 576, National Archives.

57. Military Intelligence Division, *History,* p. 322; see also Charles A. H. Thomson, *Overseas Information Service of the US Government* (Washington, D.C.: Brookings Institution, 1948), pp. 25f.

58. Daugherty and Janowitz, *Casebook,* pp. 134f.

59. Letter, General of the Army Dwight D. Eisenhower, Headquarters, US Forces, European Theater, Office of the Commanding General, in Psychological Warfare Division, "Operations in Western European Campaign," p. 1.

Chapter III Notes

1. "Lineage of Special Forces," undated mimeographed fact sheet located in G-1 archives, USAJFKCMA. Department of the Army Directive AGAO-322, 18 October 1960, consolidated the various Ranger Battalions with the 1st Special Service Force and redesignated them all as the 1st Special Forces—which became the parent unit of all Special Forces Groups.

2. Joint Chiefs of Staff, *Dictionary of US Military Terms for Joint Usage* (Washington, D.C., August 1968).

3. R. Harris Smith, *OSS: The Secret History of America's First Central Intelligence Agency* (Berkeley: University of California Press, 1972), pp. 1-2.

4. OSS Assessment Staff, *Assessment of Men: Selection of Personnel for the Office of Strategic Services* (New York: Rinehart & Co., 1948), pp. 64-65.

5. See, for example, the variance of figures in Ford, *Donovan of OSS;* Harry Rowe Ransom, *Central Intelligence and National Security* (Cambridge: Harvard University Press, 1958); Hymoff, *OSS in World War II;* Smith, *OSS;* Roosevelt, *War Report of the OSS,* 1:116.

6. Ford, *Donovan of OSS,* pp. 167-68, 338-39.

7. Roosevelt, *War Report of the OSS,* 1:205.

8. Ransom, *Central Intelligence,* pp. 64-65.

9. Department of the Army, Office of the Chief of Staff, Minutes, Meeting of the General Council, 13 November 1945. Figures extracted from the Report of the War Department Manpower Board, p. 15, USAMHI.

10. Roosevelt, *War Report of the OSS,* 1:70, 72, 80-82.

11. Corson, *Armies of Ignorance,* p. 177. In a bit of understatement in *War Report of the OSS,* Roosevelt comments that "there seemed to be a deep-seated disapproval of the organization of independent military forces on the part of the War Department" (1:223).

12. WDGS, G-2, Washington D.C., Memorandum for the Assistant Chief of Staff, G-1, subject: Comments on Memo from the COI re Organization of Guerrilla Warfare Command, 23 June 1942, from Maj. Gen. George V. Strong, Record Group 319, Army Intelligence, 370.64, box 874, National Archives.

13. Roosevelt, *War Report of the OSS,* 1:105, 223.

14. Hugh Chandler, private interview held at Fort Bragg, N. C., 8 March 1973.

15. US Army, Headquarters, Special Warfare School, *Readings in Guerrilla Warfare,* (Fort Bragg, N.C., 1 December 1960), p. 29.

16. William R. Peers and Dean Brelis, *Behind the Burma Road: The Story of America's Most Successful Guerrilla Forces* (Boston: Little, Brown & Co.,

1963), pp. 207-20. Information on Detachment 101 activities is also contained in Charles F. Romanus and Riley Sunderland, *Time Runs Out in CBI: United States Army in World War II, China-Burma-India Theater* (Washington, D.C.: Office of the Chief of Military History, Department of the Army, 1959). See also Roosevelt, *War Report of the OSS,* 2:369-92.

17. Smith, *OSS,* p. 248.

18. Roosevelt, *War Report of the OSS,* 2:x, 358.

19. The Office of Strategic Services, Operational Group Command, 1944-45, "OSS Aid to the French Resistance in World War II: Origin and Development of Resistance in France, Summary," pp. 10-11, USAJFKCMA.

20. The Office of Strategic Services, Operational Group Command, Grenoble, France, 20 September 1944, "OSS Aid to the French Resistance in World War II: Operations in Southern France, Operational Groups," pp. 1-3, USAJFKCMA; Roosevelt, *War Report of the OSS,* 2:170, 222.

21. Roosevelt, *War Report of the OSS,* 2:223; Department of the Army, Organization and Training Division, Washington, D.C., "A Study of Special and Subversive Operations," 25 November 1947, G-3 Hot File, 091.412TS, 1949, box 10, National Archives.

22. The Office of Strategic Services, Operational Group Command, Booklet, "OG—Operational Group Command," (Washington, D.C., December 1944), USAJFKCMA; Roosevelt, *War Report of the OSS,* 2:223-25.

23. The Office of Strategic Services, Operational Group Command, Grenoble, France, 20 September 1944, "OSS Aid to the French Resistance in World War II: Operations in Southern France, Operational Groups"; Special Operations Research Office, *Undergrounds in Insurgent Revolutionary and Resistance Warfare* (Washington, D.C.: American University, 1963), p. 204; Roosevelt, *War Report of the OSS,* 2:145; OSS booklet, "OG—Operational Group Command," USAJFKCMA.

24. Roosevelt, *War Report of the OSS,* 2:219.

25. Department of the Army, General Staff, G-2, "Summary of French Resistance, 6 June-31 August 1944," USAMHI.

26. Lt. Col. Henry C. Hart, "United States Employment of Underground Forces," *Military Review* 26, no. 3 (March 1947):52-56; US Army Special Warfare School, *Readings in Guerrilla Warfare,* p. 28.

27. Col. R. W. Volckmann, *We Remained: Three Years behind the Enemy Lines in the Philippines* (New York: W. W. Norton & Co., 1954); US Army Special Warfare School, *Readings in Guerrilla Warfare,* p. 28; Department of the Army, Organization and Training Division, Washington, D.C., "A Study of Special and Subversive Operations," 25 November 1947, G-3 Hot File, 091.412TS, 1949, box 10, National Archives.

28. Ford, *Donovan of OSS,* pp. 302, 340-42.

29. Ford, *Donovan of OSS,* pp. 303-4.

30. Hymoff, *OSS in World War II,* p. 341.

31. Ransom, *Central Intelligence,* pp. 71-72.

32. Ransom, *Central Intelligence,* pp. 62-63.

33. Slavko N. Bjelajac, "Unconventional Warfare in the Nuclear Era," *Orbis* 4, no. 13 (Fall 1960):323-37.

34. Charles W. Thayer, *Guerrilla* (New York: Harper & Row, 1963), p. 180.

35. Ford, *Donovan of OSS*, p. 131.

36. Hymoff, *OSS in World War II*, p. 341.

37. Hymoff, *OSS in World War II*, p. 2.

38. Smith, *OSS*, p 6.

39. Ford, *Donovan of OSS*, pp. 109, 129, 162.

40. Stewart Alsop and Thomas Braden, *Sub Rosa: The OSS and American Espionage* (New York: Reynal & Hitchcock, 1946), p. 15.

41. Herbert Riffkind, "From Rockets to Rifles: The President's Guerrilla Policy," *Review*, May-June 1962, pp. 1-12.

42. Smith, *OSS*, pp. 243-44.

43. Ransom, *Central Intelligence*, p. 66; Smith, *OSS*, pp. 34, 250-51.

44. Thayer, *Guerrilla*, pp. xvii-xviii.

45. Franklin Mark Osanka, ed., *Modern Guerrilla Warfare: Fighting Communist Guerrilla Movements, 1941-1961* (New York: Free Press of Glencoe, 1962), p. xxii.

46. Thayer, *Guerrilla*, p. 180.

47. Russell Weigley, *History of the United States Army* (New York: Macmillan Co., 1967), p. 543.

48. Thayer, *Guerrilla*, p. 181.

49. Smith, *OSS*, pp. 364-65; Ford, *Donovan of OSS*, pp. 314, 343; Hymoff, *OSS in World War II*, pp. 341-42; Alsop and Braden, *Sub Rosa*, p. 233; Allen Dulles, *The Craft of Intelligence* (New York: Harper & Row, 1963), p. 43; OPD Memo No. 6168, 30 September 1945, states that General Magruder was instructed "to continue liquidation of activities and personnel not needed for peacetime purposes," CCS 385(2-8-42), Section I, PT. 10, box 87, National Archives. A memorandum by the Chief of Staff, US Army, as part of JCS 965/2, 28 August 1945, "Withdrawal of All Service Personnel with OSS," indicated approximately 8,000 US Army officers and enlisted men on duty with OSS in July 1945, CCS 385 (2-8-42), Section I, PT. 10, box 37, National Archives.

50. Edmond Taylor, *Awakening from History* (Boston: Gambit, 1969), pp. 345f.

51. Taylor, *Awakening from History*, p. 346.

52. Roosevelt, *War Report of the OSS*, 2:255.

Chapter IV Notes

1. Ray S. Cline, *Secrets, Spies, and Scholars: Blueprint of the Essential CIA* (Washington, D.C.: Acropolis Books, 1976), p. 98.

2. Corson, *Armies of Ignorance*, p. 302.

3. Daniel Yergin, *Shattered Peace: The Origins of the Cold War and the National Security State* (Boston: Houghton Mifflin Co., 1977), p. 54.

4. For a concise summary of the early history of the CIA, see US, Congress, Senate, Select Committee to Study Governmental Operations with Respect to Intelligence Activities, *Supplementary Detailed Staff Reports on Foreign and Military Intelligence*, bk. 4, 94th Cong., 2d sess., S. Rept. 94-755, 23 April 1976, pp. 4-41. See also Tyrus G. Fain, ed., *The Intelligence Community: History, Organization, and Issues*, Public Documents Series (New York: Bowker Co., 1977), pp. 6-18; and Cline, *Secrets, Spies, and Scholars*, pp. 99-110. For a more detailed examination, see Corson, *Armies of Ignorance*, pp. 221-329.

5. Ford, *Donovan of OSS*, p. 316.

6. Dulles, *Craft of Intelligence*, p. 45.

7. Senate, *Foreign and Military Intelligence*, bk. 4, p. 28.

8. Hugh Chandler, private interview held at Fort Bragg, N.C., 8 March 1973; Hymoff, *OSS in World War II*, p. 347.

9. Senate, *Foreign and Military Intelligence*, bk. 4, p. 26.

10. The Joint Chiefs of Staff, Joint Strategic Survey Committee, Washington D.C., Letter to Lt. Gen. J. E. Hull, Operations Division, War Department, subject: Research and Analysis of PWB Activities in World War II, 22 December 1945, from Maj. Gen. L. L. Lemnitzer, US Army, Record Group 319, Army Operations, P&O 091.412 (22 August 1946) (P/W #7), National Archives.

11. Office of Director, Information Control, Office of Military Government for Germany, APO 742, US Army, Letter from Brig. Gen. Robert A. McClure, Director, to Propaganda Branch, MID War Department, Record Group 319, 091.412 (13 January 1946), box 263, WNRC. Note that after McClure left PWD/SHAEF at the war's end, he became the Director, Information Control, a related activity.

12. Joint Chiefs of Staff, Historical Section, Memo for the JCS, subject: History of Psychological Warfare During World War II, 8 February 1946, from Maj. Gen. E. F. Harding, Chief, CCS 314.7 (2-8-46), box 39, National Archives.

13. A perusal of the Army General Council Minutes for the immediate post-war period provides one with the flavor of the mind-boggling problems faced by the Army during the rush to demobilize. The General Council met weekly, was composed of the senior War Department leadership, and was chaired by either the Chief of Staff or the Deputy Chief of Staff. Minutes, USAMHI.

14. US, Congress, Senate, Select Committee to Study Governmental Operations with respect to Intelligence Activities, *Foreign and Military Intelligence*, bk. 1, 94th Cong., 2d sess., S. Rept. 95-755, 26 April 1976, p. 19.

15. Headquarters, Army Ground Forces, Washington D.C., Letter to Assistant Chief of Staff, G-2, War Department General Staff, subject: Project to Combat subversive Activities —The United States, 15 January 1946, from Maj. Gen. W. G. Wyman, G-2, Record Group 319, Army Operations, P&O 091.412 (15 January 1946), National Archives.

16. WDGS, Intelligence Division, Washington D.C., Summary Sheet, 22 May 1946, Record Group 319, Army Operations, P&O 091.412, Section IA, Case 7, National Archives.

17. Office of Military Government for Germany (US), Office of the Director of Information Control, Letter to Col. D. W. Johnston, Chief, Propaganda Branch,

MID, G-2, 21 June 1946, from Brig. Gen. Robert A. McClure, Record Group 319, Army Operations, P&O 091.412 (22 August 1946) (FW 7), National Archives.
18. WDGS, Intelligence Division, Washington, D.C., MID 912, Memorandum for the Chief of Staff, subject: Establishment of Psychological Warfare Group, Plans and Operations Division, WDGS, 22 August 1946, Record Group 319, Army Operations, P&O 091.412 (22 August 1946) (FW 7), National Archives.
19. WDGS, Plans and Operations Division, Washington, D.C., Memo for Record, subject: Establishment of Psychological Warfare Group, P&O Division, WDGS, 4 October 1946, Record Group 319, Army Operations, P&O 091.412 (27 September 1946), National Archives.
20. See note 19 above.
21. WDGS, Plans and Operations Division, Washington, D.C., handwritten notes dated 6 November 1946, Record Group 319, Army Operations, P&O 091.412, Section IA, Case 7, National Archives.
22. WDGS, Intelligence Division, Memorandum No. 100, subject: Discontinuance of Propaganda Branch, I.D., 29 November 1946, Record Group 319, Army Operations, P&O 091.412 (29 November 1946), National Archives.
23. WDGS, War Department, Memorandum No. 575-10-1, Responsibility of War Department Agencies for Psychological Warfare Functions, 10 January 1947, Record Group 319, Army Operations, P&O 091.412 (18 December 1946), National Archives.
24. Senate, *Foreign and Military Intelligence,* bk. 4, pp. 26f.; also Record Group 319, Army Operations, P&O 091.412 (12 May 1947), National Archives.
25. War Department, The Chief of Staff, Washington, D.C., Memorandum for the Director, Plans and Operations, WDGS, 19 June 1947, from Dwight D. Eisenhower, Record Group 319, Army Operations, P&O 091.412 (19 June 1947), National Archives.
26. WDGS, Plans and Operations Division, Memorandum for the Chief of Staff, subject: Psychological Warfare, 21 June 1947, from Brig. Gen. Robert A. McClure, P&O staff reaction, and Director, P&O Memo for the Chief of Staff, 29 July 1947, Record Group 319, Army Operations, 1948-52, box 9, P&O 091.412 (21 June 1947), National Archives.
27. See note 26 above.
28. See note 26 above.
29. Headquarters, Army Ground Forces, Fort Monroe, Va., Letter to Maj. Gen. Lauris Norstad, Director of Plans and Operations, WDGS, from Maj. Gen. W. G. Wyman, 14 June 1947, Record Group 319, Army Operations, P&O 091.412 (14 June 1947), Section II, Cases 16-30, National Archives.
30. WDGS, Plans and Operations Division, Washington, D.C., Letter to Maj. Gen. W. G. Wyman, Headquarters, Army Ground Forces, Fort Monroe, Va., from Maj. Gen. Lauris Norstad, 16 July 1947, Record Group 319, Army Operations, P&O 091.412 (14 June 1947), Section II, Cases 16-30, National Archives.
31. Headquarters, Army Ground Forces, Fort Monroe, Va., Letter to Maj. Gen. Lauris Norstad from Maj. Gen. W. G. Wyman, 22 July 1947, Record Group 319, Army Operations, P&O 091.412 (14 June 1947), Section II, Cases 16-30, National Archives.

32. Department of the Army, Chief of Information, Washington, D.C., Memorandum for the Director, Plans and Operations Division, subject: Psychological Warfare, 31 October 1947, from Maj. Gen. M. S. Eddy, Record Group 319, Plans and Operations Division, 1946-48, 091.3-091.7, Section I, box 28, P&O 091.412 TS (31 October 1947), National Archives.

33. War Department, Special Staff, Civil Affairs Division, New York Field Office, Memorandum for Gen. Dwight D. Eisenhower, subject: Candidates for Psychological Warfare Reserve, from Brig. Gen. Robert A. McClure, Chief, New York Field Office, 5 November 1947, Record Group 319, Army Operations, P&O 091.412 (5 November 1947), National Archives.

34 Department of the Army, The Chief of Staff, Memorandum for Secretary James V. Forrestal, subject: Psychological Warfare, from Dwight D. Eisenhower, 17 November 1947, Record Group 319, Army Operations, National Archives.

35. Senate, *Foreign and Military Intelligence,* bk. 4, pp. 27-29.

36. Senate, *Foreign and Military Intelligence,* bk. 1, pp. 48f.

37. Senate, *Foreign and Military Intelligence,* bk. 4, p. 28.

38. Department of the Army, Plans and Operations Division, Washington, D.C. Summary Sheet and Study to Chief of Staff, subject: A Study of Psychological Warfare, from Lt. Gen. A. C. Wedemeyer, Director of Plans and Operations, 10 February 1948, Record Group 319, P&O Division, 1946-48, 091.3-091.7, Section I, box 28, P&O 091.412 TS (15 January 1948), National Archives

39. See note 38 above.

40. Department of the Army, Plans and Operations Division, Washington, D.C., Memorandum for the Chief of Staff, 18 March 1948, from Lt. Gen. A. C. Wedemeyer, Director, Plans and Operations, Record Group 319, Plans and Operations Division, 1946-48, 091.3-091.7, Section I, box 28, filed with P&O 091.412 (30 November 1948), National Archives.

41. Department of the Army, Plans and Operations Division, Washington, D.C., Memorandum for the Director, Plans and Operations, subject: Proposed Trip of Brig. Gen. Robert A. McClure, 30 March 1948, from Col. William S. Biddle, Assistant Chief, Plans and Policy Group, Record Group 319, Plans and Operations Division, 1946-48, 091.3-091.7, Section I, box 28, P&O 091.412 (30 March 1948), National Archives.

42. Department of the Army, Plans and Operations Division, Washington, D.C., Letter to Brig. Gen. Robert A. McClure, Civil Affairs Division, New York Field Office, from Lt. Gen. A. C. Wedemeyer, Director of Plans and Operations, 18 June 1948, Record Group 319, Army Operations, filed with P&O 091.412 (28 May 1948), National Archives.

43. Department of the Army, Civil Affairs Division, New York Field Office, Letter to Lt. Gen. A. C. Wedemeyer, Director, Plans and Operations Division, from Brig. Gen. Robert A. McClure, Chief, New York Field Office, 8 July 1948, Record Group 319, Army Operations, P&O 091.412, National Archives.

44. Department of the Army, Plans and Operations Division, Washington, D.C., Letter to Brig. Gen. Robert A. McClure, Chief, New York Field Office, Civil Affairs Division, from Lt. Gen. A. C. Wedemeyer, Director of Plans and Oper-

ations, 17 September 1948, Record Group 319, Army Operations, P&O 091.412, National Archives.

45. See note 44 above.

46. Department of the Army, Plans and Operations Division, Washington, D.C., Memorandum for Gen. Omar Bradley, subject: Psychological Warfare, 9 August 1948, by Gen. A. C. Wedemeyer, filed with P&O 091.412 TS (1 September 1948), Record Group 319, Plans and Operations Division, 1946-48, 091.3-091.7, Section I, box 28, National Archives.

47. See note 46 above.

48. Department of the Army, Plans and Operations Division, Washington, D.C., Memorandum for General Schuyler, subject: Lt. Col. William H. Baumer, 16 August 1948, by Lt. Col. Robert M. Gant, Chief, Personnel Branch, P&O Division, filed with P&O 091.412 TS (1 September 1948), Record Group 319, Plans and Operations Division, 1946-48, 091.3-091.7, Section I, box 28, National Archives.

49. Linebarger, *Psychological Warfare,* p. 301.

50. Department of the Army, Plans and Operations Division, Washington, D.C., DF to Director, Organization and Training Division, subject: TO&E for Psychological Warfare Units, from Director, Plans and Operations, 20 September 1948; also Memorandum for Record, subject: TO&E for Psychological Warfare Units, 22 December 1948, Record Group 319, Plans and Operations Division, 1946-48, 091.3-091.7, Section I, box 28, P&O 091.412 TS (20 September 1948), National Archives.

51. Department of the Army, Plans and Operations Division, Washington, D.C., Memorandum for Deputy Chief of Staff for Plans and Combat Operations, subject: Planning for Wartime Conduct of Overt Psychological Warfare (NSC Staff Memorandum of 23 February 1949), 4 March 1949, Record Group 319, Army Operations, 1949-52, box 10, Hot Files, P&O 091.412 TS (23 February 1949), National Archives.

52. Department of the Army, Plans and Operations Division, Washington, D.C., Memorandum for the Record, subject: Briefing on NSC Meeting, 3 June 1948, Record Group 319, Army Operations, 1948-52, box 9, Hot Files, National Archives.

53. Department of the Army, Office of the Under Secretary of the Army, Washington, D.C., "The Army's Role in Current Psychological Warfare," A Report to William H. Draper, Under Secretary of the Army, by Wallace Carroll, 24 February 1949, Record Group 319, Army Operations, 1949-52, box 10, Hot Files, P&O 091.412 TS (24 February 1949), National Archives.

54. Department of the Army, Plans and Operations Division, Washington, D.C., Extract on Psychological Warfare from Deputy Chief of Staff, Combat Plans and Operations, Diary of important events occurring during Chief of Staff's recent absence, 15 March 1949, Record Group 319, Army Operations, 1949-52, box 10, Hot Files, CSUSA (15 March 1949) TS, National Archives.

55. See note 54 above.

56. Department of the Army, Deputy Chief of Staff for Plans and Combat Operations, Washington, D.C., Memorandum for Secretary of the Army Kenneth

C. Royall from Lt. Gen. A. C. Wedemeyer, 17 March 1949, Record Group 319, Army Operations, 1949–52, box 10, Hot Files, CSUSA 385 (17 March 1949) C, National Archives.

57. Department of the Army, Plans and Operations Division, Washington, D.C., Letter to Brig. Gen. Robert A. McClure from Maj. Gen. Charles L. Bolte, Director of Plans and Operations, 7 July 1949, Record Group 319, Army Operations, 1949–52, box 10, Hot Files, P&O 091.412 S (7 July 1949), National Archives.

58. Headquarters, Fort Ord, Calif., Letter from Brig. Gen. Robert A. McClure to Maj. Gen. Charles L. Bolte, Director of Plans and Operations, Department of the Army, 12 July 1949, Record Group 319, Army Operations, 1949–52, box 10, Hot Files, 091.412 S (7 July 1949), National Archives.

59. Department of the Army, Plans and Operations Division, Washington, D.C., Memorandum for Record, subject: Meeting with Secretary of the Army Gordon Gray Concerning Psychological Warfare, 11 July 1949, Record Group 319, Army Operations, 1949–52, box 10, Hot Files, CSUSA 385 C (11 July 1949), National Archives.

60. See note 59 above.

61. Department of the Army, Army Operations, Washington, D.C., Memorandum by Maj. Gen. H. R. Bull, Director, Organization and Training Division, subject: General Staff Responsibility for Planning Pertaining to New Developments in Warfare, 12 May 1949; also Memorandum by Maj. Gen. Charles L. Bolte, Director, Plans and Operations, commenting on above subject, Record Group 319, Army Operations, P&O 381 (12 May 1949), National Archives.

62. Armed Forces Information School, Carlisle Barracks, Pa., Student Committee Report, subject: Psychological Warfare and Propaganda Analysis, 9 June 1949, Record Group 319, Army Operations, P&O 091.412 (8 September 1949), National Archives.

63. Department of the Army, Plans and Operations Division, Washington, D.C., Memorandum to Organization and Training Division requesting information on psychological warfare training in being or planned, 19 August 1949; also P&O Division memo on subject, 4 October 1949, Record Group 319, Army Operations, P&O 091.412 (19 August 1949), National Archives.

64. Office of the Secretary of the Army, Washington, D.C., Memorandum from Gordon Gray to Chief of Staff, US Army, 7 February 1950, Record Group 319, Army Operations, 1949–52, Hot Files, box 10, P&O 091.412 (7 February 1950), National Archives.

65. Department of the Army, Plans and Operations Division, Washington, D.C., "Report on the Army Psychological Warfare Program," 13 February 1950, Record Group 319, Army Operations, 1949–52, Hot Files, box 10, P&O 091.412 TS (7 February 1950), National Archives.

66. See note 65 above.

67. See note 65 above.

68. Department of the Army, Office of the Secretary of the Army, Washington, D.C., Memorandum for the Chief of Staff, subject: Army Organization for Psychological Warfare, 29 May 1950, from Secretary of the Army Frank Pace, Jr.,

Record Group 319, G-3 Operations, March 1950-51, 091.412, Cases 1-20, box 154, National Archives.

69. Department of the Army, Plans and Operations Division, Washington, D.C., Memorandum for Gen. Charles L. Bolte, subject: Army Organization for Psychological Warfare, from General Schuyler, 13 February 1950, Record Group 319, Army Operations, 1949-52, Hot Files, box 10, P&O 091.412 TS (7 February 1950), National Archives.

70. Department of the Army, G-3, Operations, Washington, D.C., Memorandum to Assistant Chief of Staff, G-1, Personnel, subject: Requirement for Officers With Specialized Training, 13 March 1960, OPS 091.412 (13 March 1950); Department of the Army, Office of the Adjutant General, Washington, D.C., Letter to Commander in Chief, Far East; Commanding General, US Army, Europe; Chief, Army Field Forces; Commandant, Command and General Staff College, 17 April 1950, AGAO-S 210.61 (31 March 1950) G-3; both filed in Record Group 319, G-3 Operations, March 1950-51, 091.412, Cases 1-20, box 154, National Archives.

71. Department of the Army, G-3 Operations, Washington, D.C., Memorandum, subject: Army Program for Psychological Warfare, 13 March 1950, Record Group 319, G-3 Operations, March 1950-51, 091.412, Cases 1-20, box 154, OPS 091.412 (10 March 1950), National Archives.

72. Army Field Forces, Office of the Chief, Fort Monroe, Va., Letter to Maj. Gen. R. E. Duff, Acting Assistant Chief of Staff, G-3, from Maj. Gen. Robert C. Macon, Deputy Chief, 7 June 1950, Record Group 319, Army Operations, G-3 091.412 (Section III) (Cases 41-60) (Case 50 withdrawn, filed in Section III A), National Archives.

73. Department of the Army, G-3 Operations, Washington, D.C., Summary Sheet for Chief of Staff, subject: Psychological Warfare Organization in the Department of the Army, from Maj. Gen. Charles L. Bolte, G-3, 13 July 1950, Record Group 319, Army Operations, OPS 091.412 (Section II) (Cases 21-40) (Case 26 withdrawn, filed Section II A), 091.412 (5 July 1950) S, National Archives.

Chapter V Notes

1. US, Congress, Senate, Select Committee to Study Governmental Operations with Respect to Intelligence Activities, *Foreign and Military Intelligence,* bk. 4, 94th Cong., 2d sess., S. Rept. 94-755, 23 April 1976, p. 26.

2. WDGS, Military Intelligence Division, Washington, D.C., Memorandum to the Adjutant General, subject: Airborne Reconnaissance Units, 19 August 1946, from Maj. Gen. S. J. Chamberlain, Director of Intelligence, Record Group 319, Army Intelligence Decimal Files, 1941-48, 373.14, box 874, WNRC.

3. WDGS, Military Intelligence Division, Washington, D.C., Memorandum to Director, Organization and Training Division, subject: Airborne Reconnaissance Units, from Col. M. A. Solomon, Assistant Executive, Director of Intelligence, 6 March 1947, Record Group 319, Army Intelligence Decimal Files, 1941–48, 373.14, box 874, WNRC.

4. WDGS, Military Intelligence Division, Washington, D.C., Memorandum to Commanding General, Army Ground Forces, Fort Monroe, Va., subject: Airborne Reconnaissance Units, from Lt. Gen. C. P. Hall, Director of Organization and Training, 9 April 1947, Record Group 319, Army Intelligence Decimal Files, 1941–48, 373.14, box 874, WNRC.

5. Army Field Forces, Office of the Chief, Fort Monroe, Va., Letter from Maj. Ernest Samusson, Jr., to Col. W. R. Peers, US Army Command and Staff College, 24 June 1948, Record Group 319, Army Intelligence Decimal Files, 1941–48, 373.14, box 874, WNRC.

6. See note 5 above.

7. WDGS, Organization and Training Division, Washington, D.C., Memorandum to Director of Intelligence, subject: Ranger Group (Old Proposed Airborne Reconnaissance Company), from Maj. Gen. H. R. Bull, Acting Director, O&T Division, 13 September 1948, Record Group 319, Army Intelligence Decimal Files, 1941–48, 373.14, box 874, WNRC.

8. Army Ground Forces, Intelligence Section, Fort Monroe, Va., Memorandum for Lt. Col. Roland N. Gleszer, Intelligence Division, WDGS, Record Group 319, Army Intelligence Decimal Files, 1941–48, 373.14, box 874, WNRC. The memo was sent by an officer named "Farris," with a copy of a paper on the Ranger Group that the Intelligence Section was submitting to the Plans Section for forwarding to the WDGS.

9. Department of the Army, Organization and Training Division, Washington, D.C., "A Study of Special and Subversive Operations," 25 November 1947, Record Group 319, Army Operations, 1949–52, box 10, Hot Files, G–3, Hot File 091.412 TS (1949), National Archives.

10. See note 9 above.

11. Department of the Army, Plans and Operations Division, Washington, D.C., "Study on Guerrilla Warfare," 1 March 1949, Record Group 319, Army Operations, 1949–52, box 10, Hot Files, P&O 370.64 TS (1 March 1949), National Archives.

12. Department of the Army, Plans and Operations Division, Washington, D.C., Memorandum for the Secretary of the Army, subject: Director of Special Studies (NSC 10), from Lt. Gen. A. C. Wedemeyer, Director of Plans and Operations, 19 May 1948, Record Group 319, Army Operations, 1948–52, box 9, Hot Files, P&O 092 TS (12 May 1948), National Archives.

13. Senate, *Foreign and Military Intelligence,* bk. 4, pp. 28–30.

14. Department of the Army, Plans and Operations Division, Washington, D.C., memorandum for the Secretary of the Army, subject: Director of Special Studies (NSC 10), 19 May 1948, Record Group 319, Army Operations, 1948–52, box 9, Hot Files, P&0 092 TS (12 May 1948), National Archives.

15. Department of the Army, Plans and Operations Division, Washington, D.C., Memorandum for the Secretary of the Army, subject: Director of Special

Studies (NSC 10), from Lt. Gen. A. C. Wedemeyer, Director of Plans and Operations, 2 June 1948, Record Group 319, Army Operations, 1948-52, box 9, Hot Files, P&O 092 TS (12 May 1948), National Archives.

16. Department of the Army, Plans and Operations Division, Washington, D.C., Memorandum for the Record, subject: Briefing on NSC Meeting, 3 June 1948, Record Group 319, Army Operations, 1948-52, box 9, Hot Files, National Archives.

17. Department of the Army, Plans and Operations Division, Washington, D.C., Memorandum for the Chief of Staff, US Army, subject: Designation of Military Establishment Representatives NSC 10/2 (Office of Special Projects) (JCS 1735/14), from Lt. Gen. A. C. Wedemeyer, Director, P&O Division, 19 August 1948, Record Group 319, Army Operations, 1948-52, box 9, Hot Files, P&O 091.412 TS (31 July 1948), National Archives.

18. Department of the Army, Plans and Operations Division, Washington, D.C., Memorandum for the Secretary of the Army, subject: Office of Special Projects (NSC/10/1), from Lt. Gen. A. C. Wedemeyer, Director, Plans and Operations Division, 16 June 1948, Record Group 319, Army Operations, 1948-52, box 9, Hot Files, P&O 091.412 TS (16 June 1948), National Archives.

19. Department of the Army, Plans and Operations Division, Washington, D.C., Memorandum for Record, subject: Study on Guerrilla Warfare, 1 March 1949, Record Group 319, Army Operations, 1949-52, box 10, Hot Files, P&O 370.64 TS (1 March 1949), National Archives.

20. Corson, *Armies of Ignorance,* p. 304.

21. Corson, *Armies of Ignorance,* pp. 306f.

22. Office of Policy Coordination, Memorandum for Lt. Gen. A. C. Wedemeyer, OCSA, subject: Transmittal of OPC response to the Special Section Joint Strategic Plans Group request for information regarding the need for establishment of an NME organization for collaboration with OPC, from Frank G. Wisner, Assistant Director of Policy Coordination, 1 August 1949, Record Group 319, Army Operations, 1949-52, box 10, Hot Files CSUSA 320 (1 August 1949) TS, National Archives.

23. See note 22 above.

24. Department of the Army, Plans and Operations Division, Washington, D.C., Memorandum for Record, subject: Department of the Army Assistance to the CIA in the Field of Guerrilla Warfare, 26 July 1949, and Summary Sheet for Chief of Staff, same subject, 29 July 1949, Record Group 319, Army Operations, 1949-52, box 10, Hot Files, P&O 370.64 TS (23 June 1949), National Archives.

25. Department of the Army, Plans and Operations Division, Washington, D.C., Memorandum for Record, subject: Department of the Army Assistance to the CIA in the Field of Guerrilla Warfare, 21 November 1949, and Notes on Meeting of Representatives of CIA and NME Joint CIA/NME Training Program, Record Group 319, Army Operations, 1949-52, box 10, Hot Files, P&O 370.64 TS (21 November 1949), National Archives.

26. See note 25 above.

27. Department of the Army, Plans and Operations Division, Washington, D.C., Memorandum for the Director of Central Intelligence, subject: Request for

Documents, 18 October 1949, Record Group 319, Army Operations, 1949–52, box 10, Hot Files, P&O 370.64 TS (18 October 1949), National Archives.

28. Department of the Army, Plans and Operations Division, Washington, D.C., Memorandum for the Chief of Staff, subject: The Military Organization for Psychological and Covert Operations (JCS 1735/32), 2 November 1949, from Maj. Gen. Charles L. Bolte, Director, Plans and Operations Division, Record Group 319, Army Operations, 1949–52, box 10, Hot Files, P&O 091.412 TS (28 October 1949), National Archives.

29. See note 28 above.

30. Department of the Army, Plans and Operations Division, Washington, D.C., Memorandum for the Chief of Staff, subject: Paramilitary Training Program (JCS 1735/34), 23 November 1949, from Maj. Gen. Charles L. Bolte, Record Group 319, Army Operations, 1949–52, box 10, Hot Files, P&O 091.412 TS (16 November 1949), National Archives.

31. Department of the Army, Plans and Operations Division, Washington, D.C., Memorandum for the Chief of Staff, subject: Liaison With Unified Commands for Special Operations, 20 December 1949, from Maj. Gen. Charles L. Bolte, Director, Plans and Operations Division, Record Group 319, Army Operations, 1949–52, box 10, Hot Files, P&O 091.412 TS (17 December 1949), National Archives.

32. Headquarters, 2d Army, Fort George C. Meade, Md., Letter to Lt. Gen. Alfred M. Gruenther, 30 November 1949, from Col. C. H. Gerhardt, Record Group 319, Army Operations, 1949–52, box 10, Hot Files, filed with P&O 000.5 (30 November 1949) TS, National Archives.

33. See note 32 above; Department of the Army, Office of the Chief of Staff, Washington, D.C., Memorandum for Director, Plans and Operations Division, 5 January 1950, CSUSA 381 (5 January 1950) C, from Lt. Gen. Alfred M. Gruenther, and Plans and Operations Division Summary Sheet, subject: Plans and Organization for Underground Development, 17 January 1950, Tab "B," Planning Status in Covert Operations, P&O 000.5 (30 November 1949) TS, filed in Record Group 319, Army Operations, 1949–52, box 10, Hot Files, National Archives.

34. See note 33 above, Tab "C," proposed letter to Col. C. H. Gerhardt.

Chapter VI Notes

1. Department of the Army, G-3 Operations Division, Washington, D.C., Report on Psychological Warfare Activities—Far East Command, 31 August 1950, Record Group 319, G-3 Operations, March 1950–51, 091.412, Case 41–100, box 157, OPS 091.412 S (29 August 1950), National Archives.

2. Department of the Army, Office of the Secretary of the Army, Washington, D.C., Memorandum for Gen. J. Lawton Collins, subject: Psychological Warfare Organization in the Department of the Army, 5 July 1950, from Secretary of

the Army Frank Pace, Jr., filed with G-3 091.412 S (5 July 1950), National Archives.

3. Department of the Army, G-3 Operations Division, Washington, D.C., Summary Sheet for the Chief of Staff, Psychological Warfare Organization in the Department of the Army, 13 July 1950, from Maj. Gen. Charles L. Bolte, Assistant Chief of Staff, G-3 091.412 S (5 July 1950), National Archives.

4. Department of the Army, G-3 Operations, Washington, D.C., Memorandum for Record, subject: Delineation of Responsibilities for Psychological Warfare, 17 July 1950, by Maj. Kenneth B. Stark, Record Group 319, G-3 Operations, March 1950-51, 091.412, Case 1-20, box 154, OPS 091.412 (17 July 1950), National Archives.

5. See note 4 above.

6. Department of the Army, G-3 Operations, Washington, D.C., Letter to Lt. Gen. A. C. Wedemeyer, Commanding General, 6th Army, from Maj. Gen. Charles L. Bolte, G-3, 12 August 1950, Record Group 319, G-3 Operations, March 1950-51, 091.412, Case 1-20, box 154, 091.412 (11 August 1950), National Archives.

7. See note 5 above, Message from Brig. Gen. Robert A. McClure to Maj. Gen. C. L. Bolte, 24 August 1950.

8. Department of the Army, Office of the Secretary of the Army, Washington, D.C., Memorandum for Gen. J. Lawton Collins, subject: Army Organization for Psychological Warfare, 30 August 1950, from Secretary of the Army Frank Pace, Jr., filed with OPS 091.412 (30 August 1950), Record Group 319, G-3 Operations, March 1950-51, 091.412, Case 1-20, box 154, National Archives.

9. Department of the Army, Office of the Chief of Staff, Washington, D.C., Minutes, Meeting of the General Council, Item No. 8, Assistant Chief of Staff, G-3, 30 August 1950, USAMHI.

10. Department of the Army, G-3 Operations, Washington, D.C., Summary Sheet for Chief of Staff, subject: Department of the Army Organization for Psychological Warfare, 31 August 1950, Record Group 319, G-3 Operations, March 1950-51, 091.412, Case 41-100, box 157, OPS 091.412 (31 August 1950) S, National Archives.

11. Department of the Army, Office of the Chief of Staff, Washington, D.C., Minutes, Meeting of the General Council, Item No. 3, 13 September 1950, USAMHI.

12. Department of the Army, G-3 Operations, Washington, D.C., Summary Sheet for Chief of Staff, subject: Psychological Warfare Training, 12 September 1950, from Maj. Gen. Charles L. Bolte, G-3, National Archives.

13. Department of the Army, G-3 Operations, Washington, D.C., DF to Special Assignments Branch, Career Management Division, Office of the Adjutant General, subject: Personnel for Psychological Warfare Division, OCAFFE, 25 October 1950, from Brig. Gen. Robert A. McClure, Chief, Psychological Warfare Division, G-3, Record Group 319, G-3 Operations, G3 091.412 (19 September 1950), National Archives.

14. Department of the Army, G-3 Operations, Washington, D.C., Memorandum for Record, Minutes of Psychological Warfare Division Staff Meeting,

31 October 1950, Record Group 319, Army-Chief of Special Warfare, box 2, File 020 Staff Meetings, National Archives.

15. See note 14 above.

16. Department of the Army, G-3 Operations, Washington, D.C., Letter to Maj. Gen. Daniel Noce, Chief of Staff, EUCOM, from Brigadier General McClure, 15 January 1951, Record Group 319, Army-Chief of Special Warfare, 1951-54, box 6, 091.412 Propaganda, National Archives. General Order No. 1, Department of the Army, 17 January 1951, established the division as of 15 January 1951, General Council Minutes, 24 January 1951, USAMHI.

17. Department of the Army, Office of the Chief of Staff, Washington, D.C., Minutes, Meeting of the General Council, 31 January 1951, USAMHI; Department of the Army, Office of the Chief of Psychological Warfare, Washington, D.C., Memorandum for Record, subject: Weekly Staff Meeting, 1 February 1951, Record Group 319, Army-Chief of Special Warfare, box 2, National Archives.

18. Headquarters, Department of the Army, Special Regulations no. 10-250-1, 22 May 1951, "Organizations and Functions, Department of the Army, Office of the Chief of Psychological Warfare, Special Staff," pp. 11-12, USAJFKCMA; US, Department of Defense, *Semiannual Report of the Secretary of Defense, 1 January through 30 June 1951*, p. 92.

19. Department of the Army, Office of the Secretary of the Army, Washington, D.C., Memorandum for the Chief of Staff, subject: Importance of Army-Wide Support of the Psychological Warfare Program, from Secretary of the Army Frank Pace, Jr., 2 February 1951, Record Group 319, Psy War, Decimal File 1951-54, 384-385, box 23, filed with Psy War 385 (2 February 1951), National Archives.

20. See note 19 above.

21. See note 19 above.

22. Department of the Army, Office of the Chief of Psychological Warfare, Washington, D.C., Memorandum for Record, subject: Conversation with the Secretary of the Army, 10 May 1951, by Brig. Gen. Robert A. McClure, Chief of Psychological Warfare, Record Group 319, Army-Chief of Special Warfare, National Archives.

23. Department of the Army, Office of the Chief of Psychological Warfare, Washington, D.C., Memorandum for Record, subject: Telephone conversation with Mr. Pace, Sec/Army, 26 May 1951, Brig. Gen. Robert A. McClure, Chief of Psychological Warfare, Record Group 319, Army-Chief of Special Warfare, National Archives.

24. Department of the Army, Office of the Chief of Psychological Warfare, Washington, D.C., Message DA 92760, 31 May 1951, from Chief of Staff, US Army, to CINCFE; filed with Psy War 091.412 TS (13 June 1951), Psychological Warfare, Far East Command, Record Group 319, Army-Chief of Special Warfare, 1951-54, box 6, National Archives.

25. Department of the Army, Office of the Chief of Psychological Warfare, Washington, D.C., Message C 64846, 13 June 1951, from CINCFE to SEC ARMY; filed with Psy War 091.412 TS (16 June 1951), Psychological Warfare, Far East Command, Record Group 319, Army-Chief of Special Warfare, 1951-54, box 6, National Archives.

26. Department of the Army, Office of the Chief of Psychological Warfare, Washington, D.C., Memorandum for Record, subject: ORO Briefing for Secretary of the Army Frank Pace, Jr., 23 July 1951, Brig. Gen. Robert A. McClure, Chief of Psychological Warfare, Record Group 319, Army-Chief of Special Warfare, National Archives.

27. Department of the Army, Office of the Chief of Psychological Warfare, Washington, D.C., unnumbered cable from Gen. Matthew B. Ridgeway to Secretary of the Army Pace, 17 August 1951, filed with Psy War 091.412 FECOM TS (17 September 1951), Record Group 319, Army-Chief of Special Warfare, 1951-54, National Archives.

28. Department of the Army, Office of the Chief of Psychological Warfare, Washington, D.C., Message DA 81176, 11 September 1951, from Secretary of the Army Pace to General Ridgeway, filed with Psy War 091.412 FECOM TS (17 September 1951), Record Group 319, Army-Chief of Special Warfare, 1951-54, National Archives.

29. Department of the Army, Office of the Chief of Psychological Warfare, Washington, D.C., Memorandum for Chief, Joint Subsidiary Plans Division, JCS, subject: Psychological Warfare Policy Guidance for FECOM, Psy War 091.412 FECOM TS (17 September 1951), Record Group 319, Army-Chief of Special Warfare, 1951-54, National Archives.

30. Department of the Army, Office of the Chief of Psychological Warfare, Washington, D.C., Memorandum of Weekly Staff Meetings, 8 March 1951, Record Group 319, Army-Chief of Special Warfare, 020 Staff Meetings, box 2, National Archives.

31. Department of the Army, Office of the Chief of Psychological Warfare, Washington, D.C., Informal Report as a Result of Visit of Chief, Psychological Warfare Division, DA, 24 April 1951, Record Group 319, Army-Chief of Special Warfare, Psy War 319.1 TS (24 April 1951), box 7, National Archives.

32. Lt. Ernest Conine, "New Horizons in Psychological Warfare," *Army Information Digest* 7, no. 12 (December 1951):22; Letter, Col. Otis E. Hayes, 5 May 1969, USAJFKCMA (Public Affairs Office); Linebarger, *Psychological Warfare,* pp. 301, 303.

33. Psychological Warfare Division, "Operations in Western European Campaign," p. 13; Propaganda Branch, "Syllabus of Psychological Warfare," p. 2; Linebarger, *Psychological Warfare,* p. 45.

34. US, Department of Defense, *Semiannual Report of the Secretary of Defense, 1 January through 30 June 1951,* p. 92.

35. Linebarger, *Psychological Warfare,* pp. 301-2, 304.

36. Linebarger, *Psychological Warfare,* p. 45; Psychological Warfare Division, "Operations in Western European Campaign," p. 13; Propaganda Branch, "Syllabus of Psychological Warfare," p. 2.

37. Linebarger, *Psychological Warfare,* pp. 301-2, 304, 306-7.

38. Psychological Warfare Division, "Operations in Western European Campaign," p. 19; McClure, "Trends in Psychological Warfare," p. 10; Daugherty and Janowitz, *Casebook,* p. 132; The Intelligence School, Fort Riley, Kans., "Tactical

Psychological Warfare, The Combat Psychological Warfare Detachment," October 1946, p. 1, USAJFKCMA.

39. Department of the Army, Office of the Chief of Psychological Warfare, Washington, D.C., Memorandum for the Chief, Psychological Operations Division, subject: Report on Field Trip to HQ FECOM and Korea, Capt. James J. Kelleher, Jr., Operations Branch, Record Group 319, Army-Chief of Special Warfare, SECRET Decimal Files, 1951–54, 333–334, Psy War 333 (22 April 1952), box 14, National Archives.

40. Department of the Army, Office of the Chief of Psychological Warfare, Washington, D.C., Memorandum for Record, subject: Briefing of the Chief of Staff on Letter from Gen. Doyle O. Hickey, Chief of Staff, FECOM, and FECOM Interim Report on Comprehensive Psychological Warfare Plans, 7 August 1951, Record Group 319, Army-Chief of Special Warfare, TS Decimal Files, box 1, Psy War 020 C/Staff TS (9 August 1951), National Archives.

41. Department of the Army, Office of the Chief of Psychological Warfare, Washington, D.C., Letter to Maj. Gen. Charles A. Willoughby, Assistant Chief of Staff, G-2, GHQ FECOM, from Brig. Gen. Robert A. McClure, 10 March 1951, Record Group 319, Army-Chief of Special Warfare, SECRET Decimal Files, 1951–54, Psy War 091.412 (10 March 1951), box 6, National Archives.

42. Department of the Army, Office of the Chief of Psychological Warfare, Washington, D.C., Informal Report as a Result of Visit of Chief, Psychological Warfare Division, DA, 24 April 1951, Record Group 319, Army-Chief of Special Warfare, Psy War 319.1 TS (24 April 1951), box 7, National Archives.

43. Department of the Army, Office of the Chief of Psychological Warfare, Washington, D.C., Memorandum for Record, subject: Conference with General Edwards, Director of Operations, US Air Force, 10 May 1951, Psy War 337 (10 May 1951); Memorandum for the Chief, Joint Subsidiary Plans Division, JCS, subject: Participation by the Tactical Air Forces of the Services in Psychological Warfare, 14 June 1951, Psy War 360 (14 June 1951); Memorandum for Record, subject: Briefing of the Chief of Staff on letter from Gen. Doyle O. Hickey, Chief of Staff, FECOM, and FECOM Interim Report on Comprehensive Psychological Warfare Plans, 7 August 1951, Psy War 020 C/Staff TS (9 August 1951); Memorandum for the Secretary of the Air Force, subject: Equipment for Psychological Operations in Korea, 9 June 1951, from Robert A. Lovett, Assistant Secretary of the Army, OSA 400 Korea; Memorandum for Brig. Gen. Robert A. McClure, subject: Utilization of Aircraft in the Conduct of Psychological Warfare, 24 July 1951, by Col Frederick S. Haydon, Chief, Plans Branch, Psy War 373 S (24 July 1951); all filed in Record Group 319, Army-Chief of Special Warfare, 1951–54, National Archives.

44. Department of the Army, Office of the Chief of Psychological Warfare, Washington, D.C., Letter to Lt. Gen. Doyle O. Hickey, Chief of Staff, Far East Command, 13 July 1951, from Brig. Gen. Robert A. McClure, Record Group 319, Psy War Decimal File (C), 1951–54, 360–370.64, box 19, Psy War 360 (13 July 1951), National Archives.

45. Department of the Army, Office of the Chief of Psychological Warfare, Washington, D.C., Letter to Maj. Gen. Charles A. Willoughby, Assistant Chief of Staff, G-2, GHQ, Far East Command, from Brig. Gen. Robert A. McClure,

12 March 1951, Record Group 319, Army-Chief of Special Warfare, 1951-54, box 6, Psy War 091.412 (10 March 1951), National Archives.

46. Department of the Army, Office of the Chief of Psychological Warfare, Washington, D.C., Letter to Brig. Gen. Robert A. McClure from Maj. Gen. Charles A. Willoughby, 24 March 1951, Record Group 319, Psy War Admin Office, 1951-54, 091.412-091.714, box 8, Psy War 091.412 (24 March 1951), National Archives.

47. Department of the Army, Office of the Chief of Psychological Warfare, Washington, D.C., Letter from Lt. Gen. Doyle O. Hickey, Chief of Staff, GHQ, Far East Command, 13 January 1952, to Brig. Gen. Robert A. McClure, Record Group 319, Psy War Admin Office, 1951-54, box 1, Psy War 000.7 (13 January 1952), National Archives.

48. Department of the Army, Office of the Chief of Psychological Warfare, Washington, D.C., Letter from Brig. Gen. Robert A. McClure to Lt. Gen. Doyle O. Hickey, 28 January 1952, Record Group 319, Psy War Admin Office, 1951-54, box 1, Psy War 000.7 (13 January 1952), National Archives.

49. Department of the Army, Office of the Chief of Psychological Warfare, Washington, D.C., AFFE Cable No. EX 22958 to DEPTAR Wash, DC for Psy War, 090425Sep 53, Record Group 319, Army-Chief of Special Warfare, 1951-54, SECRET Decimal Files, 333-334, box 14, Psy War 334 S (9 September 1953), National Archives.

50. Headquarters, 8th US Army Korea, Table of Distribution No. 80-8086, Miscellaneous Group, 8086th Army Unit, undated, Record Group 319, Army-Chief of Special Warfare, 1951-54, SECRET Decimal Files, 400.112 to 413.52, box 26, Psy War 400.34 (S) (1951), National Archives; interview with Robert Bodroghy, Strategic Studies Institute, US Army War College, Carlisle Barracks, Pa., 15 May 1979. As a young Army officer, Bodroghy was a member of the LEOPARD organization.

51. Interview with Robert Bodroghy, 15 May 1979; Psy War 091 Korea (31 December 1952), Weekly Summary from Korea of Items of Operational Interest for Period 16-22 December 1952, Record Group 319, Army-Chief of Special Warfare, 1951-54, SECRET Decimal Files, 091-091.412, box 7, National Archives; HQ Far East Command Liaison Detachment (Korea), 8240th Army Unit, Guerrilla Section, Guerrilla Operations Outline, 1952, to Commanders of LEOPARD, WOLFPACK, KIRKLAND, and BAKER Section, 11 April 1952, by Lt. Col. Jay D. Vanderpool, OIC Guerrilla Division, filed with Staff Visit of Col. Bradford Butler, Jr., March 1953, Record Group 319, Army-Chief of Special Warfare, 1951-54, National Archives.

52. Department of the Army, Office of the Chief of Psychological Warfare, Washington, D.C., Memorandum for Record, subject: Notes on WOLFPACK, source: Maj. R. M. Ripley, Series No. 037760, Former Commanding Officer, by Col. Bradford Butler, Jr., Chief, Special Forces Operations and Training Branch, Special Forces Division, 29 December 1952, Record Group 319, Army-Chief of Special Warfare, 1951-54, National Archives; Interview with Robert Bodroghy, 15 May 1979.

53. See note 52 above.

54. Headquarters, Far East Command Liaison Detachment (Korea), 8240th Army Unit, Guerrilla Operations Outline, 1953, by Lt. Col. Jay D. Vanderpool, OIC Guerrilla Division, 22 January 1953, filed with Staff Visit of Col. Bradford Butler, Jr., March 1953, Record Group 319, Army-Chief of Special Warfare, 1951–54, National Archives.

55. Interview with Robert Bodroghy, 15 May 1979.

56. Headquarters, Far East Command, Letter from Maj. Gen. Charles A. Willoughby to Maj. Gen. Charles L. Bolte, subject: Covert Intelligence Activities, Korea, 12 January 1951, Record Group 319, Army-Chief of Special Warfare, 1951–54, TS Decimal files, box 5, 091 Korea, National Archives; Joint Subsidiary Plans Division, JCS, Washington, D.C., Memorandum for Chief, Joint Subsidiary Plans Division, subject: Report on Trip to FECOM, 26 November–17 December 1951, by Col. W. H. S. Wright, Record Group 319, Army-Chief of Special Warfare, 1951–54, TS Decimal Files, 323.3–333, box 9, Psy War 333 TS (20 December 1951), National Archives.

57. See note 56; also, interview with Robert Bodroghy, 15 May 1979.

58. Department of the Army, Office of the Chief of Psychological Warfare, Washington, D.C., Memorandum for the Assistant Chief of Staff, G-2, subject: Reports on Special Operations in Korea, 15 March 1951, by Brig. Gen. Robert A. McClure, Record Group 319, Psy War Admin Office, Records Branch, 1951–54, 091, box 6, Psy War 091 Korea (15 March 1951), National Archives.

59. Department of the Army, Office of the Chief of Psychological Warfare, Washington, D.C., Memorandum to Assistant Chief of Staff, G-3, subject: CINC-FE Organization for Covert Operations and Clandestine Intelligence, 3 August 1951, from Brig. Gen. Robert A. McClure, Record Group 319, Army-Chief of Special Warfare, 1951–54, TS Decimal Files, box 2, Psy War 040 CIA TS (20 July 1951), National Archives.

60. See note 59; response from G-3 was dated 2 October 1951; also, interview with Col. John B. B. Trussell (Ret.), at Carlisle Barracks, Pa., 7 May 1979; a review of the OCPW, G-2, and G-3 files reveals numerous instances of policy differences.

61. Department of the Army, Office of the Chief of Psychological Warfare, Washington, D.C., Letter to Lt. Gen. Doyle O. Hickey, Chief of Staff, GHQ, Far East Command, 25 October 1951, from Brig. Gen. Robert A. McClure, Record Group 319, Army-Chief of Special Warfare, 1951–54, 091.412 Far East, National Archives.

62. Department of the Army, Office of the Chief of Psychological Warfare, Washington, D.C., Memorandum for Gen. Mark Clark, subject: Psychological Warfare Matters, 2 May 1952, by Brig. Gen. Robert A. McClure, Record Group 319, Army-Chief of Special Warfare, 1951–54, TS Decimal Files, box 6, Psy War 091.412 TS, National Archives.

63. See note 62 above.

64. See note 62 above.

65. Department of the Army, Office of the Chief of Psychological Warfare, Washington, D.C., Memorandum for Assistant Chief of Staff, G-3, subject: Revised Discussion of Queries Concerning Guerrilla Warfare, 23 May 1952, by Brig. Gen. Robert A. McClure, Record Group 319, Army-Chief of Special Warfare, 1951–54, TS Decimal Files, box 15, Psy War 370.64 TS (23 May 1952), National

Archives; Memorandum for Col. D. V. Johnson, Assistant Chief, Plans Division, Assistant Chief of Staff, G-3, subject: Responsibilities of the Services and the Joint Chiefs of Staff for Unconventional Warfare, from Brig. Gen. Robert A. McClure, Record Group 319, Army-Chief of Special Warfare, 1951-54, TS Decimal Files, box 15, Psy War 370.64 TS (26 October 1951), National Archives.

66. Headquarters, 10th Special Forces Group Airborne, Fort Bragg, N.C., Letter to Commanding Officer, Psychological Warfare Center, Fort Bragg, N.C., subject: Situation of Special Forces Officers in FECOM, 19 May 1953, by Col. Aaron Bank, Commanding Officer, filed with Psy War 220.3 (14 May 1953), Record Group 319, Army-Chief of Special Warfare, 1951-54, National Archives; Department of the Army, Office of the Chief of Psychological Warfare, Washington, D.C., Letter to Maj. Gen. Riley F. Ennis, Assistant Chief of Staff, G-2, GHQ, FECOM, from Col. William J. Blythe, Chief, Special Forces Division, 24 November 1952, Record Group 319, Army-Chief of Special Warfare, 1951-54, National Archives; Office of the Chief of Psychological Warfare, Message DA 927709 to CINCFE, 2 January 1953, Record Group 319, Army-Chief of Special Warfare, TS Decimal Files, 1951-54, box 15, Psy War 370.64 TS (13 December 1952), National Archives; Office of the Chief of Psychological Warfare, Memorandum for Record, subject: Conversation with Gen. Maxwell D. Taylor reference Special Forces Operations in the Far East Command, Record Group 319, Army-Chief of Special Warfare, 1951-54, TS Decimal Files, box 319, Psy War 337 TS (26 December 1952), National Archives; interview with Robert Bodroghy, 15 May 1979.

67. The Joint Chiefs of Staff, Joint Subsidiary Plans Division, Washington, D.C., Memorandum for Chief, Joint Subsidiary Plans Division, subject: Report on Trip to FECOM, 26 November-17 December 1951, by Col. W. H. S. Wright, US Army, 20 December 1951, filed with Psy War 333 TS (20 December 1951), Record Group 319, Army-Chief of Special Warfare, 1951-54, TS Decimal Files, 323.3-333, box 9, National Archives.

68. Department of the Army, Office of the Chief of Psychological Warfare, Washington, D.C., Disposition Form to G-1, G-2, G-3, subject: The Status and Role of "Partisan Forces," 18 February 1953, from Brig. Gen. Robert A. McClure with G-3 response, 20 February 1953, by Maj. Gen. C. D. Eddleman, Record Group 319, Army-Chief of Special Warfare, TS Decimal Files, 1951-54, 383.7-385, box 20, Psy War 384 FE TS (18 February 1953), National Archives.

69. Department of the Army, Office of the Chief of Staff, Washington, D.C., Letter from Gen. J. Lawton Collins to Gen. Mark Clark, 19 February 1953, filed with Psy War 370.64 TS (19 February 1953), Record Group 319, Army-Chief of Special Warfare, 1951-54, TS Decimal Files, 370.2-370.64, box 15, National Archives; Headquarters, Far East Command, Office of the Commander in Chief, Letter from Gen. Mark Clark to Gen. J. Lawton Collins, 12 March 1953, filed with Psy War 370.64 TS (9 April 1953), Record Group 319, Army-Chief of Special Warfare, 1951-54, TS Decimal Files, 370.2-370.64, box 15, National Archives.

Chapter VII Notes

1. Headquarters, European Command, Letter from Maj. Gen. Daniel Noce, Chief of Staff, to Brig. Gen. Robert A. McClure, 13 December 1950, Record Group 319, Army-Chief of Special Warfare, 1951–54, TS Decimal Files, box 6, Psy War 091.412 TS (13 December 1950, 15 January 1951), National Archives.

2. Department of the Army, G-3 Operations, Washington, D.C., Letter to Maj. Gen Daniel Noce, Chief of Staff, EUCOM, from Brig. Gen. Robert A. McClure, 15 January 1951, Record Group 319, Army-Chief of Special Warfare, 1951–54, TS Decimal Files, box 6, Psy War 091.412 TS (13 December 1950, 15 January 1951), National Archives.

3. Department of the Army, Office of the Chief of Psychological Warfare, Washington, D.C., letter from Brig. Gen. Robert A. McClure to Maj. Gen. Daniel Noce, 12 June 1951, Record Group 319, Army-Chief of Special Warfare, 1951–54, TS Decimal Files, box 6, Psy War 091.412 TS (12 June 1951), National Archives.

4. See note 3 above, Headquarters, European Command, Letter from Lt. Col. R. G. Ciccolella, Chief, Psy War Section, Special Plans Branch, Operations, Plans, Organization and Training Division, to Brig. Gen. Robert A. McClure, 15 October 1951, Psy War 337, National Archives; Letter from Lt. Col. R. G. Ciccolella to McClure, 14 November 1951, Record Group 319, Psy War Admin Office, Records Branch, Decimal File (C), 1951–54, 385.2-400, box 24, Psy War 400 (14 November 1951) S, National Archives; Department of the Army, Office of the Chief of Psychological Warfare, Washington, D.C., Progress Report—1 April 1951, Record Group 319, Army-Chief of Special Warfare, 1951–54, Psy War 319.1, National Archives.

5. Department of the Army, Office of the Chief of Psychological Warfare, Washington, D.C., Letter from Brig. Gen. Robert A. McClure to Maj. Gen. Charles A. Willoughby, G-2, General Headquarters, Far East Command, 10 March 1951, Record Group 319, Army-Chief of Special Warfare, 1951–54, Psy War 091.412, National Archives; also Psy War 322 (19 February 1951), Request for Increase in Authorized Strength of Psy War Units, Psy War 322 (28 February 1951), RB&L Group for FECOM, and Psy War 322 (5 March 1951), Reduced Strength RB&L Group for EUCOM, Record Group 319, Psy War Admin Office, Records Branch, Decimal File (C), 1951–54, 322-326, box 13, National Archives.

6. Department of the Army, Office of the Chief of Psychological Warfare, Washington, D.C., Memorandum for Record, subject: Meeting called by Colonel Hopkins, JSPD, by Lt. Col. Richard Hirsch, Intelligence and Evaluation Branch, 2 August 1951, Record Group 319 Army-Chief of Special Warfare, 1951–54, TS Decimal Files, box 6, Psy War 091.412, National Archives.

7. Department of the Army, Office of the Chief of Psychological Warfare, Washington, D.C., Memorandum for Record, Staff Meeting, 6 December 1951, Record Group 319, Army-Chief of Special Warfare, 1951–54, TS Decimal Files, box 2, Psy War 020 Staff Meetings, National Archives; Memorandum for Chief of Staff, US Army, subject: Psychological Warfare Conference EUCOM, 27–28 November 1951, by Brig. Gen. Robert A. McClure, 6 December 1951, Record Group 319, Army-Chief of Special Warfare, 1951–54, Psy War 334S (6 December 1951), National Archives.

8. Department of the Army, Office of the Chief of Psychological Warfare, Washington, D.C., Memorandum for Record, Weekly Staff Meeting, 8 March 1951, Record Group 319, Army-Chief of Special Warfare, 1951–54, TS Decimal Files, box 2, Psy War 020 Staff Meetings, National Archives.

9. Interview with Col. John B. B. Trussell, US Army (Ret.), at Carlisle Barracks, Pa., 7 May 1979. Colonel Trussell, as a lieutenant colonel, was a staff officer in OCPW during the early 1950's.

10. Department of the Army, Office of the Chief of Psychological Warfare, Washington, D.C., Memorandum from Captain Hahn, US Navy, to Deputy Chief of Naval Operations, subject: Air Force Views Relating to Retardation (of Soviet Advances), 20 October 1951, Record Group 319, Army-Chief of Special Warfare, 1951–54, TS Decimal Files, box 15, Psy War 381, National Archives; see also Psy War 350.001 TS (7 January 1952), subject: Psychological Warfare Presentation for PSB, TS Decimal Files, 1951–54, box 13, and Psy War 385 TS (29 August 1951), subject: Appraisal of Capabilities of Psychological Operations in Department of Defense, TS Decimal Files, box 20, National Archives.

11. Department of the Army, Office of the Chief of Psychological Warfare, Washington, D.C., Memorandum for Chief of Staff, US Army, subject: Psychological Warfare Conference, EUCOM, 27–28 November 1951, by Brig. Gen. Robert A. McClure, 6 December 1951, Record Group 319, Army-Chief of Special Warfare, 1951–54, Psy War 334 S (6 December 1951), National Archives.

12. Department of the Army, Office of the Chief of Psychological Warfare, Washington, D.C., Letter from Maj. Kenneth B. Stark to Lt. Col. Homer E. Shields, 12 March 1951, Record Group 319, Army-Chief of Special Warfare, 1951–54, National Archives.

13. Linebarger, *Psychological Warfare,* p. 304; Letter, Col. Otis E. Hayes, Jr. (Ret.), 5 May 1969, to Office of Information, John F. Kennedy Center for Special Warfare, USAJFKCMA (Public Affairs Office); Army General School, Fort Riley, Kans., "Program of Instruction, Psychological Warfare Unit Officer Course," January 1951, p. i, USAJFKCMA.

14. Army General School, Fort Riley, Kans., "Program of Instruction for Psychological Warfare Officer Course," August 1951, p. 12, USAJFKCMA; Letter, Col. Otis E. Hayes, 5 May 1969, to Office of Information, USAJFKCMA (Public Affairs Office). Colonel Hayes was recalled to active duty in 1951 as Deputy of the Psychological Warfare Division at Fort Riley. After the Psychological Warfare Center was activated at Fort Bragg in 1952, he became the first Director of the Psychological Operations Department (in the Psychological Warfare School) and remained in that position for 18 months.

15. Department of the Army, Office of the Chief of Psychological Warfare, Washington, D.C., Progress Report, Personnel and Training Division, 1 April 1951, Record Group 319, Army-Chief of Special Warfare, 1951–54, Psy War 319.1, National Archives; Office of the Chief of Psychological Warfare, Letter to Lt. Col. John W. White, G–3 Section, Headquarters, 1st Army, Governor's Island, N.Y., from Brig. Gen. Robert A. McClure, 24 May 1951, Psy War 320.2, National Archives.

16. Department of the Army, Operations Research Office, Washington, D.C., Letter from Ellis A. Johnson, Director, to Brig. Gen. Robert A. McClure, subject:

Research for Psychological Warfare, 8 May 1951, Psy War 400.112; Office of the Chief of Psychological Warfare, Memorandum for Chief, Psychological Warfare, subject: Non-materiel Research Program, 7 February 1951, from Lt. Col. Jerome G. Sacks, Research Branch, filed with Psy War 400.112 (29 February 1951); Office of the Secretary of the Army, Memorandum for the Secretary of Defense, subject: Appraisal of Capabilities of Psychological Operations in Department of Defense, from Secretary Frank Pace, Jr., 21 September 1951, Record Group 319, Army-Chief of Special Warfare, 1951–54, TS Decimal Files, box 20, Psy War 385 TS, National Archives.

17. Department of the Army, Office of the Chief of Psychological Warfare, Washington, D.C., "Briefing for Secretary of Defense on OCPW Activities," 5 November 1951, Record Group 319, Psy War Admin Office, Records Branch, Decimal File (C), 1951–54, 334–337, Psy War 337 S (5 November 1951), National Archives.

18. Department of the Army, Office of the Chief of Psychological Warfare, Washington, D.C., Memorandum to Office of the Chief of Staff of the Army, subject: Reduction of Military and Civilian Personnel in the Chief of Staff area, 27 August 1951, Record Group 319, Army-Chief of Special Warfare, SECRET Decimal Files, 1951–54, 092–230, box 9, Psy War 230 (17 August 1951), National Archives; interview with Col. John B. B. Trussell, 9 May 1979.

19. Interview with Col. John B. B. Trussell, 9 May 1979.

20. Department of the Army, Office of the Chief of Psychological Warfare, Washington, D.C., Weekly Staff Meeting, 8 March 1951, Record Group 319, Army-Chief of Special Warfare, 1951–54, TS Decimal Files, box 2, National Archives.

21. Letter, Brig. Gen. Russell W. Volckmann (Ret.), 21 March 1969, to Office of Information, John F. Kennedy Center for Special Warfare, US-AJFKCMA (Public Affairs Office); Letters, Col. Aaron Bank (Ret.), 17 February 1968 and 3 April 1968, to Office of Information, John F. Kennedy Center for Special Warfare, USAJFKCMA (Public Affairs Office).

22. Letter, Volckmann, 21 March 1969 (see note 21 above).

23. Letters, Volckmann and Bank (see note 21 above).

24. Letter, Col. Aaron Bank (Ret.), 23 February 1969, to Office of Information, John F. Kennedy Center for Special Warfare, USAJFKCMA (Public Affairs Office).

25. Department of the Army, Office of the Chief of Psychological Warfare, Washington, D.C., Minutes of Staff Meetings, 29 March 1951 and 19 July 1959, Record Group 319, Army-Chief of Special Warfare, 1951–54, TS Decimal Files, box 2, National Archives. These frequent changes of division chief designations were probably due to the relative date of rank, or seniority, among the colonels brought into the Special Operations Division.

26. See note 24 above.

27. Department of the Army, Office of the G–3, Washington, D.C., Memorandum for Director, O&T Division, subject: Responsibilities of Army with Respect to Guerrilla Warfare, 20 March 1951, by Maj. Gen. Maxwell D. Taylor, Record Group 319, Army-Chief of Special Warfare, 1951–54, TS Decimal Files, 370.2–370.64, box 15, Psy War 370.64 TS (20 March 1951), National Archives.

28. Department of the Army, Office of the Chief of Psychological Warfare, Washington, D.C., Minutes of Weekly Staff Meeting, 8 March 1951, Record Group 319, Army-Chief of Special Warfare, 1951–54, TS Decimal Files, box 2, National Archives.

29. Department of the Army, Office of the Chief of Psychological Warfare, Washington, D.C., Memorandum for the Assistant Chief of Staff, G–2, subject: Reports on Special Operations in Korea, 15 March 1951, by Brig. Gen. Robert A. McClure, Record Group 319, Psy War Admin Office, Records Branch, 1951–54, box 6, Psy War 091 Korea (15 March 1951), National Archives.

30. Department of the Army, Office of the Chief of Psychological Warfare, Washington, D.C , Minutes of Weekly Staff Meeting, 29 March 1951, Record Group 319, Army-Chief of Special Warfare, 1951–54, TS Decimal Files, box 2, National Archives.

31. Headquarters, The Infantry School, Fort Benning, Ga., Memorandum to the Commanding General, Infantry Center, subject: Analysis and Suggestions re Gen. J. Lawton Collins' Conference, 5 April 1951, from Lt. Col. Russell W. Volckmann, 9 April 1951, filed with Psy War 337 TS (16 April 1951), Record Group 319, Army-Chief of Special Warfare, 1951–54, TS Decimal Files, box 12, National Archives.

32. See note 31 above.

33. See note 31 above.

34. Department of the Army, Office of the Chief of Psychological Warfare, Washington, D.C., Memorandum for Gen. Maxwell D. Taylor, Assistant Chief of Staff, G–3, subject: Definitions Relating to Psychological Warfare, Special Operations and Guerrilla Warfare, 17 April 1951, Record Group 319, Army-Chief of Special Warfare, 1951–54, Psy War 370.64 (17 April 1951), National Archives.

35. Department of the Army, Office of the Chief of Psychological Warfare, Washington, D.C., Summary Sheet of Chief of Staff, subject: Gen. J. Lawton Collins' Conference at the Infantry Center, 5 April 1951, from Col. Edward Glavin, Acting Chief of Psychological Warfare (summary sheet prepared by Lt. Col. Russell W. Volckmann), 16 April 1951, Record Group 319, Army-Chief of Special Warfare, 1951–54, TS Decimal Files, Psy War 337 (16 April 1951), National Archives.

36. See note 35 above; see also Department of the Army, Office of the Chief of Psychological Warfare, Washington, D.C., Briefing Notes, Conference with G–1, –2, –3, –4, and AFF re Training in the Field of Special (Forces) Operations, 21 June 1951, Record Group 319, Army-Chief of Special Warfare, 1951–54, TS Decimal Files, box 12, Psy War 337 TS (21 June 1951), National Archives. The studies resulting from this action, in addition to "Army Responsibilities in Report to Special (Forces) Operations," were "Theater Special Forces Command and (Z.I.) Special Forces Training Command"; "Special Forces Ranger Units—and— Special Forces Ranger Units, Recruiting and Training of Personnel"; "Rear Area Defense"; and "Executive Agent for the Joint Chiefs of Staff for Matters Pertaining to Guerrilla Warfare."

37. Department of the Army, Office of the Chief of Psychological Warfare, Washington, D.C., Memorandum for Gen. C. D. Eddleman, subject: Utilization of Lodge Bill Recruits in Special (Forces) Operations, 23 May 1951, from Brig. Gen.

Robert A. McClure, Record Group 319, Army-Chief of Special Warfare, 1951–54, TS Decimal Files, 370.2–370.64, box 15, Psy War 373.2 TS (23 May 1951), National Archives.

38. See note 37 above.

39. Department of the Army, Office of the Chief of Psychological Warfare, Washington, D.C., Memorandum to Assistant Chief of Staff, G-3, subject: Staff Studies, "Special Forces Ranger Units" and "Special Forces Ranger Units, Recruiting and Training of Personnel," 12 June 1951, from Brig. Gen. Robert A. McClure, Record Group 319, Army-Chief of Special Warfare, 1951–54, TS Decimal Files, 270.2–370.64, box 15, Psy War 370.64 (12 June 1951), National Archives.

40. Department of the Army, Office of the Chief of Psychological Warfare, Washington, D.C., Briefing Notes, Conference with G-1, -2, -3, -4 and AFF re Training in the Field of Special (Forces) Operations, 21 June 1951, Record Group 319, Army-Chief of Special Warfare, 1951–54, TS Decimal Files, box 12, Psy War 337 TS (21 June 1951), National Archives. Additionally, Lieutenant Colonel Volckmann had earlier reiterated to McClure the conclusion "that a need exists for a training command or center that will bring together the many segments of special (forces) operations under a program that will fully develop doctrine, policies, techniques, and tactics . . . and that will develop equipment and supplies." This came after a trip, directed by McClure, to observe training and instruction at the CIA's "School Number One," the Ranger Training Center, and the Infantry Center—all at Fort Benning. Office of the Chief of Psychological Warfare, Memorandum for Brig. Gen. Robert A. McClure, subject: Findings and Recommendations re Special Operations Training, Fort Benning, Ga., 24 April 1951, by Lt. Col. Russell W. Volckmann, Record Group 319, Army-Chief of Special Warfare, 1951–54, TS Decimal Files, 370.2–370.64, box 15, Psy War 370.64 TS (3 May 1951), National Archives.

41. Department of the Army, Office of the Chief of Psychological Warfare, Washington, D.C., Memorandum for Brig. Gen. Robert A. McClure, subject: Ranger Units, 17 July 1951, from Col. Wendell W. Fertig, Chief, Special Operations, Record Group 319, Psy War Admin Office, Records Branch, Decimal File (C), 1951–54, 322–326, box 13, Psy War 322 S (17 July 1951), National Archives.

42. See note 41 above; see also Eliot A Cohen, *Commandos and Politicians: Elite Military Units in Modern Democracies* (Cambridge: Center for International Affairs, Harvard University, 1978), pp. 56–58.

43. Department of the Army, Office of the Chief of Psychological Warfare.

44. Adjutant General, Army Field Forces, Letter to Adjutant General, Department of the Army, subject: Training of Individuals and Units of the Army in Special (Forces) Operations, 23 August 1951, Record Group 319, Army-Chief of Special Warfare, 1951–54, box 6, 091.412 TS Propaganda (23 August 1951), National Archives.

45. Department of the Army, Office of the Chief of Psychological Warfare, Washington, D.C., Memorandum for Record, subject: Conference to Resolve Ranger Program, 24 August 1951, by Col. Aaron Bank, Special Operations Division, Record Group 319, Psy War 337 (24 August 1951), National Archives. The

principals attending the conference were General Taylor, General Bradford, G-3, AFF, and General McAuliffe, G-1.

46. Department of the Army, Office of the Chief of Psychological Warfare, Washington, D.C., Memorandum for Assistant Chief of Staff, G-3, subject: Request for Spaces in the Active Army, 28 September 1951, from Brig. Gen. Robert A. McClure, Record Group 319, Psy War Admin Office, Records Branch, Decimal File (C), 1951-54, 311.5-319.1, box 11, Psy War 320.2 (28 September 1951), National Archives.

47. Department of the Army, Office of the Chief of Psychological Warfare, Washington, D C., Memorandum to Assistant Chief of Staff, G-3, subject: Table of Organization and Equipment 33-510 (proposed) for Special Forces Group (Abn), 13 November 1952, with draft 1st Ind letter to OCAFF, Record Group 319, Army-Chief of Special Warfare, 1951-54, TS Decimal Files, box 8, Psy War 320.3 TS (30 September 1952), National Archives.

48. Headquarters, European Command, Letter to Brig. Gen. Robert A. McClure, 12 November 1952, from Brig. Gen. Willard K. Liebel, Chief, Support Plans Branch, J-3, Psy War 240 (12 November 1952); Office of the Chief of Psychological Warfare, Letter to Brigadier General Liebel, 8 December 1952, from McClure, Psy War 290 (8 December 1952); Office of the Chief of Psychological Warfare, Letter to General Liebel from General McClure, 19 December 1952, Psy War 290 (19 December 1952); all filed in Record Group 319, Army-Chief of Special Warfare, 1951-54, TS Decimal Files, box 6, National Archives.

49. Cohen, *Commandos and Politicians,* particularly his discussion of "The Specialist Function," pp. 30f.

50. Department of the Army, Office of the Chief of Psychological Warfare, Washington, D C., Memorandum for Brig. Gen. Robert A. McClure, subject: Findings and Recommendations re Special Operations Training, Fort Benning, Ga., from Lt. Col. Russell W. Volckmann, 24 April 1951, Record Group 319, Army-Chief of Special Warfare, 1951-54, TS Decimal files, 370.2-370.64, box 15, Psy War 370.64 TS (3 May 1951), National Archives. Volckmann had been directed by McClure to visit Fort Benning to review the training and instruction at the CIA's "School Number One," the Ranger Training Center, and the Infantry School, with emphasis on the special operations instruction, then report to him his findings and recommendations (see memorandum from McClure to Volckmann, 19 March 1951, filed with above reference). See also General McClure's and Colonel Bank's discussion with AFF concerning a training center, Department of the Army, Office of the Chief of Psychological Warfare, Washington, D.C., Minutes of Weekly Staff Meeting, 16 August 1951, Record Group 319, Army-Chief of Special Warfare, 1951-54, TS Decimal Files, 020 Staff Meeting, box 2, National Archives.

51. See note 50 above, especially Minutes of Weekly Staff Meeting, 16 August 1951.

52. Central Intelligence Agency, Office of Policy Coordination, Washington, D.C., Memorandum for Brig. Gen. Robert A. McClure, through the Joint Subsidiary Plans Division, JCS, subject: Joint CIA-DA Guerrilla Warfare Training, from Kilbourne Johnston, Deputy Assistant Director for Policy Coordination, 17

August 1951, Record Group 319, Psy War, Decimal File (C), 1951-54, 360-370.64, box 19, Psy War 370.64 (21 August 1951) S, National Archives.

53. Department of the Army, Office of the Chief of Psychological Warfare, Washington, D.C., Agreement between Frank G. Wisner, Assistant Director for Policy Coordination, CIA, and Brig. Gen. Robert A. McClure, Chief of Psychological Warfare—Staff, DA, on the Respective Roles and Responsibilities of CIA/OPC and Psy War Division, Special Staff, Department of the Army, in the Field of Unconventional Warfare, 17 July 1951, Record Group 319, Army-Chief of Special Warfare, 1951-54, TS Decimal Files, box 2, 020 CIA, National Archives; Office of the Chief of Psychological Warfare, Memorandum for the Chief, Joint Subsidiary Plans Division, JCS, subject: Coordination of Army Psychological Warfare Materiel Research Activities with CIA, 25 March 1952, from Brig. Gen. Robert A. McClure, and reply from CIA, 23 April 1952, Record Group 319, Psy War Admin Office, box 25, Psy War 400.112 (25 March 1952) C, National Archives.

54. Department of the Army, Office of the Chief of Psychological Warfare, Washington, D.C., Minutes of Meeting, 5 September 1951, Record Group 319, Army-Chief of Special Warfare, 1951-54, TS Decimal Files, box 12, Psy War 337 TS (5 September 1951), National Archives.

55. Department of the Army, Office of the Chief of Psychological Warfare, Washington, D.C., Letter to Lt. Gen. Charles L. Bolte, Commander in Chief, US Army, Europe, from Brig. Gen. Robert A. McClure, 1953 undated (probably late February or early March 1953), Record Group 319, Psy War Admin Office, Records Branch, 1951-54, 020-40, box 3, Psy War 040 CIA (undated) 53, National Archives.

56. Department of the Army, Office of the Chief of Psychological Warfare, Washington, D.C., Summary Sheet for Chief of Staff, subject: Staff visit to Europe, 13 September 1951, from Brig. Gen. Robert A. McClure, Record Group 319, Army-Chief of Special Warfare, 1951-54, TS Decimal Files, 323.3-333, box 9, Psy War 333 Europe TS (12 September 1951), National Archives.

57. Central Intelligence Agency, Office of the Director, Washington, D.C., Letter to Maj. Gen. A. R. Bolling, Assistant Chief of Staff, G-2, Department of the Army, 10 March 1952, from Walter B. Smith, Director, filed with Record Group 319, Army-Chief of Special Warfare, 1951-54, TS Decimal Files, box 15, Psy War 370.64, Guerrilla Warfare, National Archives.

58. See note 57 above.

59. Department of the Army, Office of the Chief of Psychological Warfare, Washington, D.C., Memorandum for Gen. J. Lawton Collins, Chief of Staff, subject: Staff Visit to Europe, from Brig. Gen. Robert A. McClure, 10 September 1951, Record Group 319, Army-Chief of Special Warfare, 1951-54, TS Decimal Files, 323.3-333, box 9, Psy War 333 (10 September 1951), National Archives.

60. The CIA's statement appeared in a memorandum dated 6 June 1952, an enclosure to JCS 1969/73, Memorandum for Chairman, JCS, subject: Overseas CIA Logistical Support Bases; see Office of the Chief of Psychological Warfare, Memorandum for the Chief of History, subject: Summary of Major Events and Problems, Psy War 314.7 TS (15 August 1953); see also Psy War 314.7 (6 January 1953), History of DA Activities, for OCPW's explanation of why the JCS disap-

proved its Special Forces Operations Plan for Europe; both are filed in Record Group 319, Army-Chief of Special Warfare, 1951-54, TS Decimal Files, 311-319.1, box 7, National Archives.

61. Department of the Army, Office of the Chief of Psychological Warfare, Washington, D.C., Memorandum for Brig. Gen. Paul D. Harkins, subject: JSPC 808/112, Command Relationships between the CIA/OPC Organization and the Armed Forces in Actual Theaters of War Where American Forces Are Engaged (29 December 1952), from Brig. Gen. Robert A. McClure, Chief of Psychological Warfare, 30 December 1952, Record Group 319, Army-Chief of Special Warfare, 1951-54, TS Decimal Files, 000.1-020, box 1, National Archives. General Harkins was the "Army Planner," a senior officer responsible for presenting the Army's position on JCS actions.

62. Department of the Army, Office of the Chief of Psychological Warfare, Washington, D.C., Air Force Presentation to the Psychological Strategy Board on 10 January 1952. filed with Record Group 319, Army-Chief of Special Warfare, 1951-54, TS Decimal Files, 337-350.05, box 13, Psy War 350.001 TS (7 January 1952), National Archives.

63. Department of the Army, Office of the Chief of Psychological Warfare, Washington, D.C., Discussions of Questions by the Under Secretary of the Army concerning Army Role in Guerrilla and Unconventional Warfare, in response to a Memorandum to the Vice Chief of Staff, subject: Guerrilla Warfare, 11 April 1952, filed with Psy War 320.64 TS (3 May 1952) (12 May 1952), TS Decimal Files, 1951-54, box 15, National Archives.

64. Department of the Army, Office of the Chief of Psychological Warfare, Washington, D.C., Minutes of Meeting, 5 September 1951, Record Group 319, Army-Chief of Special Warfare, 1951-54, TS Decimal Files, box 12, Psy War 337 TS (5 September 1951), National Archives.

65. Department of the Army, Office of the Chief of Psychological Warfare, Washington, D.C., Memorandum for Gen. J. Lawton Collins, Chief of Staff, subject: Staff Visit to Europe, from Brig. Gen. Robert A. McClure, 12 September 1951, Record Group 319, Army-Chief of Special Warfare, 1951-54, TS Decimal Files, 323.3-333, box 9, Psy War 333 (10 September 1951), National Archives.

66. Department of the Army, Office of the Chief of Psychological Warfare, Washington, D.C., Memorandum for the Chief of Staff, US Army, subject: Unconventional Warfare (Special Forces Operations) Discussions Held at EUCOM and SHAPE, from Brig. Gen. Robert A. McClure, 5 December 1951, Record Group 319, Army-Chief of Special Warfare, 1951-54, TS Decimal Files, 370.2-370.64, box 15, Psy War 370.64 TS (5 December 1951), National Archives.

67. Department of the Army, Office of the Chief of Psychological Warfare, Washington, D.C., Memorandum to the Chief of Military History, subject: Summary of Major Activities of OCPW for Period 9 September 1951 to 31 December 1952, 7 April 1953. JCS Decision 1969/18, 27 March 1952, Responsibilities of the Services and the Joint Chiefs of Staff for Guerrilla Warfare, assigned to the Army primary responsibility for guerrilla warfare in combat operations on land. The decision also assigned to the Army primary responsibility for developing, in coordination with the other services and subject to JCS policy direction, the doctrine, tactics, techniques, procedures, and equipment employed by guerrilla forces in

combat operations on land, and for training these forces with the assistance of the other services. Record Group 319, Army-Chief of Special Warfare, 1951–54, TS Decimal File, 311–319.1, box 7, Psy War 314.7 (6 January 1953), National Archives.

68. General Collins' directive remained in effect for 9 months until March 1952. At that time, after considerable interservice battling, the JCS assigned the Army primary responsibility for guerrilla warfare. See note 67 above; see also the briefing by Brig. Gen. Bullock (McClure's replacement as Chief, OCPW) to the Chief, Army Field Services, at Fort Monroe, Va., 5 October 1953, Record Group 319, Army-Chief of Special Warfare, 1951–54, TS Decimal Files, 337–350.05, box 13, Psy War 337 TS (2 October 1953), National Archives.

69. Department of the Army, Organization and Training Division, G–3, Washington, D.C., Memorandum for the Chief of Psychological Warfare, subject: Training of Individuals and Units of the Army in Special (Forces) Operations, 14 September 1951, from Brig. Gen. D. A. D. Ogden, G–3, 370.2 TS (23 August 1951), filed with Record Group 319, Army-Chief of Special Warfare, 1951–54, TS Decimal Files, 370.2–370.64, box 15, Psy War 370.2 TS (14 September 1951), National Archives.

70. Department of the Army, Office of the Chief of Psychological Warfare, Washington, D.C., Response to G–3, 370.2 TS (14 September 1951), subject: Training of Individuals and Units of the Army in Special (Forces) Operations, from Brig. Gen. Robert A. McClure, 5 October 1951, Record Group 319, Army-Chief of Special Warfare, 1951–54, TS Decimal Files, 370.2–370.64, box 15, filed with Psy War 370.2 TS (14 September 1951), National Archives. The minutes of the 13 September 1951 weekly OCPW staff meeting show that a plan for a Center for Psychological Warfare and Special Operations Training was being worked on, with the intent of making the necessary suggestions to AFF, who in turn could recommend to G–3 that such a center be established—an interesting, but not uncommon, bit of bureaucratic maneuvering for a pet project; Record Group 319, Army-Chief of Special Warfare, 1951–54, TS Decimal Files, box 2, Psy War 020 Staff Meetings, National Archives.

71. See note 70 above, OCPW response to G–3, 5 October 1951.

72. Department of the Army, Office of the Chief of Psychological Warfare, Washington, D.C., "Special Forces Operations," by Col. Russell W. Volckmann, 26 October 1951, filed in Psy War 372.2 Operations, National Archives.

73. See note 72 above.

74. Department of the Army, Office of the Chief of Psychological Warfare, Washington, D.C., "Briefing for Secretary of Defense on OCPW Matters," 5 November 1951, by Brig. Gen. Robert A. McClure, Record Group 319, Psy War Admin Office, Records Branch, Decimal File (C), 1951–54 334–337, box 15, Psy War 337 S (5 November 1951), National Archives.

75. See Note 74 above.

76. Department of the Army, Office of the Chief of Psychological Warfare, Washington, D.C., Memorandum for Col. D. V. Johnson, Assistant Chief, Plans Division, Office of the Assistant Chief of Staff, G–3, subject: Responsibilities of the Services and the Joint Chiefs of Staff for Unconventional Warfare, 26 October 1951, from Brig. Gen. Robert A. McClure, Record Group 319, Army-Chief of

Special Warfare, 1951-54, TS Decimal Files, 370.2-370.64, box 15, Psy War 370.64 TS (26 October 1951), National Archives.

77. Department of the Army, Training Circular 31-20-1, *The Role of US Army Special Forces*, 22 October 1976. In *Commandos and Politicians*, Eliot Cohen states that "the US Army contributed to the downfall of Special Forces by creating two Ranger battalions [in 1974-75]. These units fit the specialist model: They are relatively small forces trained for such missions as the rescue of hostages (along the lines of Israel's Entebbe Raid)" (Cohen, p. 88). These types of missions, as well as other unilateral (no indigenous personnel) Ranger or Commando-like "direct action" activities, have, however, become part of the Special Forces' growing repertoire of capabilities (Cohen somewhat inelegantly calls Special Forces "guerrilla/commandos, preparing for a variety of military odd jobs," p. 25). Cohen discusses the desire among elite units to acquire new missions and additional personnel, and concludes: "The mission of elite troops must be as rigorously defined as possible: a niche must be carved out for them and they must be kept within it" (p. 97).

78. Department of the Army, Office of the Chief of Psychological Warfare, Washington, D.C., Minutes of Weekly Staff Meeting, 8 November 1951, Record Group 319, Army-Chief of Special Warfare, 1951-54, TS Decimal Files, box 2, 020 Staff Meetings, National Archives.

79. Department of the Army, Office of the Chief of Psychological Warfare, Washington, D.C., Memorandum for the Record, subject: Survey for Psychological Warfare Center, 19 November 1951, by Col. Wendell W. Fertig, Chief, Special Operations Division; Memorandum for Brig. Gen. Robert A. McClure, subject: Status of Special Forces Training Center, 3 December 1951, by Col. Wendell W. Fertig; both filed in Psy War 322C (3 December 1951), Record Group 319, Psy War Admin Office, Records Branch, Decimal Files (C), 1951-54, National Archives. The personnel who made the initial survey of Fort Benning and Fort Bragg during the period 13 to 15 November 1951 were Col. Aaron Bank and Maj. Kenneth B. Stark of OCPW, Col. Edward Glavin of AFF, and Maj. Taylor of the G-3 Division, Psy War Section, 3d Army.

80. Department of the Army, Office of the Chief of Psychological Warfare, Washington, D.C., Memorandum for Brig. Gen. Robert A. McClure, subject: Status of Special Forces Training Center, 3 December 1951, by Col. Wendell W. Fertig, Psy War 322C (3 December 1951), Record Group 319, Psy War Admin Office, Records Branch, Decimal File (C), 1951-54, National Archives; see also OCPW Minutes of Weekly Staff Meeting, 6 December 1951, Record Group 319, Army-Chief of Special Warfare, 1951-54, TS Decimal Files, box 2, 020 Staff Meetings, National Archives.

81. Department of the Army, Office of the Chief of Psychological Warfare, Washington, D.C., Minutes of Weekly Staff Meeting, 6 December 1951, Record Group 319, Army-Chief of Special Warfare, 1951-54, TS Decimal Files, box 2, 020 Staff Meetings, National Archives.

82. See note 81 above; see also Minutes of Weekly Staff Meetings, 25 October 1951 and 8 November 1951, Record Group 319, Army-Chief of Special Warfare, 1951-54, TS Decimal Files, box 2, 020 Staff Meetings, National Archives.

83. Office of the Post Engineer, Fort Bragg, N.C., Memorandum for Record, subject: Establishment of Psychological Warfare Center, 12 December 1951, by A. W. Hart, Division Chief, Record Group 319, Army-Chief of Special Warfare, File 123 Money and Savings, National Archives; Office of the Chief of Psychological Warfare, Memorandum for Record, subject: Fort Bragg Survey, 17 December 1951, from Lt. Col. Melvin R. Blair, Special Operations Division, Record Group 319, Army-Chief of Special Warfare, File 061.2 Army and Military Surveys, National Archives; Office of the Chief of Psychological Warfare, Minutes of Weekly Staff Meeting, 20 December 1951, Record Group 319, Army-Chief of Special Warfare, 1951-54, TS Decimal Files, 020 Staff Meetings, National Archives. The survey team that selected Smoke Bomb Hill consisted of Col. Edward Glavin, AFF; Lt. Col. Melvin R. Blair and Maj. Kenneth B. Stark, OCPW; Lt. Col. John O. Weaver, Psychological Warfare Division, Army General School, Fort Riley; and Lt. Col. Brock and Maj. Taylor, 3d Army.

84. Department of the Army, Office of the Chief of Psychological Warfare, Washington, D.C., Memorandum for Brig. Gen. Robert A. McClure, subject: Psychological Warfare Presentation for PSB, 7 January 1952, from Col. Wendell W. Fertig, Record Group 319, Army-Chief of Special Warfare, 1951-54, TS Decimal Files, 337-350.05, box 13, Psy War 350.01 TS (7 January 1952), National Archives; Office of the Chief of Psychological Warfare, Memorandum to the Assistant Chief of Staff, G-3, subject: Funds for a Psychological Warfare Center, 14 January 1952, from Brig. Gen. Robert A. McClure, Psy War 123 (14 January 1952), National Archives; Office of the Chief of Psychological Warfare, Memorandum for the Assistant Chief of Staff, G-2, subject: Compromise of Classified Information, 22 January 1952, from Brig. Gen. Robert A. McClure, Record Group 319, Psy War Admin Office, Records Branch, Decimal File (C), 1951-54, 370.64-380.01, box 20, Psy War 380.01 C (22 January 1952), National Archives. The breach of security that annoyed McClure was the following sentence from the 21 January 1952 issue of *Newsweek:* "The Army will soon open a secret guerrilla warfare and sabotage school for military personnel and CIA agents at Fort Bragg, N.C." McClure insisted that this information had been handled within OCPW as a TOP SECRET matter, with dissemination on a "need-to-know" basis, and he therefore requested an investigation to determine the source of the leak. Although the G-2 refused to follow through on the request, the incident reveals the sensitive manner in which Special Forces activities were being handled by OCPW at this time and helps explain in part why so little publicity was given to Special Forces, including no mention of this activity in the title of the proposed center at Fort Bragg.

85. Department of the Army, Office of the Chief of Psychological Warfare, Washington, D.C., Memorandum to the Assistant Chief of Staff, G-3, subject: Utilization of Active Army Spaces Allocated for FY 1952 and FY 1953, 6 February 1952, from Brig. Gen. Robert A. McClure, Record Group 319, Psy War Admin Office, Records Branch, Decimal File (C), 1951-54, 319.5-320.3, box 12, Psy War 320.2 (6 February 1952), National Archives.

86. See note 85 above, Comment No. 2 from Brig. Gen. G. J. Higgins, Chief, Organization and Training Division, G-3, 15 February 1952.

87. Department of the Army, Assistant Chief of Staff, G-3, Washington, D.C., Summary Sheet for Chief of Staff, US Army, subject: Establishment of Psychological Warfare and Special Forces Center, 3 March 1952, from Maj. Gen. C. D. Eddleman, Deputy Assistant Chief of Staff, G-3, Record Group 319, Army-Chief of Special Warfare, 1951–54, TS Decimal Files, box 8, Psy War 322 TS (3 March 1952), National Archives. The total personnel needs for the center itself were stated as 362, of which 312 would be military and 50 civilian. Twenty-nine spaces (27 military and 2 civilian) from the Psychological Warfare Division, Army General School, Fort Riley, would be transferred to the new center at Fort Bragg.

88. Department of the Army, Office of the Chief of Psychological Warfare, Washington, D.C., Memorandum for the Chief, Joint Subsidiary Plans Division, JCS, subject: Activation of Psychological Warfare Center at Fort Bragg, N.C., from Brig. Gen. Robert A. McClure, Record Group 319, Psy War Admin Office, Records Branch, Decimal File (C), 1951–54, 319.5–320.3, box 13, Psy War 322 (7 April 1952), National Archives.

Chapter VIII Notes

1. Department of the Army, Office of the Chief of Psychological Warfare, Washington, D.C., Memorandum for the Deputy Chief of Staff for Operations and Administration, subject: Activation and Mission of the Psychological Warfare Center, from Brig. Gen. Robert A. McClure, 22 May 1952, Record Group 319, Psy War Admin Office, Records Branch, Decimal File (C), 1951–54, 322–326, box 13, Psy War 322 (22 May 1952), National Archives. Department of the Army General Order No. 37, 14 April 1952, established the Psychological Warfare Center as a Class I activity and installation, effective 10 April 1952 (extract filed with above reference). A copy of the Recommended Table of Distribution for the Psychological Warfare Center can be found with Psy War 320.3 (16 April 1952), National Archives.

2. Office, Chief of Army Field Forces, Fort Monroe, Va., Letter, subject: Psychological Warfare Doctrine Development and Instruction, 29 May 1952, US-AJFKCMA; Letter, Col. Otis E. Hays, 5 May 1969, USAJFKCMA (Public Affairs Office). An advance party from the Psychological Warfare Division, Army General School, consisting of Lt. Col. John O. Weaver with five officers and seven enlisted men was scheduled to arrive at Fort Bragg on 27 April 1952; the remainder of this division (eight officers and four enlisted men) was scheduled to move not later than 15 May 1952. See Army Field Forces letter, subject: Psy War Center, 30 April 1952, to Commanding General, 3d Army, filed with Psy War 322 (1 May 1952), National Archives.

3. Headquarters, Psychological Warfare Center, Fort Bragg, N.C., Memorandum No. 14, "Organization and Functions Manual, Headquarters, Psychological Warfare Center," 12 November 1952, p. 3, USAJFKCMA.

4. Letter, Col. Otis E. Hays, 5 May 1969, USAJFKCMA (Public Affairs Office).

5. Headquarters, Psychological Warfare Center, Fort Bragg, N.C., "Administrative Information Handbook, Psychological Warfare Seminar, 17-19 December 1952," December 1952, p. 2. USAJFKCMA.

6. Department of the Army, Organization and Training Division, G-3, Washington, D.C., DF to Psy War, subject: Establishment of the Psychological Operations School, 27 August 1952, G-3 352 (6 August 1952), filed with Psy War 322 (25 September 1952), National Archives.

7. Headquarters, Psychological Warfare Center, Fort Bragg, N.C., Letter to the Chief of Psychological Warfare, subject: Activation of the Psychological Warfare School, 12 September 1952, USAJFKCMA; Office of the Chief of Psychological Warfare, Memorandum to the Assistant Chief of Staff, G-3, subject: Establishment of the Psychological Warfare School, 25 September 1952, Psy War 322 (25 September 1952), National Archives.

8. The Psychological Warfare School, Fort Bragg, N.C., "Guide for Staff and Faculty," April 1953, p. 10, USAJFKCMA. Additional detail on the mission of the school can be found in the Psychological Warfare Center's Memorandum No. 14, "Organization and Functions Manual," and "Administrative Information Handbook," USAJFKCMA.

9. Letter, Col. Otis E. Hays, 5 May 1969, USAJFKCMA (Public Affairs Office).

10. Headquarters, Psychological Warfare Center, Memorandum No. 14, "Organization and Functions Manual," p. 52, USAJFKCMA.

11. US, Department of Defense, *Semiannual Report of the Secretary of Defense, 1 January through 30 June 1953*, p. 140.

12. US, Department of Defense, *Semiannual Report of the Secretary of Defense, 1 January through 30 June 1952*, p. 92.

13. Department of the Army, Office of the Chief of Psychological Warfare, Washington, D.C., Memorandum for the Chief of Information, subject: Proposed Contingency Press Release Regarding Psy War Center, 17 June 1952, from Brig. Gen. Robert A. McClure, Psy War 000.7 (16 June 1952); and Memorandum for G-3, subject: Proposed Press Release Regarding the Psychological Warfare Center, 1 July 1952, from Col. Wendell W. Fertig, Acting Chief, OCPW, Psy War 000.7 (1 July 1952); both in Record Group 319, Psy War Admin Office, 1951-54, box 1, National Archives. General McClure told the Chief of Information in his 17 June 1952 memorandum that the mission of Special Forces was classified confidential; thus it was "considered unwise to make any reference thereto in the proposed contingency release." When Col. C. H. Karlstad assumed command of the center, the story noting this event in the Fort Bragg newspaper made no reference to Special Forces operations. Later, the Chief of Information suggested that the press release include reference to Special Forces "to prevent undue probing by the news services into Special Forces activities at Fort Bragg, N.C." By late August 1952, after several weeks of correspondence between G-2, G-3, the Chief of Information, OCPW, and Army Field Forces, a specific policy on the matter still had not been resolved. Nor had the problem been solved by January 1953, when the Special Forces Division initiated action to downgrade from Confidential to Re-

stricted certain aspects of the Special Forces Program (see Psy War 380.01, Record Group 319, Psy War Admin Office, Records Branch, Decimal File (C), 1951-54, 370.64-380.01, box 20, National Archives.

14. Department of the Army, Office of the Chief of Psychological Warfare, Washington, D.C., Memorandum for the Chief, Special Forces Division, subject: Student Handbook—"The Psychological Warfare School," 13 August 1952, from Lt. Col. Marvin J. Waters, Operations and Training Branch; Memorandum for Col. Wendell W. Fertig, subject: Psy War Center Student Handbook, 14 August 1952, from Col. William J. Blythe, Chief, Special Forces Division; Memorandum for Colonel Blythe, subject: Student Handbook—"The Psychological Warfare School," 21 August 1952, from Lt. Col. Melvin R. Blair; all filed under Psy War 332, Army Service Schools, National Archives. Colonel Blair complained that "not a single word is devoted to the role of Special Forces" in chapter I of the Handbook, although "approximately 50% of the Staff and Faculty personnel and student body will be Special Forces personnel."

15. Headquarters, Psychological Warfare Center, Memorandum No. 14, "Organization and Functions Manual," p. 49. USAJFKCMA.

16. See note 15 above, p. 34; see also the Psychological Warfare Center, Fort Bragg, N.C., *Psy War,* 1954, p. 1, USAJFKCMA.

17. Psychological Warfare Center, *Psy War,* USAJFKCMA. Apparently the Board gave little attention to Special Forces operations: In the above publication, which outlined activities of the Board since its inception, there was no mention of any unconventional warfare projects, nor were there any Special Forces members on the Board as of early 1954. *Psy War* purports "to tell the story of the US Army's Psychological Warfare Center," but nowhere in the 99-page book is any reference made to the Special Forces Group or instructional department that constituted integral elements of the center. Undoubtedly, this was again the result of security-consciousness, perhaps carried to an extreme, concerning Special Forces activities.

18. Headquarters, Department of the Army, Washington, D.C., Training Circular No. 13, "Military Aspects of Psychological Warfare," 8 June 1953, pp. 6f., USAJFKCMA; Psychological Warfare Center, *Psy War,* pp. 35-69, USAJFKCMA.

19. Melvin Russell Blair, "Toughest Outfit in the Army," *Saturday Evening Post,* 228 (12 May 1956): 40-41; Department of the Army, Office of the Chief of Psychological Warfare, Washington, D.C., Orientation Conference for TI&E (Troop Information and Education) Officers, subject: "Current Developments in the Field of Special Forces Operations" (15 January 1952), by Lt. Col. Melvin R. Blair, Record Group 319, Psy War Admin Office, Records Branch, Decimal File (C), 1951-54, 334-337, box 15, Psy War 337 (C) (10 January 1952), National Archives; Department of the Army, Office of the Chief of Psychological Warfare, Washington, D.C., Letter to the Chief, Army Field Forces, subject: Special Forces Orientation for Training Directive and Reception Centers, 24 June 1952, Record Group 319, Psy War, Decimal File (C), 1951-54, 352.16-354.2, box 18, Psy War 353 (24 June 1952), National Archives; also OCPW letter, subject: Orientation Conferences for Service Schools and Selected Headquarters and Installations, to Chief, Army Field Forces, 1 August 1952, Record Group 319, Psy War, Decimal

File (C), 1951-54, 352.16-354.2, box 18, Psy War 353 (1 August 1952), National Archives.

20. Department of the Army, Office of the Chief of Psychological Warfare, Washington, D.C., Orientation Conference, "Current Developments in the Field of Special Forces Operations," to be presented to service schools, Army Headquarters, and selected installations during the period 1 October 1952-March 1953, by Lt. Col. Melvin R. Blair, Record Group 319, Psy War Admin Office, Records Branch, Decimal File (C) 334-337, 1951-54, box 15, Psy War 337 S (24 September 1952), National Archives; also Psy War 353 (6 November 1952), Orientation Material for Use in Connection with Selection of Volunteers for Special Forces, Record Group 319, Psy War, Decimal File (C), 1951-54, 352.16-354.2, box 18, National Archives; and Psy War 335 C (10 January 1952), Orientation Conference for TI&E (Troop Information and Education) Officers, subject: "Current Developments in the Field of Special Forces Operations" (15 January 1952), by Lt. Col. Melvin R. Blair, Record Group 319, Psy War Admin Office, Records Branch, Decimal File (C), 1951-54, 334-337, box 15, National Archives.

21. See note 20 above, Psy War 337 TS (16 April 1951), Psy War 337 C (10 January 1952), and Psy War 337 (24 September 1952), National Archives.

22. See note 20 above, Psy War 353 (6 November 1952), National Archives.

23. See note 20 above, Psy War 290 TS (8 December 1952) and Psy War 390 TS (19 December 1952), National Archives.

24. Department of the Army, Office of the Adjutant General, Washington, D.C., Letter, subject: Activation of a Unit of the General Reserve, 19 May 1952, AGAO-I, Department of the Army, Washington, D.C., TO&E 33-2 (proposed), 14 April 1952, cited in US Army Combat Developments Command, Special Warfare Agency, Combat Developments Study: Organization for US Army Special Forces, August 1964, USAJFKCMA; Department of the Army, Office of the Chief of Special Forces, Washington, D.C., DF to G3, Organization Branch, subject: Activation of Special Forces Units, 2 May 1952, from Brig. Gen. Robert A. McClure, Record Group 319, Psy War Admin Office, Records Branch, Decimal File (C), 1951-54, 322-326, box 13, Psy War 322 (1 May 1952), National Archives.

25. Letter, Col. Aaron Bank, 17 February 1968, USAJFKCMA (Public Affairs Office).

26. The Psychological Warfare Center, Fort Bragg, N.C., Comments by Members Attending Organization and Training Conference, 9 July 1952, USAJFKCMA. Attendees included representatives from OCPW, AFF, 3d Army, and the Psychological Warfare Center. Colonel Bank strongly urged that the Special Forces Group TO&E's be declassified; present classification restricted publicity in Army publications, and the men could not even tell others their correct unit designation, other than the Psychological Warfare Center—which limited their pride in their unit, Bank believed.

27. Headquarters, The Psychological Warfare Center, Fort Bragg, N.C., Letter to Brig. Gen. Robert A. McClure from Col. C. H. Karlstad, Commanding Officer, 12 September 1952, filed with Record Group 319, Army-Chief of Special Warfare, 1951-54, Psy War 322, National Archives. Karlstad asked McClure for assistance in getting the 7 US training divisions to fulfill their allotted quotas of 35

volunteers per month for Special Forces. McClure followed through on the request rapidly and wrote back to Karlstad on 22 September that the situation should soon improve.

28. Department of the Army, Office of the Chief of Psychological Warfare, Washington, D.C., Staff Study to Chief of Staff, US Army, subject: Staff Study on Intensification of Lodge Bill Recruitment Program, 8 August 1952, from Brig. Gen. Robert A. MClure, Record Group 319, Army-Chief of Special Warfare, 1951-56, TS Decimal Files, 337-350.05, box 13, Psy War 342 TS (8 August 1952), National Archives. The reasons for this low rate were many: The many married people and German nationals who applied were not eligible; the citizens of NATO member nations who applied were not eligible; many applicants were disqualified on mental and physical grounds; and many applicants changed their minds during the long time required for security checks.

29. Department of the Army, Office of the Chief of Psychological Warfare, Washington, D C., Memorandum to the Chief, Legislative Liaison, subject: Program for Liaison with the Congress, Tab A, "Intensification of Lodge Bill Recruitment Program," from Col. Wendell W. Fertig, Acting Chief, OCPW, 15 August 1952, Record Group 319, Army-Chief of Special Warfare, 1951-54, TS Decimal Files, box 2, Psy War 032.1, National Archives. Tab A, prepared by Col. William J. Blythe, Special Forces Division, projected the overall need for Lodge bill personnel as 4,875 for Special Forces and 40 for psychological warfare units.

30. Headquarters, The Psychological Warfare Center, Fort Bragg, N.C., Letter to Brig. Gen. Robert A. McClure, from Col. C. H. Karlstad, 25 November 1952, Record Group 319, Army-Chief of Special Warfare, 1951-54, National Archives.

31. Letter, Col. Aaron Bank, 17 February 1968, USAJFKCMA (Public Affairs Office).

32. Department of the Army, Office of the Chief of Psychological Warfare, Washington, D C., Training Circular, Special Forces Group (Airborne), 13 May 1952, Record Group 319, Psy War Admin Office, Records Branch, Decimal File (C), 1951-54, 322-326, box 13, Psy War 322 (13 May 1952), National Archives.

33. Special Warfare Agency, "Organization for Special Forces," pp. II-10-II-13.

34. Letters, Col. Aaron Bank, 17 February 1968 and 3 April 1968, USAJFKCMA (Public Affairs Office).

35. Letter, Brig. Gen. Russell W. Volckmann, 21 March 1969, USAJFKCMA (Public Affairs Office).

36. Headquarters, The Psychological Warfare Center, Fort Bragg, N.C., Comments by Members Attending Organization and Training Conference, 9 July 1952, USAJFKCMA.

37. Department of the Army, Office of the Chief of Psychological Warfare, Washington, D.C., Memorandum to the Chief, Plans and Policy Branch, OCPW, from Col. Oliver Jackson Sands, Jr., US Army Reserve, 7 July 1952, Record Group 319, Army-Chief of Special Warfare, 1951-54, TS Decimal Files, box 6, National Archives. Colonel Sands' memorandum forwarded a study that he had undertaken during his 2 weeks of duty in OCPW, the subject of which was "to study the position of the Office of the Chief of Psychological Warfare in the National Estab-

lishment." Recognizing the limitations of time and breadth in his endeavor, Sands suggested that the study "be used to stimulate thinking among those who are more closely connected with the problem."

38. Department of the Army, Office of the Chief of Psychological Warfare, Washington, D.C., "Tactical Psychological Warfare in the Korean Conflict: An Informal Commentary on Propaganda Operations of the 8th US Army, 1950-51," by Col. Donald F. Hall, 1 April 1954, Record Group 319, Army-Chief of Special Warfare, 1951-54, Secret Decimal Files, 091-091.412, box 7, Psy War 091 Korea, National Archives. Colonel Hall was the Psychological Warfare Officer for the 8th Army in Korea from 9 November 1952 to 14 January 1954, then later served in that capacity at Headquarters, Army Field Forces. Most of the comments and recommendations in his report were limited to the tactical aspects of psychological warfare.

39. See note 38 above.

40. Daniel Lerner, *Sykewar: Psychological Warfare against Germany, D-Day to VE-Day* (New York: George W. Stewart, 1949), pp. 67-93.

41. See note 37 above, Psy War 090.412 TS (7 July 1952). McClure's handwritten comment regarding Colonel Sand's report is instructive: "This is an interesting report although I do not concur that Propaganda and Special Forces Operations are so completely different as to require separation particularly when (a) all other services have same combination, (b) JSPD has dual responsibility, (c) black covert and white propaganda are split between State and OPC."

Chapter IX Notes

1. Daugherty and Janowitz, *Casebook,* pp. 137f., write: "In the military establisment in Washington, staff planning activities involving psychological warfare ceased with the end of World War II hostilities." The authors infer that nothing was done at the Department of the Army until creation of the OCPW. McClure himself was prone to exaggerate somewhat the authorship of OCPW's achievements. As an example, planning for both the Radio Broadcasting and Leaflet Group and Loudspeaker and Leaflet Company concepts was under way in G-3 before the outbreak of war in 1950 and before the creation of OCPW; but McClure would claim later that those ideas, based on World War II experience, originated in OCPW.

2. I am indebted to Prof. Theodore Ropp, Duke University, for this insight.

3. In an economy move, Army Field Forces recommended in October 1953 that the Psychological Warfare Center be deactivated and the responsibility for psychological warfare training transferred back to the Army General School at Fort Riley. Under this plan, all Special Forces schooling would have been conducted within units, rather than in a separate school. After a long and impassioned appeal by OCPW the result was a Psychological Warfare Center that survived, but

at reduced strength. See Office of the Chief of Army Field Forces, Fort Monroe, Va., Letter to Assistant Chief of Staff, G-3, Department of the Army, subject: Future of Psychological Warfare Center, 12 October 1953, filed with Psy War 322, Psy War Center C (30 October 1953), Record Group 319, Psy War Admin Office, Records Branch, Decimal File (C), 1951-54, 322-326, box 13, National Archives.

4. A letter to his friend Lt. Gen. Charles L. Bolte expressed McClure's feelings about leaving OCPW: "To my unexpected surprise and with no little consternation, I have received orders transferring me to Iran to lead the Military Mission. After 10½ of the past 12 years in this particular field and with the added emphasis being placed thereon by the White House, I fail to appreciate G-1's policy. I asked the Chief if there was anything behind it and he assured me there was not. The inference is that I have been in this field too long and there was no future for me as long as I continue in a specialized activity. There are already some rumblings in Defense and across the river but nevertheless I am selling my house and packing up." Office of the Chief of Psychological Warfare, Letter to Lt. Gen. Charles L. Bolte, Commander in Chief, US Army, Europe, 4 March 1953, Record Group 319, Psy War Admin Office, Records Branch, 1951-54, 020-40, box 3, Psy War 040 CIA (undated) 53, National Archives. Ironically, McClure had decried the scarcity of general officers in the Army with psychological warfare or special operations experience. He tried to increase the number of general officers assigned to these specialized activities, including a general officer to head the Psychological Warfare Center. But he was unsuccessful in these attempts, and now he—probably the most experienced general officer in any of the services—was being forced to leave the field that he had devoted so much of his career to building up. See Office of the Chief of Psychological Warfare, Memorandum for the Deputy Chief of Staff for Operations and Administration, subject: Assignment of General Officers to Psychological Warfare Activities, 30 October 1952, from Brig. Gen. Robert A. McClure; McClure's Memorandum for Record, subject: Conversation with General McAuliffe reference General Officers, 26 December 1952; and Memorandums for Record, 2 March 1953 and 6 March 1953, subject: Selection of Commander for the Psychological Warfare Center, by Lt. Col. William Trabue, Executive, OCPW; all filed with Psy War 210.3, Record Group 319, Army-Chief of Special Warfare, National Archives.

SOURCES

Section I—Research Aids

The research for this study began, naturally enough, at the US Army John F. Kennedy Center for Military Assistance, Fort Bragg, N.C. The center's archives were found in three separate locations: the Institute for Military Assistance Library, the center G-1, and the center Public Affairs Office. Within recent years, the G-1 files have been transferred to the Public Affairs Office, and are maintained there by the center historian, Mrs. Beverly Lindsey. Mrs. Lindsey also has a file of correspondence with many of the key officers at the center in the early 1950's, and and keeps some historical documents in her private collection. The personal files of Mr. John Farrell, Combat Developments, Institute for Military Assistance, were helpful. The Institute library is small but specialized in its collection of special warfare secondary sources. While important materials about the establishment of the Psychological Warfare Center were uncovered, the primary sources of the center's archives are not well organized and pertain primarily to the post-1952 years. One must search elsewhere for more detailed information about the center's historical roots.

At the US Army Military History Institute (USAMHI), Carlisle Barracks, Pa., key staff personnel who were most helpful to the author were Miss Joyce Eakin, Assistant Director, Library Services, and Dr. Richard Sommers, Archivist. Miss Eakin has special MHI bibliographies for US Rangers and Special Forces in her files, is knowledgeable about institute holdings, and can provide valuable contacts at both the Center of Military History (CMH) and the National Archives in Washington, D.C. Dr. Sommers maintains the papers and oral histories of numerous senior Army officers; those of Robert A. McClure, Ray Peers, and William P. Yarborough were particularly useful for my work. The MHI Special Bibliographic Series, number 13, volumes 1 and 2, Oral History, contain references to these and other officers, as well as a cross-index of key topics. The institute also has a complete set of the Army General Council Minutes for the period 1942 to 1952. The council met weekly, was composed of the senior War Department leadership, and was chaired by either the Chief of Staff or Deputy Chief of Staff. These minutes were particularly useful in providing an overview of the major decisions and events leading to establishment of the Office of the Chief of Psychological

Warfare (OCPW) in 1951. Similarly, the War Department's *History of the Military Intelligence Division, 7 December 1941–2 September 1945,* which can be found in the MHI, provides some useful leads to the Army's psychological warfare activities during World War II.

Miss Hannah Zeidlik, General Reference Branch, Center of Military History, Washington, D.C., provided CMH special bibliographies on psychological warfare and Special Forces, as well as assistance in locating materials on these topics in the CMH card catalog and files. Of note were copies of OCPW semiannual and annual historical summaries for the early 1950's, which provided valuable leads to pursue in the Department of the Army records, National Archives.

At the National Archives, William Cunliffe and Ed Reese, Modern Military Branch, were the key archivists who helped to ferret out information on US psychological and unconventional warfare from 1941 to 1952; John Taylor was most helpful with Office of Strategic Services (OSS) records. Indeed, these collections in the National Archives provided the foundation upon which this study is based. Foremost in importance were the records of the War Department General and Special Staff (Record Group 165) and those of the Army Staff (Record Group 319). Records of the following staff agencies were instrumental in tracing the history of psychological and unconventional warfare activities within the Army: the Military Intelligence Division (MID), G–2 (Special Studies Group), 1941; the Psychological Warfare Branch, Military Intelligence Service, G–2, 1941–42; the Propaganda Branch, G–2, 1943–45; the Psychological Warfare Branch, Plans and Operations Division (P&O), 1947; the Psychological Warfare Division, Office of the Assistant Chief of Staff, G–3, 1950; and the Office of the Chief of Psychological Warfare, Special Staff, 1951–54. These last records were crucial in determining policies, key personalities, and decisions leading to the formation of Special Forces and creation of the Psychological Warfare Center at Fort Bragg. The footnotes for each chapter of the text provide more comprehensive reference to all of the records.

Section II—Primary Sources

National Archives

Records of the Army Staff (Record Group 319).
   G–3 Operations, March 1950–51, 091.412 series, boxes 154–58.
   Plans and Operations Division, 1946–48, 091.412 series, including Top Secret files.
   Army Operations, 1948–52, 091.412 series, Top Secret "Hot Files," particularly boxes 9 and 10. Includes Plans and Operations Division and G–3 Operations records on psychological and unconventional warfare and interface with the CIA.

Office of the Chief of Psychological Warfare, 1951–54.
    Unclassified and Confidential Decimal File, 13 feet, 40 boxes.
    Secret Decimal Correspondence File, 6 feet, 30 boxes.
    Top Secret Decimal Correspondence File, 6 Feet, 22 boxes.
Army Intelligence Decimal Files, 1941–48, Washington National Records
    Center (WNRC), Suitland, Md., particularly series 370.5 (1–31–42)
    to 373.2, box 874; series 322.001 (10–31–42) to 322.03 (1–1–43), box
    576; series 091.4 (9–20–43) to 091.412 (1–1–47), box 262; series
    091.412 (121.31–46) to 091.412 Counterpropaganda, box 263.

Records of the Joint Chiefs of Staff (Record Group 218). See series 385,
    1946–53, boxes 147–56, for information on psychological and uncon-
    ventional warfare.

Records of the War Department General and Special Staff (Record Group 165).
    Military Intelligence Division (G–2), Propaganda Branch Correspondence,
        1939–45, boxes 326–44. Contains reports, directives, bulletins, and
        other papers dealing with psychological warfare and propaganda activ-
        ities in overseas theaters. 6 feet.
    Office of the Director of Intelligence (G–2), 1906–49.
        The Psychologic Section contains classified propaganda manuals and
        other records relating to propaganda and psychological warfare, 1918–
        26. 2 feet.
    Operations and Plans Directorate (OPD), OPD 000.24 Section I (Cases
        1–39), OPD 000.24 Section II (Cases 40–61), September 1943–
        January 1944, and OPD 000.24 Section III (Case 62–   ), February
        1944–December 1945. Contains excellent material on interaction be-
        tween OPD, G–2, and other offices, establishment of Propaganda
        Branch, G–2, and organization for psychological warfare in the War
        Department General Staff (WDGS).

US Army John F. Kennedy Center for Military Assistance

Army General School, Fort Riley, Kans. Instructional Text, "Tactical Psycho-
    logical Warfare, The Combat Psychological Warfare Detachment," October
    1946.
Army General School, Fort Riley, Kans. "Program of Instruction for Psychological
    Warfare Officer Course," August 1951.
Army General School, Fort Riley, Kans. "Program of Instruction, Psychological
    Warfare Unit Officer Course," January 1951. Believed to be the first formal
    course in psychological warfare taught in the United States.
Department of the Army, Office of the Chief of Information. *Special Warfare, US
    Army: An Army Specialty.* Washington, D.C., 1962.
The Ground General School, Fort Riley, Kans. Special Text No. 8, "Strategic
    Psychological Warfare," 15 February 1949.

Headquarters, Department of the Army, Washington, D.C. Training Circular No. 13, "Military Aspects of Psychological Warfare," 8 June 1953. Gives definitions and organization for psychological warfare at national and Department of the Army levels. Outlines mission and organizations of the Radio Broadcasting and Leaflet Group and the Loudspeaker and Leaflet Company.

Headquarters, Department of the Army, Washington, D.C. Special Regulations No. 10-250-1, "Organization and Functions, Office of the Chief of Psychological Warfare, Special Staff," 22 May 1951.

Headquarters, John F. Kennedy Center for Military Assistance, Fort Bragg, N.C. Undated fact sheet, "Lineage of Special Forces" (mimeographed).

Headquarters, The Psychological Warfare Center, Fort Bragg, N.C. "Administrative Information Handbook, Psychological Warfare Seminar, 17-19 December 1952," December 1952. Gives detailed mission of the Psychological Warfare School and an outline of some of its early academic subjects. Also contains map outlining physical organization of the center.

Headquarters, The Psychological Warfare Center, Fort Bragg, N.C. Letter to Chief, Psychological Warfare, Department of the Army, subject: "Activation of the Psychological Warfare School," 12 September 1952. The center's appeal to the Department of the Army to give the Psychological Warfare School a formal service school status rather than a provisional status.

Headquarters, The Psychological Warfare Center, Fort Bragg, N.C. Memorandum No. 14, "Organization and Functions Manual, Headquarters, The Psychological Warfare Center," 12 November 1952. The earliest formal document published by the Psychological Warfare Center that I have been able to find—the basic organizational directive for the center.

The Institute for Military Assistance Library, Fort Bragg, N.C. "Examples of UW." A folder of reports and speeches on various aspects of unconventional warfare. Includes the 1956 speech by Ray Peers to the Special Warfare School, one of the most comprehensive speeches I have read on the details of a guerrilla warfare organization (OSS Detachment 101, Burma).

The Office of Strategic Services. "OSS Aid to the French Resistance in World War II." The following individual reports were assembled in 1944-45 under the direction of Col. Joseph Lincoln. They are basically post-action reports of OSS activities and operations taken verbatim from unit and personal journals. These reports represent the richest lode of information I have seen on the details of actual OSS organization, techniques, training, personnel, and operations in Europe.

"Origin and Development of Resistance in France: Summary."

"Jedburghs: DOUGLAS II, Number 61, through JULIAN II, Number 67."

"Operations in Southern France: Operational Group."

"American Participation in MASSINGHAM Operations Mounted in North Africa: Jedburghs."

"Corsica: Operation Tommy."

"Poles in France Used by the Resistance: A Report on the Organization of Poles in France by SOE/OSS to Create a Guerrilla Force for Augmenting the Activities of French Resistance Elements."

"DF Section."

"Massive Supply Drops."

"Missions: F-Section."

"F-Section Circuits: Reports by Participating American Personnel of OSS."

"F-Section: Reports by OSS Participants."

"SO-RF Section Missions: Introduction and First Quarter, 1944."

"SO-RF Section Missions: Second Quarter, 1944."

"Missions and Sabotage: RF Section, Third Quarter, 1944."

Operations Research Office (ORO), The Johns Hopkins University.

Technical Memorandum ORO-T-64 (AFFE), "UN Partisan Warfare in Korea, 1951-1954," June 1956. A study performed by a team from ORO that traveled to Korea, examined records, and conducted interviews. Attempts to evaluate magnitude and effectiveness of US partisan warfare activities. IMA Library archives.

Propaganda Branch, Intelligence Division, War Department General Staff, The Pentagon, Washington, D.C. "Revised Draft War Department Field Manual, FM 30-60," September 1946.

Propaganda Branch, Intelligence Division, War Department General Staff, The Pentagon, Washington, D.C. "A Syllabus of Psychological Warfare," October 1946.

The Psychological Warfare School, Fort Bragg, N.C. "Guide for Staff and Faculty," April 1953. Contains organization and functions of the school, boards, and committees; information on preparation of instruction and instructional material; and information on administration of students and academic evaluation.

The Psychological Warfare Center, Fort Bragg, N.C. *Psy War,* 1954.

The first publication that gives some details on the background, training, and activities of the individual units assigned to the Psychological Warfare Center. Contains unit organization and chain of command charts. No mention is made of the Special Forces Department in the Psychological Warfare School or of the Special Forces Group.

The Psychological Warfare School, Fort Bragg, N.C. "Student Handbook," September 1953. Contains mission and organization of school, academic and administrative information pertaining to students, and a valuable organization chart of the Psychological Warfare Center dated 1 August 1953.

Public Affairs, Office, John F. Kennedy Center for Military Assistance, Fort Bragg, N.C. Letters from:

Brig. Gen. Russell W. Volckmann (Ret.), with one enclosure, 21 March 1969.

Col. Otis E. Hays, Jr., (Ret.) with five enclosures, 5 May 1969.

Col. Aaron Bank (Ret.), 17 February 1968, 3 April 1968, and 27 February 1973.

These letters not only contained valuable information but also provided important leads on the origins of the Psychological Warfare Center.

Section III—Secondary Sources

Aerospace Studies Institute. *Guerrilla Warfare and Airpower in Korea, 1950–53.* Maxwell Air Force Base, Ala.: US Air University, 1964.

Alcorn, Robert Hayden. *No Bugles for Spies: Tales of the OSS.* New York: David McKay Co., 1962.

Alsop, Stewart, and Braden, Thomas. *Sub Rosa: The OSS and American Espionage.* New York: Reynal & Hitchcock, 1946.

Altieri, James J. *Darby's Rangers.* Fisher-Harrison Corporation, 1977.

Beaumont, Roger A. *Military Elites.* Indianapolis and New York: Bobbs-Merrill Co., 1974.

Bjelajac, Slavko N. "Unconventional Warfare in the Nuclear Era." *Orbis* 4, no. 13 (Fall 1960):323–37.

Blair, Melvin Russell. "Toughest Outfit in the Army." *Saturday Evening Post,* 228 (12 May 1956).

Blaufarb, Douglas S. *The Counterinsurgency Era: US Doctrine and Performance, 1950 to the Present.* New York: Free Press, 1977.

Cline, Ray S. *Secrets, Spies, and Scholars: Blueprint of the Essential CIA.* Washington: Acropolis Books, 1976.

Cohen, Eliot A. *Commandos and Politicians: Elite Military Units in Modern Democracies.* Cambridge: Center for International Affairs, Harvard University, 1978.

Colby, William. *Honorable Men: My Life in the CIA.* New York: Simon & Schuster, 1978.

Conine Ernest. "New Horizons in Psychological Warfare." *Army Information Digest* 7, no. 12 (December 1952):21–27.

Corson, William R. *The Armies of Ignorance: The Rise of the American Intelligence Empire.* New York: Dial Press, 1977.

Daughterty, William E., and Janowitz, Morris. *A Psychological Warfare Casebook.* Baltimore: The Johns Hopkins Press, 1958.

Deitchman, Seymour J. *Limited War and American Defense Policy: Building and Using Military Power in a World at War.* Cambridge: MIT Press, 1969.

Dulles, Allen. *The Craft of Intelligence.* New York: Harper & Row, 1963.

Dyer, Murray. *The Weapon on the Wall: Rethinking Psychological Warfare.* Baltimore: The John Hopkins Press, 1959.

Elliot-Bateman, Michael, ed. *The Fourth Dimension of Warfare.* Vol. 1. New York: Praeger, 1970.

Fain, Tyrus G.; Plant, Katherine C.; and Milloy, Ross. *The Intelligence Community: History, Organization, and Issues.* Public Documents Series. New York: Bowker Co., 1977.

Fayetteville Observer. Fayetteville, N.C., March–June 1952.

Foot, M. R. D. *Resistance: An Analysis of European Resistance to Nazism, 1940–1945.* London: Eyre Metheuen.

Ford, Corey, *Donovan of OSS.* Boston: Little, Brown & Co., 1970.

Hall, Donald F. "Organization for Combat Propaganda." *Army Information Digest* 6, no. 5 (May 1951):11–16.

Harkins, Philip. *Blackburn's Headquarters.* New York: W. W. Norton & Co., 1955.

Hart, Henry C. "US Employment of Underground Forces." *Military Review* 26, no. 3 (March 1947):50–56.

Hazen, William E., and Wilson, Barbara Anne. *The Purposes and Practices of Guerrilla Warfare: A Structured Anthology.* 4 vols. Washington: The American University Center for Research in Social Systems, 1969.

Heilbrunn, Otto. *Warfare in the Enemy's Rear.* New York: Praeger, 1963.

Holley, I. B., Jr. *Ideas and Weapons.* Hamden, Conn.: Archon Books, 1971.

Hymoff, Edward. *The OSS in World War II.* New York: Ballantine Books, 1972.

Ladd, James D. *Commandos and Rangers of World War II.* London: McDonald & Janes, 1978.

Lerner, Daniel. *Sykewar: Psychological Warfare against Germany, D-Day to VE-Day.* New York: George W. Steward, 1949.

Linebarger, Paul M. A. *Psychological Warfare.* New York: Duell, Sloan & Pearce, 1948.

Matloff, Maurice, ed. *Army Historical Series, American Military History.* Washington, D.C.: Office of the Chief of Military History, Department of the Army, 1969.

McClure, Robert A. "Trends in Army Psychological Warfare." *Army Information Digest* 7, no. 2 (February 1952):8–14.

Morgan, William J. *The OSS and I.* New York: W. W. Norton & Co., 1957.

Osanka, Franklin Mark, ed. *Modern Guerrilla Warfare: Fighting Communist Guerrilla Movements, 1941–1961.* New York: Free Press of Glencoe, 1962.

OSS Assessment Staff. *Assessment of Men: Selection of Personnel for the Office of Strategic Services.* New York: Reinehart & Co., 1948.

Padover, Saul K., and Lasswell, Harold D. "Psychological Warfare." *Headline Series,* no. 86 (20 March 1951), pp. 14f.

Peers, William R., and Brelis, Dean. *Behind the Burma Road: The Story of America's Most Successful Guerrilla Forces.* Boston: Little, Brown & Co., 1963.

Prouty, L. Fletcher. *The Secret Team: The CIA and Its Allies in Control of the United States and the World.* Englewood Cliffs, N.J.: Prentice-Hall, Inc., 1973.

Ransom, Harry Howe. *Central Intelligence and National Security.* Cambridge: Harvard University Press, 1958.

Riffkind, Herbert. "From Rockets to Rifles: The President's Guerrilla Policy." *Review,* May–June 1962, pp. 1–12.

Romanus, Charles F., and Sunderland, Riley. *Time Runs Out in CBI: United States Army in World War II; China-Burma-India Theater.* Washington, D.C.: Office of the Chief of Military History, Department of the Army, 1959.

Roosevelt, Kermit, ed. *War Report of the OSS.* 2 vols. New York: Walker & Co., 1976.

Ropp, Theodore. *War in the Modern World.* New York: Collier Books, 1959.

Smith, R. Harris. *OSS: The Secret History of America's First Central Intelligence Agency.* Berkeley: University of California Press, 1972.

Special Operations Research Office. *Undergrounds in Insurgent Revolutionary and Resistance Warfare*. Washington, D.C.: American University, 1963.

Tarr, David W. *American Strategy in the Nuclear Age*. New York: Macmillan Co., 1966.

Taylor, Edmond, *Awakening from History*. Boston: Gambit, 1969.

Taylor, Maxwell D. *The Uncertain Trumpet*. New York: Harper & Row, 1960.

Thayer, Charles W. *Guerrilla*. New York: Harper & Row, 1963.

Thomson, Charles A. H. *Overseas Information Service of the US Government*. Washington, D.C.: Brookings Institution, 1948.

Truscott, L. K., Jr. *Command Missions: A Personal Story*. New York: E. P. Dutton & Co., 1954.

US Army. Headquarters, Special Warfare School. *Readings in Guerrilla Warfare*. Fort Bragg, N.C., December 1960.

US Congress. Senate, Select Committee to Study Governmental Operations with Respect to Intelligence Activities. *Final Report*. Books 1, 4. Washington, D.C.: Government Printing Office, 1976.

US Department of Defense. *Semiannual Report of the Secretary of Defense, Semiannual Reports of the Secretary of the Army, Secretary of the Navy, and Secretary of the Air Force, 1949 through 1958*. Washington, D.C.

US War Department. General Staff, Military Intelligence Division G-2. *History of the Military Intelligence Division, 7 December 1941–2 September 1945*. Washington, D.C., 1946.

Volckmann, R. W. *We Remained: Three Years behind the Enemy Lines in the Philippines*. New York: W. W. Norton & Co., 1954.

Weigley, Russell. *History of the US Army*. New York: Macmillan Co., 1967.

Yergin, Daniel. *Shattered Peace: The Origins of the Cold War and the National Security State*. Boston: Houghton Mifflin Co., 1977.

GLOSSARY

AFF	Army Field Forces
AFHQ	Allied Forces Headquarters
AG	Adjutant General
AGF	Army Ground Forces
ARC	Aerial Resupply and Communications (Wings, USAF)
CCRAK	Covert, Clandestine, and Related Activities
CCS	Combined Chiefs of Staff
CIA	Central Intelligence Agency
CIAA	Office of Coordinator of Inter-American Affairs
CIA/OPC	Central Intelligence Agency/Office of Policy Coordination
CIG	Central Intelligence Group
CINCEUR	Commander in Chief, Europe
CINCFE	Commander in Chief, Far East
CMH	Center of Military History
COI	Coordinator of Information
CSUSA	Chief of Staff, US Army
DA	Department of the Army
EUCOM	European Command
FBI	Federal Bureau of Investigation
FEC/LG	Far East Command Liaison Group
FECOM	Far East Command
FIS	Foreign Information Service (COI)
FM	Field Manual
GHQ	General Headquarters
GHQ FECOM	General Headquarters, Far East Command
HQ	Headquarters
HQ FECOM	Headquarters, Far East Command
JACK	Joint Advisory Commission Korea
JCS	Joint Chiefs of Staff
JPWC	Joint Psychological Warfare Committee
JSPD	Joint Subsidiary Plans Division
L&L	Loudspeaker and Leaflet (Company)
MHI	US Army Military History Institute
MID	Military Intelligence Division
MIS	Military Intelligence Service

MO	Morale Operations
MRB	Mobile Radio Broadcasting (Company)
NCO	noncommissioned officer
NME	National Military Establishment
NSC	National Security Council
O&T	Organization and Training (Division)
OCPW	Office of the Chief of Psychological Warfare
OG	Operational Group (Command)
OG's	Operational Groups (OSS)
ONI	Office of Naval Intelligence
OPC	Office of Policy Coordination
OPD	Operations and Plans Directorate
ORO	Operations Research Office
OSO	Office of Special Operations
OSS	Office of Strategic Services
OWI	Office of War Information
P&O	Plans and Operations (Division)
PSB	Psychological Strategy Board
PW	psychological warfare
PWB	Psychological Warfare Branch
PWB/AFHQ	Psychological Warfare Branch, Allied Forces Headquarters
PWD	Psychological Warfare Division
PWD/SHAEF	Psychological Warfare Division, Supreme Headquarters, Allied Expeditionary Force
PWO	Psychological Warfare Operations
PWS	Psychological Warfare Section
R&A	Research and Analysis (COI)
RB&L	Radio Broadcasting and Leaflet (Group)
SANACC	State-Army-Navy-Air Force Coordinating Committee
SFHQ	Special Forces Headquarters
SHAEF	Supreme Headquarters, Allied Expeditionary Force
SO	Special Operations
SOE	Special Operations Executive (Great Britain)
SSU	Strategic Services Unit
SWNCC	State-War-Navy Coordinating Committee
TD	Table of Distribution
TO&E	Table of Organization and Equipment
UN	United Nations
UNPFK	United Nations Partisan Forces in Korea
USA	US Army
USAF	US Air Force
USAFE	US Air Force, Europe
WDGS	War Department General Staff
WNRC	Washington National Records Center

INDEX

Printed in the United States
22895LVS00003B/176